JN095099

お詫びと訂正
「渉外取引・会社運営等で必要な 英文定款・議事録等の作成に関する実践と書式」

本書に，下記の誤り等がございました。読者の皆様に深くお詫び申し上げますとともに，謹んで下記のとおり訂正と補足をさせていただきます。

日本加除出版株式会社

記

■209 頁〈例 87〉の記載例
　211 頁〈例 89〉の記載例と入れ替える

以上

お詫びと訂正

「海外取引・会社運営等で必要な
英文定款・議事録等の作成に関する実務と書式」

本書に、下記の誤り等がございました。読者の皆様に深くお詫び申し上げますとともに、謹んで下記のとおり訂正と補足をさせていただきます。

日本加除出版株式会社

記

■209 頁〈例87〉の記載例

211 頁〈例89〉の記載例と入れ替える

以上

涉外取引・会社運営等で必要な

英文定款・議事録等の作成に関する実践と書式

株式会社・合同会社・一般社団法人等で活用する定款、議事録、決算期変更、発行可能株式総数の変更、増資、減資、合併、清算、就業規則等における日英文例及び解説

石田佳治／山北英仁　著

日本加除出版株式会社

はしがき

近年，国際化に伴い日本に外国会社が子会社を設立したり，日本企業が海外展開をしたり，外国人投資家を意識したIR展開がなされたりと，定款や議事録を英文化する機会が生じている。また，企業が社内公用語を英語にする動きもある。

英文定款は，株主や社員など定款に応じてその構成員となる者に外国人を期待する場合に必要になり，具体的には「海外の取引先から会社の概要の確認のため提出を求められた場合」，「日本法人の海外子会社を設立する場合」，「海外と合弁会社を作る場合」，「外国会社の子会社が日本で登記する場合，外国人が日本で法人を設立する場合」（対法務局：日文，対顧客：英文），「日本法人の海外支店を設立する場合」（英文）に必要となる。

また，株主総会，取締役会の英文議事録は，外資系企業，外国企業との共同事業，合併事業などの場合，株主や取締役に外国人がいる場合等に必要になり，外国会社の日本法人などでは必ず作成される。

その他，英文の規則関係は「日本の法人に外国人従業員がいる場合」，「外国で外国人を雇用する場合」に必要になる。

本書では英文で定款，議事録等の会社関係の文書を作成しなければならない場合に必要とされる英文・日本文を，実際の書式を基に解説するとともに収録している。法律文書はスタイルを理解してしまえばバリエーションの多い文芸翻訳などよりはずっと簡単であるが，法律文書であるが故に正確に作成することも求められる。

著者の石田は長年渉外司法書士協会において，契約書など英文法律・法的文書の勉強会の講師等を務めたり，様々な法律・法的文書を作成したりと，実務に密接に関わってきた。また，著者の山北は司法書士・行政書士として長年渉外事案に携わってきた。本書は両名が実際使用した文例を取りまとめ，収録したもので，実務に活用しやすい内容となっている。

英文の理解，習得には実践が不可欠である。渉外・企業法務関係では実践で研鑽を重ねることが理解への近道となる。

なお，個々の事件により明記すべき内容は異なるので，その点は文例を書き替えて活用してほしい。渉外事件を扱う司法書士，弁護士を中心とした実務家，企業，その他関係者において，広く活用していただければと願う次第である。

2020年８月

著　　者

凡　　例

本書中，法令名等の表記については，原則として省略を避けたが，括弧内においては以下の略号を用いた。

【法令等】

会社　　　会社法
労基　　　労働基準法
一般法人　一般社団法人及び一般財団法人に関する法律

【先例】

・平18・３・31民商782号民事局長通達
　→　平成18年３月31日法務省民商第782号法務省民事局長通達

目　次

〈例〉一覧

第1章　法律文書の書き方

企業内で日本語と英語の双方で作成しなければならない文書には，契約書，議事録，定款・規則・規約・規程，証明書，確認書・通知書等があるが，本章では契約書以外の議事録，定款・規則・規約・規程及び証明書，確認書・通知書等について，その性質，内容，書き方に関し総論的に述べる。

1　議事録

(1)　議事録の作成

日本文と英文の議事録の双方を作成しなければならない場合は，外資系企業，外国企業との共同事業，合併事業などの場合である。これらの場合には議事の参加者や議事録の読み手に外国人がいるので，それらの者が読んで明確に内容を把握できるよう法律的に正確な英語で書かなければならない。

議事録の例としては外資系企業や合弁事業における株主総会議事録，取締役会議事録や日本企業と外国企業の間の共同事業（共同研究，共同開発，共同販売など）の議事録などがある。

実務としては作成者が指名されて日英両文で議事録を作成し，議事録署名者の署名を経た後，必要な部数のコピーを取って出席者及び通知を受け取る者に配布し，オリジナルをファイルするという作業となる。

日本語で作成したものを英訳するよりは，最初に英文で作成したものを日本語訳する方が正確になるので，外資系企業などの社内実務ではそのように行われている。

議事録を取る会議の出席者は，通常日本人と外国人の双方であり，会議は英語で行われる。議事録を作成する者が指名され，その者が議事を聴取しつつ作成する。録音する場合もある。議事録作成者はあらかじめ議題及び出席者氏名を確認しておかなければならない。

(2)　議事録の項目

(a)　冒頭に議事録の標題が書かれる。議事録は単に「minutes of meeting」としないで，その内容が分かるようにする。「minutes of Ordinary general Shareholders meeting of ABC Corporation」（ABCコーポレーション定時株主総会議事録），「minutes of First Board of Directors meeting in 2021 Fiscal Year of ABC Corporation」（ABCコーポレーション2021事業年度第１回取締役会議事録）というような標題である。

(b)　次に会議の開催日時と開催場所を書く。開催日は曜日まで書く。時刻は開会と閉会の時刻を書く。「Date and Time: Monday, February 1,2021, From 10 a.m. to 12 a.m.（開催日時：2021年２月１日㈪午前10時-12時）というように書く。

開催場所は住所だけでなく開催場所の社名と開催室名まで書く。「Place of meeting: The First Conference Room at ABC Corporation Head Office at 2 Ginza 2-chome,Chuo-ku, Tokyo, Japan」（開催場所：東京都中央区銀座２丁目２番地 ABCコーポレーション本社第１会議室）というように書く。

(c)　次に出席者名を書く。「Attendants: Mr.James Sandars（President and CEO of ABC Corporation), Ms.Marissa Tompson（Vice President of ABC Corporation), Mr.Ichiro Kohno（Director of ABC Corporation)」（出席者：ABCコーポレーション社長兼最高執行役員ジェームス・サンダース氏，ABCコーポレーション副社長マリッサ・トンプソンソン氏，ABCコーポレーション取締役甲野一郎氏）というように，出席者の肩書は出席者の氏名の後に併記する。

株主総会のように出席者が多数の場合は大株主を数名，代表として列挙し，その後にその他の株主として記載する。株主が保有する（又は代理する。）株式数を併記する。「Attendants:Mr.Samuel Sanders owing 100,000 shares of ABC Corporation, Ms.Maririn Monroe owing 200,000 shares of ABC Corporation,Ms.Mariko Okada representing 300,000 shares of ABC Corporation,and other 10 shareholders owing in total 100,000 shares of ABC Corporation（出席者：ABCコーポレーション株式10万株を所有する株主サミュエル・サンダース氏，同20万株を所有する株主マリリン・モンロー氏，同30万株を代理する岡田まり子氏及び総計10万株を所有するその他10名の株主）というような書き方である。

(d)　次に会議の議長の選出と会議の成立を書く。株主総会であれば，通常，会社の代表取締役が議長になるから，それを書く。議長が開会を宣することも書く。「In accordance with the provision of Articles of Corporation of the Company,the President and Reprezentative Director Mr.James Sanders took the chair of the meeting and announced the opening of the meeting, starting that the number of shares of attendants formed a quorum.」（定款の定めに従って会社の代表取締役社長ジェームス・サンダース氏が議長となり，出席者の株式数が定足数に達していることを告げて，開会を宣した。）というように書く。

(e)　続いて議事進行（Proceedings）を議題（Agenda，議題が一つだけの時はAgendum）ごとに可決，否決と書いていく。「After proposed agendum was detailedly explained, the chairperson put the proposal to a vote.」（提案された議題について詳細に説明されたのち，議長は議場に対し賛否を諮った。）と書いたあと，可決の場合は，「The proposed agendum was unanimously approved.」（提案は満場一致で可決された。）又は「the proposed agendum was approved by a vote of 51 to 49.」（提案は51票対49票で可決された。）というように書けばよい。否決の場合は「The agendum was rejected against the proposal by a vote of 51 to 49.」（提案は51票対49票で否決された。）というように書く。

修正の動議があった場合は，「A motion for amendment to the proposal was made.」（原案に対し修正の動議があった。）と書いて，その修正案の賛否の結果を書く。

(f)　全ての議題が終了したら，議長の閉会宣言を，「All the agenda were voted and since there was no other business to discuss, the chairperson declared that the meeting was adjourned.」（全ての議題

が票決され，他に論議すべき案件もなかったので，議長は閉会を宣した。）というように書く。

議事録には，以上のように記載した後，議長及び議事録署名人（取締役など）の署名欄が記載される。

以上は株主総会の場合の議事録の書き方の例であるが，同じような要領で取締役会やその他の会議（委員会など）の議事録も書ける。議事録には会議名，日時，場所，出席者，議題，議事進行，決議結果などを簡潔に書くことである。

2　定款，規則，規約等の書き方

⑴　定　款

定款は会社やその他の法人において作られる基本的な規則であり，その組織，活動，構成員について述べるものである。会社の定款は会社の設立に当たって作成され，株主は定款の条項を了解して出資を行う。特定非営利法人や社団法人等の定款はそれぞれ法人の設立に当たって作成され，その社員は定款の条項を了解して社員となる。財団法人においては定款に相当するものは寄付行為とされる書面であって，これを設立しようとする者は寄付行為を了解して設立をする。財団法人には民法による財団法人のほか，宗教法人，学校法人，医療法人，社会福祉法人など特別法によって規定されているものがある。定款の記載事項には絶対的記載事項（法律上必要とされている事項）と任意的記載事項があるが，株式会社等では更に相対的記載事項（記載された時のみ効力が生ずる。）もある。

通常，定款にはその会社や法人の名称，本店所在地，事業目的，構成員，組織，運営等が絶対的記載事項として書かれるが，必要に応じその他の任意的記載事項や相対的記載事項が書かれることもある。

株主や社員など定款に応じてその構成員となる者に外国人を期待する場合は，それらの者が内容を理解できるよう定款を日本語と英語の両言語で作成しなければならない。

近時，国際化に伴いそのような場合が増加している。

(2) 規　則

就業規則，給与賞与規程，退職金規程，発明規程，知的財産規程等の会社諸規定は，使用者である会社と労働者である従業員の間の関係を律するものとして作成され運用される。就業規則は使用者が事業場における労働者の規律や労働条件について定める規則であって，使用者の恣意的な規定を制限するため，10人以上の労働者を使用する使用者は就業規則の作成とその労働行政当局への届出を義務付けられている（労基89条。なお10名以下であれ作成するのが望ましい。）。

給与賞与規程や退職金規程は，労働条件中の勤務対価の条件を労働契約に代えて表すものとして，多くの企業で作成されている。

発明規程や知的財産規程は労働者の創造する発明や知的財産を会社が必要とする場合にこれを会社が取得するための規定で，研究開発に従事する労働者に適用するために多くの会社で作成されている。

これらの規則は現在のように外国人労働者の雇用が増加してきている状況の下では日本語と英語の両言語で作成，運用しなければならないニーズが生じている。

規則の書き方としては，これらの規則は多くは使用者と労働者の権利，義務，禁止，許可の行為を規定するものであるから，英文はそのような表現で書かれる。即ち，権利表現としての「be entitled to」又は「shall have the right to」（○○することができる。），義務表現としての「shall」（○○しなければならない。），許可表現としての「may」（○○することができる。），禁止表現としての「shall not」（○○してはならない。）のいずれかで書かれる。上記に加え，権利の否定（「be not entitled to」若しくは「shall have no right to」（○○することができない。）），義務の否定（「shall not be obligated to」（○○する義務がない。）），許可の否定（「may not」（○○することができない。）），禁止の否定（「shall not be abstain from」（○○することを禁止されない。））で条項が書かれることが多い。

多くの場合，既定の条文の主語は「Employer」（使用者）や「Worker (Employee)」（労働者）といった行為者であるが，行為者の権利，義務，許可，禁止を規定した後に，その行為や目的語を主語にして受動態の表現で引き続く規定が書かれることもある。例えば「Worker is entitled to receive compensation for his or her work. Such compensation may be received beforehand at the end of the month perior to the working month.」（労働者は労働賃金を受け取る権利を有する。当該賃金は労働月の前月末に前払いで受け取ることができる。）というような書き方である。

(3)　規　約

多くの会員を有して会を運営している場合には規約が作成される。クレジットカード会員規約，百貨店友の会会員規約，レンタカー利用会員規約等の例である。いずれの会の運営者と会員を当事者とする，サービスの提供における会員の権利，義務，禁止，許可及び運営者の権利，義務，禁止，許可を文章で表現したものであるから前述した規則に類似している。

多数の会員の中には日本に居住する外国人も相当数いるから，内容の理解のために会員規約は日英両言語で書かれなければならない。実際に多くの会員規約は，日英両語で書かれ，運用されている。

第2章 株式会社

1 設 立

株式会社の設立手続には，発起設立と募集設立の２種類がある。発起設立には，会社が設立に際して発行する株式の全部を発起人が引き受けるもので（会社25条１項１号），募集設立は，設立時発行引受株式の一部を発起人が引き受け，残りにつき株式を引き受ける者を募集する（同条１項２号）方法である。

発起人は，自然人，法人のいずれでもよく，また，員数の制限はないので一人でも足りることになる。そこで，実務的には，少なくとも発起人一人がいればよいため発起設立の方法をとる設立が大多数である。募集設立の場合には，旧来手続と同様に，銀行の別段預金に株式払込金を振り込み，払込取扱銀行の払込金保管に関する証明書の発行手続を踏まなくてはならず，手続が重くなるため実務的な設立方法としては避けられている。

(1) 発起設立

発起設立手続の流れとしては，

① 発起人による定款の作成（会社26条）
② 公証人による定款の認証（会社30条）
③ 設立時発行株式に関する事項の決定（会社32条）
④ 検査役の選任・調査（会社33条）
⑤ 発起人による出資の履行（会社34条）
⑥ 設立時役員等の選任・解任（会社38条～45条）
⑦ 設立時取締役等の調査（会社46条）
⑧ 設立登記の申請（会社49条）

となるのであるが，手続を簡便にし，早急に会社を立ち上げビジネスを開始したいという要請のため，③については定款上で決定し，④については，現物出資等の変態設立事項を認めず，金銭のみとしてスキップしており，⑥についても定款上で決定し，⑦も変態設立事項に関するものでスキップするため，実務的には，①，②，⑤，⑧の手続を踏むことになる。

(2)　募集設立

募集設立手続の流れとしては，

①　発起人による定款の作成（会社26条）
②　公証人による定款の認証（会社30条）
③　設立時募集株式に関する事項の決定（会社58条）
④　設立時募集株式の申込み（会社59条）
⑤　設立時募集株式の割合（会社60条）
⑥　設立時募集株式の引受け・払込み（会社34条）
⑦　払込金の証明（会社64条）
⑧　創立総会（会社65条）
⑨　設立時取締役等の選任及び解任（会社88条～91条）
⑩　設立登記の申請（会社49条）

といった手続を踏むことになる。

例1は，パキスタン人二人が発起人となり，日本で株式会社を設立したときの定款である。彼らは日本でビジネス活動するために会社を興すのであるから，日本での在留資格が必要になる。彼らのための在留資格は，「経営・管理」の在留資格が該当する。その資格取得要件の一つに，資本金の額又は出資の総額が500万円以上であること，とあるため，多くの外国人の会社設立は資本金500万円以上となっていることが多い。

〈例１　定款〉

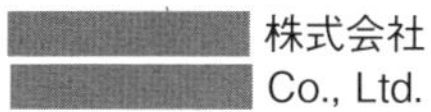

株式会社
Co., Ltd.

定　　款
ARTICLES OF INCORPORATION

第１章　総　　則
CHAPTER 1　GENERAL PROVISIONS

（商　号）
第１条　当会社は，　株式会社と称し，英文では　Co., Ltd.と表示する。
Article 1 (Trade name)
The company shall be called "　Kabushiki-Kaisha" and in English "　Co., Ltd."

（目　的）
第２条　当会社は，次の事業を営むことを目的とする。
1．不動産の売買，仲介，賃貸及び管理
2．中古自動車，中古自動車部品，付属品の仕入，販売及び輸出入
3．各種自動二輪車，原動機付自転車の仕入，販売及び輸出入
4．食料品の販売及び輸出入
5．語学教室の運営
6．食料品店及びレストランの経営
7．前各号に付帯する一切の業務

Article 2 (Purposes)
Purposes of the company shall be to engage in the following businesses:
1. Management, lease, brokerage and sale of real estate.
2. Purchase, sale, import and export of used automobiles and those parts.
3. Purchase, sale, import and export of various two-wheeled motor vehicles.
4. Purchase, sale, import and export of foods.
5. Operation of language school.
6. Operation of grocery shop and restaurant.
7. Any and all businesses incidental to the foregoing.

（本店の所在地）
第３条　当会社は，本店を埼玉県　市に置く。
Article 3 (Location of head office)
The company shall have its head office in　-shi, Saitama.

（公告方法）
第４条　当会社の公告は，官報に掲載してする。

Article 4 (Method of public notices)
Public notices of the company shall be carried in Official Gazette (Kampo) published by the Japanese Government.

第2章 株　　式
CHAPTER 2 SHARES

(発行可能株式総数)
第5条 当会社の発行可能株式総数は，1万株とする。
Article 5 (Total number of shares authorized to be issued)
The total number of shares authorized to be issued by the Company shall be 10,000 shares.

(株券の不発行)
第6条 当会社の株式については，株券を発行しない。
Article 6 (Non-issuance of share certificate)
Share certificate of the company shall not be issued.

(株式の譲渡制限)
第7条 当会社の発行する株式を譲渡によって取得するには，株主総会の承認を要する。
Article 7 (Restriction on transfer of shares)
Transfers of shares of the company shall be subject to approval by the shareholders meeting.

(基準日)
第8条 当会社は，毎事業年度末日の最終の株主名簿に記載された議決権を有する株主をもって，その事業年度の定時株主総会において権利を行使することができる株主とする。
2 前項のほか，株主又は登録株式質権者として権利を行使することができる者を確定するため必要があるときは，取締役は，臨時に基準日を定めることができる。ただし，この場合には，その日を2週間前までに公告するものとする。
Article 8 (Standard date)
The company shall deem shareholders who possess voting rights and registered on the final shareholders record book at the end of every financial year to be the shareholders who may exercise their rights at the annual general meeting of shareholders for such term.
2. Other than the preceding paragraph, when it is necessary to determine shareholders and registered pledgees who may exercise their rights, directors may set the record date on a temporary basis. In such a case, it shall give public notice of such date no later than two weeks prior to such date.

第3章 株 主 総 会
CHAPTER 3 GENERAL MEETING OF SHAREHOLDERS

(株主総会の招集)
第9条 当会社の定時株主総会は，毎事業年度末日の翌日から3か月以内に招集し，臨時株主総会は，必要に応じて招集する。
2 株主総会は，法令に別段の定めがある場合を除くほか，社長がこれを招集する。
3 株主総会を招集するには，会日より3日前までに，議決権を有する各株主に対して招集通知を発するものとする。ただし，招集通知は，書面ですることを要しない。
Article 9 (Convening of shareholders meeting)
The annual general meeting of shareholders of the company shall be convened within three (3) months from the immediately succeeding day of the last day of each financial year, and an extraordinary general meeting shall be convened whenever necessary.
2. Unless otherwise provided by laws and regulations, the president shall convene a general

meeting of shareholders.
3. In a case of convening a general meeting of shareholders, the notice shall be given to the shareholders who possess voting rights no later than three (3) days prior to the day of meeting, however, the notice is not necessary to be in a written form.

（議長及び決議の方法）
第10条　株主総会は，社長が議長となる。
2　株主総会の決議は，法令又は定款に別段の定めがある場合を除き，出席した議決権を行使することができる株主の議決権の過半数をもって行う。
Article 10 (Chairmanship and method of resolution)
The president shall assume chairmanship at a general meeting of shareholders.
2 Unless otherwise provided by laws and regulations or the articles of incorporation, resolution at the ordinary shareholders meeting shall be made by a majority of the votes of the shareholders present at such meeting who possess the voting rights.

（株主総会議事録）
第11条　株主総会の議事については，議事録を作成し，議事の経過の要領及び結果その他法令で定める事項を記載して株主総会の日から10年間本店に備え置くものとする。
Article 11 (Minutes of shareholders meeting)
The minutes of shareholders meeting shall be made stating a summary of proceeding and the result and other matters specified by law of the meeting, and shall be kept for 10 years in the head office of the company.

第４章　取締役及び代表取締役
CHAPTER 4　DIRECTORS AND REPRESENTATIVE DIRECTOR

（取締役の定員）
第12条　当会社には，１名以上の取締役を置く。
Article 12 (Number of directors)
The company shall have no less than one (1) director.

（取締役の選任方法）
第13条　当会社の取締役を選任する株主総会の決議は，議決権を行使することができる株主の議決権の３分の１以上を有する株主が出席し，出席した当該株主の議決権の過半数をもって行う。
2　前項の選任については，累積投票の方法によらない。
Article 13 (Method of election of directors)
Resolutions for the election of directors shall be made by the majority of the votes of the shareholders present at the meeting where the shareholders holding a majority of one third or more of the votes of the shareholders entitled to exercise their votes at such shareholders meeting are present.
2. The election in the preceding paragraph shall not be by cumulative voting.

（取締役の任期）
第14条　取締役の任期は，選任後10年以内に終了する事業年度のうち最終のものに関する定時株主総会の終結の時までとする。
2　増員又は補欠により選任された取締役の任期は，前任者又は他の在任取締役の任期の残任期間と同一とする。
Article 14 (Term of office of directors)
The term of office of directors shall be until the close of the annual general meeting of shareholders for the financial year last to come within 10 years from their selection of office.
2. The term of office of a director elected to fill a vacancy or to increase the number of directors, shall be equal to the remaining term of office of the predecessor or the other

directors currently in office.

（代表取締役及び社長）
第15条　当会社に取締役を２名以上置く場合には，取締役の互選により代表取締役１名以上を定め，そのうち１名を社長とする。
２　当会社に置く取締役が１名の場合には，その取締役を社長とする。
３　社長は，当会社を代表して，会社の業務を執行する。
Article 15 (Representative Director and President)
In the event that there are two or more directors, the company shall have one or more representative directors by the mutual vote of directors and representative director shall be president.
2. In the event that there is one (1) director, the director shall be president.
3. President shall represent the company and executes the operations.

第５章　計　　算
CHAPTER 5　ACCOUNTS

（事業年度）
第16条　当会社の事業年度は，毎年４月１日から翌年３月31日までの年１期とする。
Article 16 (Financial year)
The financial year of the company shall commence on April 1st every year and end on March 31st of the next year.

（剰余金の配当）
第17条　剰余金の配当は，毎事業年度末日現在における最終の株主名簿に記載された株主又は登録株式質権者に対して行う。
Article 17 (Dividends of surplus)
Dividends of surplus shall be paid to shareholders or registered pledgees appearing in the shareholders' register as of the last day of each financial year.

第６章　附　　則
CHAPTER 6　SUPPLEMENTAL PROVISIONS

（設立に際して発行する株式の数）
第18条　当会社の設立時発行株式の数は１千株とし，その払込価額は１株につき金５千円とする。
Article 18 (The total number of shares to be issued upon incorporation of company) The total number of shares to be issued upon incorporation of the company shall be 1,000 shares, and the paid-in value per share is 5,000 yen.

（設立に際して出資される財産の価額及び資本金）
第19条　当会社の設立に際して出資される財産の価額は，金500万円とする。
２　当会社の成立後の資本金の額は，金500万円とする。
Article 19 (Value of asset funded and capital upon incorporation of company)
The value of asset funded upon incorporation of company is 5,000,000 yen.
2. The company's capital is 5,000,000 yen at incorporation.

（発起人の名称，住所，割当てを受ける株式数及びその払込金額）
第20条　当会社の発起人の名称，住所，割当てを受ける株式の数及びその払込金額は，次のとおりである。

パキスタン，アボッターバード，マンディアン，ジナッハバード，ナンバー■ストリート，■

600株　金3,000,000円
東京都港区麻布　目　番　号
400株　金2,000,000円
Article 20 (Promoter's name, address, number of subscribed shares and its value)
The name of, address of, the number of shares subscribed by, the promoter is as follows:
House NO.　Street NO　Jinnahabad, Mandian, Abbottabad, Pakistan

600 shares, 3,000,000 yen
, Azabu -chome, Minato-ku, Tokyo

400 shares, 2,000,000 yen

(設立時取締役及び設立時代表取締役)
第22条　当会社の設立時取締役及び設立時代表取締役は，次のとおりである。
設立時取締役
設立時代表取締役
Article 22 (Director and Representative Director at incorporation)
Director at incorporation:
Representative Director at incorporation:

(設立当初の本店所在場所)
第23条　当会社の設立当初の本店は，埼玉県　市　番地　に置く。
Article 23 (Address of the head office)
The address of the head office at incorporation is -, , -shi, Saitama.

(定款に定めのない事項)
第24条　本定款に定めのない事項については，会社法その他の法令の定めるところによる。
Article 24 (Any matter not stipulated herein)
Any matter not stipulated herein shall be settled by the Japan company law or other applicable laws and regulations.

以上，　株式会社設立のため，発起人　及び　の定款作成代理人である司法書士　は，電磁的記録である本定款を作成し，これに電子署名をする。
For the incorporation of　Co., Ltd., the articles of incorporation are prepared in the form of electromagnetic record and　, Shiho-shoshi, affixes his digital signature thereto as the agent of the promoter,　and　.

年８月９日
Date: August 9,

発起人
発起人
Promoter:
Promoter:

上記発起人の定款作成代理人　司法書士
Agent of the above　Shiho-shoshi

〈例2 委任状（公証人に対する定款認証についての委任状）〉

Signature

委任状
Power of Attorney

東京都■区■二丁目■番■号■F
司法書士 ■
■rd Floor, ■ Building, ■, ■chome, ■ku, Tokyo
■, Shihoshoshi

私は，上記の者を代理人と定め，次の権限を委任する。
I hereby appoint the person mentioned above as my attorney to perform the following:

1. ■株式会社の設立に際し，添付のとおり電磁的記録であるその原始定款を作成する手続に関する一切の件
To take any and all procedures necessary to make the original Articles of Incorporation of ■ Co., Ltd. in the form of electromagnetic record as attached.

2. 前号記載の原始定款につき公証人の認証を受ける行為及び定款謄本の交付請求及び受領に関する一切の件
To take any and all necessary actions to obtain authentication of a notary to the original Articles of Incorporation in the preceding clause and to request and receive a certified copy of the Articles of Incorporation.

■ 月 日
, ■

発起人 パキスタン，アボッターバード，マンディアン，■，ナンバー■ストリート，ハウスナンバー■
■
Promoter : House NO.■, Street NO■, ■, Mandian, Abbottabad, Pakistan ■

Signature

次頁に掲載する**例3**は，パキスタン人の身元（住所，氏名，生年月日）を宣誓し，当該国官憲となるパキスタン公証人が認証した書面である。日本の印鑑証明書に代替することになるものである。日本の印鑑証明書は，本人を印鑑により間接証明するものであるが，公証人による本人の署名の認証は，公証人の面前での本人の署名であるので直接証明としてより証明力が高いものと思われる。

なお，この宣誓供述書は，定款認証時の委任状，取締役の就任承諾書及び会社印鑑届出書に添付する印鑑証明書に代替する証明書として使用することができる。

〈例3　パキスタン公証人認証の宣誓供述書〉

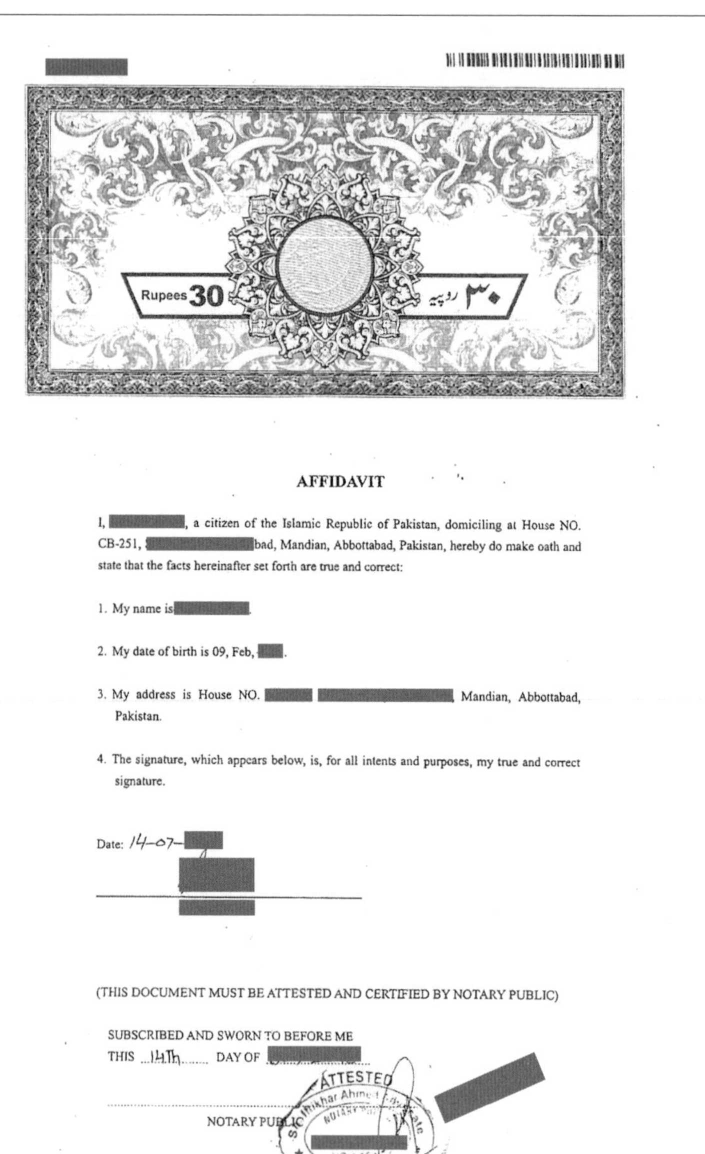

Rupees 30 روپیہ ۳۰

AFFIDAVIT

I, [redacted], a citizen of the Islamic Republic of Pakistan, domiciling at House NO. CB-251, [redacted]bad, Mandian, Abbottabad, Pakistan, hereby do make oath and state that the facts hereinafter set forth are true and correct:

1. My name is [redacted].

2. My date of birth is 09, Feb, [redacted].

3. My address is House NO. [redacted] [redacted], Mandian, Abbottabad, Pakistan.

4. The signature, which appears below, is, for all intents and purposes, my true and correct signature.

Date: 14-07-[redacted]

(THIS DOCUMENT MUST BE ATTESTED AND CERTIFIED BY NOTARY PUBLIC)

SUBSCRIBED AND SWORN TO BEFORE ME
THIS ...14Th...... DAY OF [redacted]

ATTESTED

NOTARY PUBLIC

〈例４　払込証明書〉

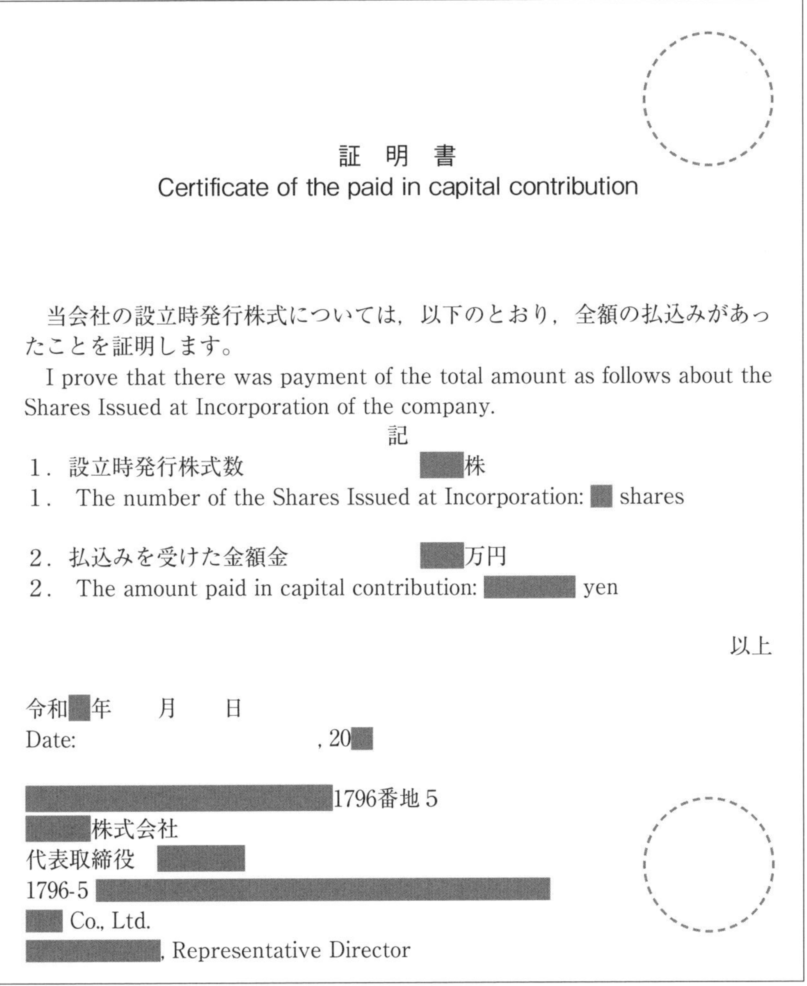

証 明 書
Certificate of the paid in capital contribution

当会社の設立時発行株式については，以下のとおり，全額の払込みがあったことを証明します。
I prove that there was payment of the total amount as follows about the Shares Issued at Incorporation of the company.

記

1．設立時発行株式数　　　■■株
1．The number of the Shares Issued at Incorporation: ■ shares

2．払込みを受けた金額金　　　■■万円
2．The amount paid in capital contribution: ■■■■ yen

以上

令和■年　月　日
Date:　　　, 20■

■■■■1796番地５
■■株式会社
代表取締役　■■■
1796-5 ■■■■
■■ Co., Ltd.
■■■■, Representative Director

発起人等が非居住者（外国人等日本の居住していない者）による場合に，日本に居住している発起人や取締役就任予定者が不在のときは，金融機関の別段預金を利用することになる。**例５**はその場合の金融機関に対する委託書の書式である。

〈例５　株式払込事務取扱委託書〉

Appointment as Agent for Handling of Operation
pertaining to the Payment for the Shares
in Relation to Incorporation without Public Offering

発起設立時の株式払込事務取扱委託書

Date（日付）：

To: The ████████ Banking Corporation Limited
████銀行　御中

Address（所在地）：
Name of Company（委託者）：
Name of Representative Incorporator（代表者名）：
Signature of Representative Incorporator（代表者サイン）：

Dear Sirs,

We hereby appoint your bank（"Bank"）as the agent for handling of following operation pertaining to the shares of our company.
We herein confirm that we shall remain fully responsible for any events arising from the matters handled by the Bank, as far as the Bank complies with its designated internal procedures and deems its handling as justifiable.

下記の要領により，当社株式に関する事務の取扱を貴行に委託します。尚，貴行所定の取扱に従い，正当と認めて取り扱った事項について事故が生じた場合には，全て当社において処理します。

Matters to be Handled 委託事項	To receive the capital funds to be paid-in in relation to incorporation of kabushiki kaisha（K.K.）without public offering 株式会社の発起設立に関する払込金受入事務
Total number of Shares issued 発行株式の総数	Shares 株
Paid-in Amount per Share １株の払込金額	JPY
Total Paid-in Amount 払込金額の総額	JPY
Time Limit for Payment 払込期限	/　/　(dd/mm/yyyy) 平成　年　月　日　まで

Issuance of Certificate 証明書の発行	The Bank shall issue and deliver, without delay, 2 (two) copies of "Certificate of Receipt of Capital Funds" ("Haraikomikin Ukeire Shoumeisho") as of .... (dd/mm/yyyy) (on or after the last day of Time Limit for Payment). 「払込金受入証明書」２通を平成年月日付（払込期限の最終日またはそれ以後の日）をもって作成し，速やかに当社に交付する。
Transfer of the Paid-in Amount 株式払込金の振替	Transfer of the funds to our company's account shall be made, in principle, on the same day of the payment 当社への振替は，原則として払込が行われた日の当日とする。
Handling Charges and Out-of-Pocket Expenses 取扱手数料および実費	
Attachments 添付書類	(1) Articles of Incorporation (copy) 定款（写） (2) Certificate of Personal Seal of the Representative Incorporator, or any document equivalent thereto 発起人代表個人の印鑑証明書またはそれと同等の書類 (3) Minutes of Incorporators' Meeting (copy) 発起人会議事録（写） (4) Schedule of Shares Underwritten (specifying the names of incorporators, paid-in amount per share, the number and the amount of paid-in shares) 引受株数明細票（発起人名，１株の払込金額，払込株数および払込金額を記載したもの）
Remarks 備考	

〈例6 取締役及び代表取締役の就任承諾書〉

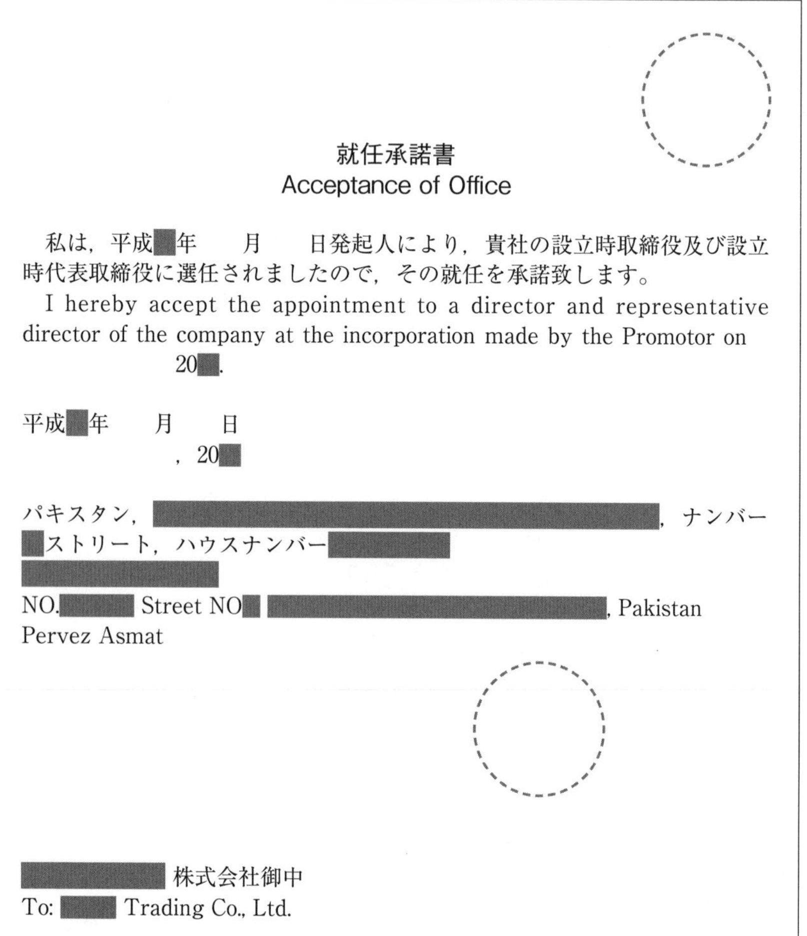

就任承諾書
Acceptance of Office

私は，平成■年　月　日発起人により，貴社の設立時取締役及び設立時代表取締役に選任されましたので，その就任を承諾致します。

I hereby accept the appointment to a director and representative director of the company at the incorporation made by the Promotor on 　　　　20■.

平成■年　月　日
　　　　, 20■

パキスタン，■■■，ナンバー■ストリート，ハウスナンバー■■■
■■■
NO.■ Street NO■ ■■■, Pakistan
Pervez Asmat

■■■株式会社御中
To: ■■■ Trading Co., Ltd.

〈例７　設立登記申請のための委任状〉

委 任 状

Power of Attorney

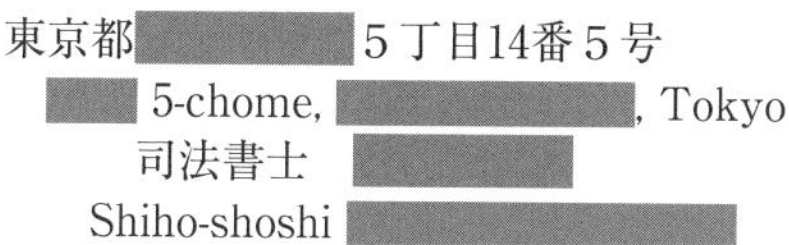

東京都　　　５丁目14番５号

　　5-chome, 　　　, Tokyo

司法書士

Shiho-shoshi

私は，上記の者を代理人と定め，次の権限を委任する。

I hereby appoint the person mentioned above as my attorney-in-fact and agent and authorize him to perform the following:

1．当会社の設立登記の申請に関する一切の件

1．Handle all matters relating to the application for company recording of the incorporation of 　　　 inc.

2．原本還付の請求並びに受領に関する件

2．Request a return of original documents and receive them.

平成　　年　　月　　日

,

東京都　　　四丁目５番４号

　　　２階

株式会社

代表取締役

2F, 　　　 Bldg.,

5-4, 4-chome, 　　　, Tokyo

　　　 inc.

Representative Director

例8は厚生労働省のモデル就業規則に労働基準法改正を反映し加筆したものである。

〈例8－1　就業規則（モデル）〉

第1章　総則
（目的）
第1条　この就業規則（以下「規則」という。）は，労働基準法（以下「労基法」という。）第89条に基づき，__________株式会社の労働者の就業に関する事項を定めるものである。
2　この規則に定めた事項のほか，就業に関する事項については，労基法その他の法令の定めによる。
（適用範囲）
第2条　この規則は，__________株式会社の労働者に適用する。
2　パートタイム労働者の就業に関する事項については，別に定めるところによる。
3　前項については，別に定める規則に定めのない事項は，この規則を適用する。
（規則の遵守）
第3条　会社は，この規則に定める労働条件により，労働者に就業させる義務を負う。また，労働者は，この規則を遵守しなければならない。

第2章　採用，異動等
（採用手続）
第4条　会社は，入社を希望する者の中から選考試験を行い，これに合格した者を採用する。
（採用時の提出書類）
第5条　労働者として採用された者は，採用された日から____週間以内に次の書類を提出しなければならない。
①　住民票記載事項証明書
②　自動車運転免許証の写し（ただし，自動車運転免許証を有する場合に限る。）
③　資格証明書の写し（ただし，何らかの資格証明書を有する場合に限る。）
④　その他会社が指定するもの
2　前項の定めにより提出した書類の記載事項に変更を生じたときは，速やかに書面で会社に変更事項を届け出なければならない。
（試用期間）
第6条　労働者として新たに採用した者については，採用した日から____か月間を試用期間とする。
2　前項について，会社が特に認めたときは，使用期間を短縮し，又は設けないことがある。

3 試用期間中に労働者として不適格と認めた者は，解雇することがある。ただし，入社後14日を経過した者については，第49第２項に定める手続によって行う。

4 試用期間は，勤続年数に通算する。

（労働条件の明示）

第７条 会社は，労働者を採用するとき，採用時の賃金，就業場所，従事する業務，労働時間，休日，その他の労働条件を記した労働条件通知書及びこの規則を交付して労働条件を明示するものとする。

（人事異動）

第８条 会社は，業務上必要がある場合に，労働者に対して就業する場所及び従事する業務の変更を命ずることがある。

2 会社は，業務上必要がある場合に，労働者を在籍のまま関係会社へ出向させることがある。

3 前２項の場合，労働者は正当な理由なくこれを拒むことはできない。

（休職）

第９条 労働者が，次のいずれかに該当するときは，所定の期間休職とする。

① 業務外の傷病による欠勤が____か月を超え，なお療養を継続する必要があるため勤務できないとき ____年以内

② 前号のほか，特別な事情があり休職させることが適当と認められるとき 必要な期間

2 休職期間中に休職事由が消滅したときは，原則として元の職務に復帰させる。ただし，元の職務に復帰させることが困難又は不適当な場合には，他の職務に就かせることがある。

3 第１項第１号により休職し，休職期間が満了してもなお傷病が治癒せず就業が困難な場合は，休職期間の満了をもって退職とする。

第３章 服務規律

（服務）

第10条 労働者は，職務上の責任を自覚し，誠実に職務を遂行するとともに，会社の指示命令に従い，職務能率の向上及び職場秩序の維持に努めなければならない。

（遵守事項）

第11条 労働者は，以下の事項を守らなければならない。

① 許可なく職務以外の目的で会社の施設，物品等を使用しないこと。

② 職務に関連して自己の利益を図り，又は他より不当に金品を借用し，若しくは贈与を受ける等不正な行為を行わないこと。

③ 勤務中は職務に専念し，正当な理由なく勤務場所を離れないこと。

④ 会社の名誉や信用を損なう行為をしないこと。

⑤ 在職中及び退職後においても，業務上知り得た会社，取引先等の機密を漏洩しないこと。

⑥ 酒気を帯びて就業しないこと。
⑦ その他労働者としてふさわしくない行為をしないこと。

（職場のパワーハラスメントの禁止）

第12条 職務上の地位や人間関係などの職場内の優越的な関係を背景とした，業務上必要かつ相当な範囲を超えた言動により，他の労働者の就業環境を害するようなことをしてはならない。

（セクシュアルハラスメントの禁止）

第13条 性的言動により，他の労働者に不利益や不快感を与えたり，就業環境を害するようなことをしてはならない。

（個人情報保護）

第14条 労働者は，会社及び取引先等に関する情報の管理に十分注意を払うとともに，自らの業務に関係のない情報を不当に取得してはならない。

2 労働者は，職場又は職種を異動あるいは退職するに際して，自らが管理していた会社及び取引先等に関するデータ・情報書類等を速やかに返却しなければならない。

（始業及び終業時刻の記録）

第15条 労働者は，始業及び終業時にタイムカードを自ら打刻し，始業及び終業の時刻を記録しなければならない。

（遅刻，早退，欠勤等）

第16条 労働者は遅刻，早退若しくは欠勤をし，又は勤務時間中に私用で事業場から外出する際は，事前に直属上司に対し申し出るとともに，承認を受けなければならない。ただし，やむを得ない理由で事前に申し出ることができなかった場合は，事後に速やかに届出をし，承認を得なければならない。

2 前項の場合は，第 条に定めるところにより，原則として不就労分に対応する賃金は控除する。

3 傷病のため継続して３日以上欠勤するときは，医師の診断書を提出しなければならない。

第４章 労働時間，休憩及び休日

（労働時間及び休憩時間）

第17条 労働時間は，１週間については40時間，１日については８時間とする。

2 始業・終業の時刻及び休憩時間は，次のとおりとする。ただし，業務の都合その他やむを得ない事情により，これらを繰り上げ，又は繰り下げることがある。この場合，前日までに労働者に通知する。

始業・終業時刻	休憩時間
始業 午前９時00分	12時00分から午後１時00分まで
終業 午後６時00分	

（休日）

第18条　休日は，次のとおりとする。
① 土曜日及び日曜日
② 国民の祝日（日曜日と重なったときは翌日）
③ 年末年始（12月29日～1月3日）
④ 夏季休日（8月14日～8月16日）
2　業務の都合により会社が必要と認める場合は，あらかじめ前項の休日を他の日と振り替えることがある。

（時間外及び休日労働等）

第19条　業務の都合により，第17条の所定労働時間を超え，又は第18条の所定休日に労働させることがある。
2　前項の場合，法定労働時間を超える労働又は法定休日における労働については，あらかじめ会社は労働者の過半数代表者と書面による労使協定を締結するとともに，これを所轄の労働基準監督署長に届け出るものとする。
3　妊娠中の女性，産後1年を経過しない女性労働者（以下「妊産婦」という）であって請求した者及び18歳未満の者については，第2項による時間外労働又は休日若しくは深夜（午後10時から午前5時まで）労働に従事させない。
4　災害その他避けることのできない事由によって臨時の必要がある場合には，第1項から前項までの制限を超えて，所定労働時間外又は休日に労働させることがある。ただし，この場合であっても，請求のあった妊産婦については，所定労働時間外労働又は休日労働に従事させない。

第5章　休暇等

（年次有給休暇）

第20条　採用日から6か月間継続勤務し，所定労働日の8割以上出勤した労働者に対しては，10日の年次有給休暇を与える。その後1年間継続勤務するごとに，当該1年間において所定労働日の8割以上出勤した労働者に対しては，下の表のとおり勤続期間に応じた日数の年次有給休暇を与える。

勤続期間	6か月	1年 6か月	2年 6か月	3年 6か月	4年 6か月	5年 6か月	6年 6か月以上
付与日数	10日	11日	12日	14日	16日	18日	20日

2　前項の規定にかかわらず，週所定労働時間30時間未満であり，かつ，週所定労働日数が4日以下（週以外の期間によって所定労働日数を定める労働者については年間所定労働日数が216日以下）の労働者に対しては，下の表のとおり所定労働日数及び勤続期間に応じた日数の年次有給休暇を与える。

週所定労働日数	1年間の所定労働日数	勤続期間						
		6か月	1年6か月	2年6か月	3年6か月	4年6か月	5年6か月	6年6か月以上
4日	169日～216日	7日	8日	9日	10日	12日	13日	15日
3日	121日～168日	5日	6日	6日	8日	9日	10日	11日
2日	73日～120日	3日	4日	4日	5日	6日	6日	7日
1日	48日～ 72日	1日	2日	2日	2日	3日	3日	3日

3 第1項又は第2項の年次有給休暇は，労働者があらかじめ請求する時季に取得させる。ただし，労働者が請求した時季に年次有給休暇を取得させることが事業の正常な運営を妨げる場合は，他の時季に取得させることがある。

4 前項の規定にかかわらず，労働者代表との書面による協定により，各労働者の有する年次有給休暇日数のうち5日を超える部分について，あらかじめ時季を指定して取得させることがある。

5 第1項及び第2項の出勤率の算定に当たっては，下記の期間については出勤したものとして取り扱う。
① 年次有給休暇を取得した期間
② 産前産後の休業期間
③ 育児・介護休業法に基づく育児休業及び介護休業した期間
④ 業務上の負傷又は疾病により療養のために休業した期間

6 付与日から1年以内に取得しなかった年次有給休暇は，付与日から2年以内に限り繰り越して取得することができる。

7 前項について，繰り越された年次有給休暇とその後付与された年次有給休暇のいずれも取得できる場合には，繰り越された年次有給休暇から取得させる。

8 会社は，毎月の賃金計算締切日における年次有給休暇の残日数を，当該賃金の支払明細書に記載して各労働者に通知する。

（年次有給休暇の時間単位での付与）

第21条 労働者代表との書面による協定に基づき，前条の年次有給休暇の日数のうち，1年について5日の範囲で次により時間単位の年次有給休暇（以下「時間単位年休」という。）を付与する。

⑴ 時間単位年休付与の対象者は，すべての労働者とする。
⑵ 時間単位年休を取得する場合の，1日の年次有給休暇に相当する時間数は，以下のとおりとする。
① 所定労働時間が5　時間を超え6　時間以下の者…6　時間
② 所定労働時間が6　時間を超え7　時間以下の者…7　時間
③ 所定労働時間が7　時間を超え8　時間以下の者…8　時間
⑶ 時間単位年休は1時間単位で付与する。
⑷ 本条の時間単位年休に支払われる賃金額は，所定労働時間労働した場合に支払われる通常の賃金の1時間当たりの額に，取得した時間単位年

休の時間数を乗じた額とする。

(5)　上記以外の事項については，前条の年次有給休暇と同様とする。

（産前産後の休業）

第22条　6週間（多胎妊娠の場合は14週間）以内に出産予定の女性労働者から請求があったときは，休業させる。

2　産後8週間を経過していない女性労働者は，就業させない。

3　前項の規定にかかわらず，産後6週間を経過した女性労働者から請求があった場合は，その者について医師が支障ないと認めた業務に就かせることがある。

（母性健康管理の措置）

第23条　妊娠中又は出産後1年を経過しない女性労働者から，所定労働時間内に，母子保健法（昭和40年法律第141号）に基づく保健指導又は健康診査を受けるために申出があったときは，次の範囲で時間内通院を認める。

①　産前の場合

妊娠23週まで………………4週に1回

妊娠24週から35週まで……2週に1回

妊娠36週から出産まで……1週に1回

ただし，医師又は助産師（以下「医師等」という。）がこれと異なる指示をしたときには，その指示により必要な時間

②　産後（1年以内）の場合

医師等の指示により必要な時間

2　妊娠中又は出産後1年を経過しない女性労働者から，保健指導又は健康診査に基づき勤務時間等について医師等の指導を受けた旨申出があった場合，次の措置を講ずる。

①　妊娠中の通勤緩和措置として，通勤時の混雑を避けるよう指導された場合は，原則として____時間の勤務時間の短縮又は____時間以内の時差出勤を認める。

②　妊娠中の休憩時間について指導された場合は，適宜休憩時間の延長や休憩の回数を増やす。

③　妊娠中又は出産後の女性労働者が，その症状等に関して指導された場合は，医師等の指導事項を遵守するための作業の軽減や勤務時間の短縮，休業等の措置をとる。

（育児時間及び生理休暇）

第24条　1歳に満たない子を養育する女性労働者から請求があったときは，休憩時間のほか1日について2回，1回について30分の育児時間を与える。

2　生理日の就業が著しく困難な女性労働者から請求があったときは，必要な期間休暇を与える。

（育児・介護休業，子の看護休暇等）

第25条　労働者のうち必要のある者は，育児・介護休業法に基づく育児休業，介護休業，子の看護休暇，介護休暇，育児・介護のための所定外労働，時間外労働及び深夜業の制限並びに所定労働時間の短縮措置等（以下「育児・介護休業等」という。）の適用を受けることができる。

2　育児・介護休業等の取扱いについては，「育児・介護休業等に関する規則」で定める。

（慶弔休暇）

第26条　労働者が申請した場合は，次のとおり慶弔休暇を与える。

① 本人が結婚したとき　7日
② 妻が出産したとき　5日
③ 配偶者，子又は父母が死亡したとき　5日
④ 兄弟姉妹，祖父母，配偶者の父母又は兄弟姉妹が死亡したとき　3日

（病気休暇）

第27条　労働者が私的な負傷又は疾病のため療養する必要があり，その勤務しないことがやむを得ないと認められる場合に，病気休暇を3日与える。

（裁判員等のための休暇）

第28条　労働者が裁判員若しくは補充裁判員となった場合又は裁判員候補者となった場合には，次のとおり休暇を与える。

① 裁判員又は補充裁判員となった場合　必要な日数
② 裁判員候補者となった場合　必要な時間

第6章　賃金

（賃金の構成）

第29条　賃金の構成は，次のとおりとする。

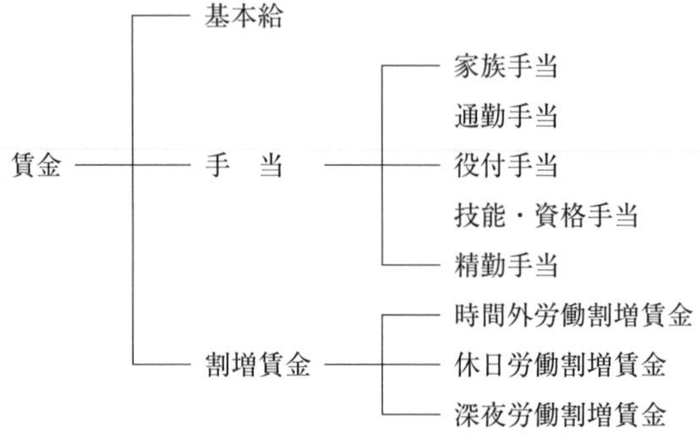

（基本給）

第30条　基本給は，本人の職務内容，技能，勤務成績，年齢等を考慮して各人別に決定する。

（家族手当）

第31条　家族手当は，次の家族を扶養している労働者に対し支給する。

① 18歳未満の子
　1人につき　月額　____円
② 65歳以上の父母
　1人につき　月額　____円

（通勤手当）

第32条 通勤手当は，月額______円までの範囲内において，通勤に要する実費に相当する額を支給する。

（役付手当）

第33条 役付手当は，以下の職位にある者に対し支給する。

部長 月額 ____円
課長 月額 ____円
係長 月額 ____円

2 昇格によるときは，発令日の属する賃金月から支給する。この場合，当該賃金月においてそれまで属していた役付手当は支給しない。

3 降格によるときは，発令日の属する賃金月の次の賃金月から支給する。

（割増賃金）

第34条 時間外労働に対する割増賃金は，次の割増賃金率に基づき，次項の計算方法により支給する。

(1) 1か月の時間外労働の時間数に応じた割増賃金率は，次のとおりとする。この場合の1か月は毎月____日を起算日とする。

① 時間外労働45時間以下……25%
② 時間外労働45時間超～60時間以下……35%
③ 時間外労働60時間超……50%
④ ③の時間外労働のうち代替休暇を取得した時間……35%（残り15%の割増賃金は代替休暇に充当する。）

(2) 1年間の時間外労働の時間数が360時間を超えた部分については，40%とする。この場合の1年は毎年____月____日を起算日とする。

(3) 時間外労働に対する割増賃金の計算において，上記(1)及び(2)のいずれにも該当する時間外労働の時間数については，いずれか高い率で計算することとする。

2 割増賃金は，次の算式により計算して支給する。

① 時間外労働の割増賃金

（時間外労働が1か月45時間以下の部分）

$$\frac{\text{基本給}+\text{役付手当}+\text{技能・資格手当}+\text{精勤手当}}{\text{1か月の平均所定労働時間数}}\times 1.25\times \text{時間外労働の時間数}$$

（時間外労働が1か月45時間超～60時間以下の部分）

$$\frac{\text{基本給}+\text{役付手当}+\text{技能・資格手当}+\text{精勤手当}}{\text{1か月の平均所定労働時間数}}\times 1.35\times \text{時間外労働の時間数}$$

（時間外労働が1か月60時間を超える部分）

$$\frac{\text{基本給}+\text{役付手当}+\text{技能・資格手当}+\text{精勤手当}}{\text{1か月の平均所定労働時間数}}\times 1.50\times \text{時間外労働の時間数}$$

（時間外労働が1年360時間を超える部分）

$$\frac{\text{基本給}+\text{役付手当}+\text{技能・資格手当}+\text{精勤手当}}{\text{1か月の平均所定労働時間数}}\times 1.40\times \text{時間外労働の時間数}$$

② 休日労働の割増賃金（法定休日に労働させた場合）

$$\frac{\text{基本給}+\text{役付手当}+\text{技能・資格手当}+\text{精勤手当}}{\text{1か月の平均所定労働時間数}}\times 1.35\times\text{休日労働の時間数}$$

③ 深夜労働の割増賃金（午後10時から午前5時までの間に労働させた場合）

$$\frac{\text{基本給}+\text{役付手当}+\text{技能・資格手当}+\text{精勤手当}}{\text{1か月の平均所定労働時間数}}\times 0.25\times\text{深夜労働の時間数}$$

（休暇等の賃金）

第35条 年次有給休暇の期間は，所定労働時間労働したときに支払われる通常の賃金を支払う。

2 産前産後の休業期間，育児時間，生理休暇，母性健康管理のための休暇，育児・介護休業法に基づく育児休業期間，介護休業期間，子の看護休暇期間及び介護休暇期間，慶弔休暇，病気休暇，裁判員等のための休暇の期間は，無給 ／ 通常の賃金を支払うこと とする。

3 第9条に定める休職期間中は，原則として賃金を支給しない（____か月までは____割を支給する。

（臨時休業の賃金）

第36条 会社側の都合により，所定労働日に労働者を休業させた場合は，休業1日につき労基法第12条に規定する平均賃金の6割を支給する。この場合において，1日のうちの一部を休業させた場合にあっては，その日の賃金については労基法第26条に定めるところにより，平均賃金の6割に相当する賃金を保障する

（欠勤等の扱い）

第37条 欠勤，遅刻，早退及び私用外出については，基本給から当該日数又は時間分の賃金を控除する。

2 前項の場合，控除すべき賃金の1時間あたりの金額の計算は以下のとおりとする。

(1) 月給の場合
基本給÷1か月平均所定労働時間数

(2) 日給の場合
基本給÷1日の所定労働時間数

（賃金の計算期間及び支払日）

第38条 賃金は，毎月____日に締め切って計算し，翌月____日に支払う。ただし，支払日が休日に当たる場合は，その前日に繰り上げて支払う。

2 前項の計算期間の中途で採用された労働者又は退職した労働者については，月額の賃金は当該計算期間の所定労働日数を基準に日割計算して支払う。

（賃金の支払と控除）

第39条 賃金は，労働者に対し，通貨で直接その全額を支払う。

2 前項について，労働者が同意した場合は，労働者本人の指定する金融機関の預貯金口座又は証券総合口座へ振込により賃金を支払う。

3　次に掲げるものは，賃金から控除する。
①　源泉所得税
②　住民税
③　健康保険，厚生年金保険及び雇用保険の保険料の被保険者負担分
④　労働者代表との書面による協定により賃金から控除することとし1社宅入居料，財形貯蓄の積立金及び組合費

（賃金の非常時払い）

第40条　労働者又はその収入によって生計を維持する者が，次のいずれかの場合に該当し，そのために労働者から請求があったときは，賃金支払日前であっても，既往の労働に対する賃金を支払う。
①　やむを得ない事由によって1週間以上帰郷する場合
②　結婚又は死亡の場合
③　出産，疾病又は災害の場合
④　退職又は解雇により離職した場合

（昇給）

第41条　昇給は，勤務成績その他が良好な労働者について，毎年＿＿月＿＿日をもって行うものとする。ただし，会社の業績の著しい低下その他やむを得ない事由がある場合は，行わないことがある。

2　顕著な業績が認められた労働者については，前項の規定にかかわらず昇給を行うことがある。

3　昇給額は，労働者の勤務成績等を考慮して各人ごとに決定する。

（賞与）

第42条　賞与は，原則として，下記の算定対象期間に在籍した労働者に対し，会社の業績等を勘案して下記の支給日に支給する。ただし，会社の業績の著しい低下その他やむを得ない事由により，支給時期を延期し，又は支給しないことがある。

算定対象期間	支給日
＿＿月＿＿日から＿＿月＿＿日まで	＿＿月＿＿日
＿＿月＿＿日から＿＿月＿＿日まで	＿＿月＿＿日

2　前項の賞与の額は，会社の業績及び労働者の勤務成績などを考慮して各人ごとに決定する。

第7章　定年，退職及び解雇

（定年等）

第43条　労働者の定年は，満60歳とし，定年に達した日の属する月の末日をもって退職とする。

2　前項の規定にかかわらず，定年後も引き続き雇用されることを希望し，解雇事由又は退職事由に該当しない労働者については，満65歳までこれを継続雇用する。

（退職）

第44条　前条に定めるもののほか，労働者が次のいずれかに該当するときは，

退職とする。
① 退職を願い出て会社が承認したとき，又は退職願を提出して____日を経過した
とき
② 期間を定めて雇用されている場合，その期間を満了したとき
③ 第９条に定める休職期間が満了し，なお休職事由が消滅しないとき
④ 死亡したとき
2　労働者が退職し，又は解雇された場合，その請求に基づき，使用期間，業務の種類，地位，賃金又は退職の事由を記載した証明書を遅滞なく交付する。

（解雇）

第45条　労働者が次のいずれかに該当するときは，解雇することがある。
① 勤務状況が著しく不良で，改善の見込みがなく，労働者としての職責を果たし得ないとき。
② 勤務成績又は業務能率が著しく不良で，向上の見込みがなく，他の職務にも転換できない等就業に適さないとき。
③ 業務上の負傷又は疾病による療養の開始後３年を経過しても当該負傷又は疾病が治らない場合であって，労働者が傷病補償年金を受けているとき又は受けることとなったとき（会社が打ち切り補償を支払ったときを含む。）。
④ 精神又は身体の障害により業務に耐えられないとき。
⑤ 試用期間における作業能率又は勤務態度が著しく不良で，労働者として不適格であると認められたとき。
⑥ 第56条第２項に定める懲戒解雇事由に該当する事実が認められたとき。
⑦ 事業の運営上又は天災事変その他これに準ずるやむを得ない事由により，事業の縮小又は部門の閉鎖等を行う必要が生じ，かつ他の職務への転換が困難なとき。
⑧ その他前各号に準ずるやむを得ない事由があったとき。
2　前項の規定により労働者を解雇する場合は，少なくとも30日前に予告をする。予告しないときは，平均賃金の30日分以上の手当を解雇予告手当として支払う。ただし，予告の日数については，解雇予告手当を支払った日数だけ短縮することができる。
3　前項の規定は，労働基準監督署長の認定を受けて労働者を00第１項第４号に定める懲戒解雇にする場合又は次の各号のいずれかに該当する労働者を解雇する場合は適用しない。
① 日々雇い入れられる労働者（ただし，１か月を超えて引き続き使用されるに至った者を除く。）
② ２か月以内の期間を定めて使用する労働者（ただし，その期間を超えて引き続き使用されるに至った者を除く。）
③ 試用期間中の労働者（ただし，14日を超えて引き続き使用されるに至った者を除く。）
4　第１項の規定による労働者の解雇に際して労働者から請求のあった場合

は，解雇の理由を記載した証明書を交付する。

第８章　退職金

（退職金の支給）

第46条　勤続＿＿年以上の労働者が退職し又は解雇されたときは，この章に定めるところにより退職金を支給する。ただし，自己都合による退職者で，勤続＿＿年未満の者には退職金を支給しない。また，０第２項により懲戒解雇された者には，退職金の全部又は一部を支給しないことがある。

２　継続雇用制度の対象者については，定年時に退職金を支給することとし，その後の再雇用については退職金を支給しない。

（退職金の額）

第47条　退職金の額は，退職又は解雇の時の基本給の額に，勤続年数に応じて定めた下表の支給率を乗じた金額とする。

勤続年数	支給率
５年未満	1.0
５年～10年	3.0
11年～15年	5.0
16年～20年	7.0
21年～25年	10.0
26年～30年	15.0
31年～35年	17.0
36年～40年	20.0
41年～	25.0

２　第９条により休職する期間については，会社の都合による場合を除き，前項の勤続年数に算入しない。

（退職金の支払方法及び支払時期）

第48条　退職金は，支給事由の生じた日から＿＿か月以内に，退職した労働者（死亡による退職の場合はその遺族）に対して支払う。

第９章　安全衛生及び災害補償

（健康診断）

第49条　労働者に対しては，採用の際及び毎年１回（深夜労働に従事する者は６か月ごとに１回），定期に健康診断を行う。

２　前項の健康診断のほか，法令で定められた有害業務に従事する労働者に対しては，特別の項目についての健康診断を行う。

３　第１項及び前項の健康診断の結果必要と認めるときは，一定期間の就業禁止，労働時間の短縮，配置転換その他健康保持上必要な措置を命ずることがある。

（健康管理上の個人情報の取扱い）

第50条　事業者は労働者の心身の状態に関する情報を適正に取り扱う。

（安全衛生教育）

第51条 労働者に対し，雇入れの際及び配置換え等により作業内容を変更した場合，その従事する業務に必要な安全及び衛生に関する教育を行う。

2 労働者は，安全衛生教育を受けた事項を遵守しなければならない。

（災害補償）

第52条 労働者が業務上の事由又は通勤により負傷し，疾病にかかり，又は死亡した場合は，労基法及び労働者災害補償保険法（昭和22年法律第50号）に定めるところにより災害補償を行う。

第10章 職業訓練

（教育訓練）

第53条 会社は，業務に必要な知識，技能を高め，資質の向上を図るため，労働者に対し，必要な教育訓練を行う。

2 労働者は，会社から教育訓練を受講するよう指示された場合には，特段の事由がない限り教育訓練を受けなければならない。

3 前項の指示は，教育訓練開始日の少なくとも____週間前までに該当労働者に対し文書で通知する。

第11章 表彰及び制裁

（表彰）

第54条 会社は，労働者が次のいずれかに該当するときは，表彰することがある。

① 業務上有益な発明，考案を行い，会社の業績に貢献したとき。

② 永年にわたって誠実に勤務し，その成績が優秀で他の模範となるとき。

③ 永年にわたり無事故で継続勤務したとき。

④ 社会的功績があり，会社及び労働者の名誉となったとき。

⑤ 前各号に準ずる善行又は功労のあったとき。

2 表彰は，原則として会社の創立記念日に行う。また，賞状のほか賞金を授与する。

（懲戒の種類）

第55条 会社は，労働者が次条のいずれかに該当する場合は，その情状に応じ，次の区分により懲戒を行う。

① けん責　　始末書を提出させて将来を戒める。

② 減給　　　始末書を提出させて減給する。ただし，減給は1回の額が平均賃金の1日分の5割を超えることはなく，また，総額が1賃金支払期における賃金総額の1割を超えることはない。

③ 出勤停止　始末書を提出させるほか，____日間を限度として出勤を停止し，その間の賃金は支給しない。

④ 懲戒解雇　予告期間を設けることなく即時に解雇する。この場合において，所轄の労働基準監督署長の認定を受けたときは，解雇予告手当（平均賃金の30日分）を支給しない。

（懲戒の事由）

第56条　労働者が次のいずれかに該当するときは，情状に応じ，けん責，減給又は出勤停止とする。
①　正当な理由なく無断欠勤が＿＿日以上に及ぶとき。
②　正当な理由なくしばしば欠勤，遅刻，早退をしたとき。
③　過失により会社に損害を与えたとき。
④　素行不良で社内の秩序及び風紀を乱したとき。
⑤　0，0，0に違反したとき。
⑥　その他この規則に違反し又は前各号に準ずる不都合な行為があったとき。

2　労働者が次のいずれかに該当するときは，懲戒解雇とする。ただし，平素の服務態度その他情状によっては，第45条に定める普通解雇，前条に定める減給又は出勤停止とすることがある。
①　重要な経歴を詐称して雇用されたとき。
②　正当な理由なく無断欠勤が　日以上に及び，出勤の督促に応じなかったとき。
③　正当な理由なく無断でしばしば遅刻，早退又は欠勤を繰り返し，＿＿回にわたって注意を受けても改めなかったとき。
④　正当な理由なく，しばしば業務上の指示・命令に従わなかったとき。
⑤　故意又は重大な過失により会社に重大な損害を与えたとき。
⑥　会社内において刑法その他刑罰法規の各規定に違反する行為を行い，その犯罪事実が明らかとなったとき（当該行為が軽微な違反である場合を除く。）。
⑦　素行不良で著しく社内の秩序又は風紀を乱したとき。
⑧　数回にわたり懲戒を受けたにもかかわらず，なお，勤務態度等に関し，改善の見込みがないとき。
⑨　0，0，エラー！　参照元が見つかりません。，エラー！　参照元が見つかりません。に違反し，その情状が悪質と認められるとき。
⑩　許可なく職務以外の目的で会社の施設，物品等を使用したとき。
⑪　職務上の地位を利用して私利を図り，又は取引先等より不当な金品を受け，若しくは求め若しくは供応を受けたとき。
⑫　私生活上の非違行為や会社に対する正当な理由のない誹謗中傷等であって，会社の名誉信用を損ない，業務に重大な悪影響を及ぼす行為をしたとき。
⑬　正当な理由なく会社の業務上重要な秘密を外部に漏洩して会社に損害を与え，又は業務の正常な運営を阻害したとき。
⑭　その他前各号に準ずる不適切な行為があったとき。

第12章　公益通報者保護

（公益通報者の保護）

第57条　会社は，労働者から組織的又は個人的な法令違反行為等に関する相談又は通報があった場合には，別に定めるところにより処理を行う。

第13章　副業・兼業
（副業・兼業）
第58条　労働者は，勤務時間外において，他の会社等の業務に従事することができる。
2　労働者は，前項の業務に従事するにあたっては，事前に，会社に所定の届出を行うものとする。
3　第１項の業務に従事することにより，次の各号のいずれかに該当する場合には，会社は，これを禁止又は制限することができる。
①　労務提供上の支障がある場合
②　企業秘密が漏洩する場合
③　会社の名誉や信用を損なう行為や，信頼関係を破壊する行為がある場合
④　競業により，企業の利益を害する場合

附　則
（施行期日）第１条　この規則は，平成____年____月____日から施行する。

（出典：厚生労働省ホームページ「モデル就業規則（平成31年３月）」を著者一部加筆）

〈例8－2 就業規則（モデル，英文）〉

Chapter 1 General Provisions

(Purposes)

Article 1 The rules of employment (hereinafter referred to as "the rules of employment") provide stipulations pertaining to employment for the workers at ＿＿＿＿＿ K.K. Corporation conforming to Article 89 of the Labor Standards Act (hereinafter referred to as "Labor Standards Act").

2. The Labor Standards Act and other labor laws apply to all matters pertaining to employment including what is stipulated in these rules.

(Scope of application)

Article 2 These rules of employment shall apply to all workers employed by K.K. Corporation.

2. The matters pertaining to employment of part time workers are stipulated in a different set of rules.

3. The matters that are not stipulated in the different set of rules set forth in the preceding provision, are governed by these rules of employment.

(Compliance with the rules)

Article 3 A company has an obligation to employ workers under the terms and conditions of employment set out in these rules of employment. The workers must comply with the rules of employment.

Chapter 2 Hiring and Transfers

(Procedures for Hiring)

Article 4 A company shall conduct screening tests for the applicants and hire those who pass such tests.

(Documents to be submitted at the time of hiring)

Article 5 A person who is hired as a worker is required to submit the following documents within ＿＿＿ weeks from the day he/she is hired.

① Certificate of items stated in the resident register;
② Copy of Driver's Licence (for those who have a driver's licence);
③ Copy of Certificates of qualifications (for those who have certificates of qualifications);
④ Other documents specified by the company;

2. In the event that any changes occur in any documents set out in the preceding clause after submission, the workers must immediately notify of such changes to the company in written form;

(Probationary Employment Period)

Article 6 A probationary employment period of ＿＿＿ months from the day of being hired shall apply to a newly hired worker.

2. The probationary period prescribed in the preceding paragraph may be shortened or eliminated in the case where the company approves such an action.
3. During the probationary period, a company may dismiss those who are assessed as unfit for employment. For those who are employed more than 14 days from the commencement of their employment, the company must follow the procedures pursuant to paragraph 2 of Article 49.
4. The probationary period shall be added to the period of service.

(Clear Declaration of Terms and Conditions of Employment)

Article 7 In the event of hiring a worker, a company is required to clearly declare the terms and conditions of employment in writing by issuing a notice with regard to the terms and conditions of employment which states matters, such as wages, the location of employment, regulations in service, working hours, days off, in conjunction with the rules of employment.

(Personnel Transfer)

Article 8 A company may order a worker to change his/her regulations in service and/or locations of his/her employment if it is necessary for the business operation.
2. A company may loan a worker to a different company related to the company who originally hired him/her while his/her employment remains under the original company, when necessary.
3. In the case of the preceding paragraph, a worker is not permitted to reject the order without rightful reasons.

(Leave of Absence)

Article 9 If a worker falls under any of the following categories, he/she shall be granted a leave of absence for the specified duration.
① In the case where a worker has been absent due to injury or illness outside the course of duties for more than ______ month (s), and he/she requires further treatment and cannot work. (within ______ year (s))
② n addition to the case of the preceding provision, where there are special circumstances in which allowing a leave of absence is considered to be appropriate. (the period required: ______)
2. In the case where the reasons for leave of absence are resolved during such leave of absence, as a basic rule, the workers shall return to work in the position he/she held before taking the leave. However, in the case where it is difficult or inappropriate for the workers to return to the position, he/she held before taking the leave, the company may assign him/her to a different position.
3. In the event that a worker who is on leave of absence pursuant to

the first paragraph of 1, fails to recover from the injury or illness and still finds it difficult to return to work after spending the full term of the leave of absence, he/she shall retire immediately after the full term of leave of absence.

Chapter 3 Regulations in service

(Regulations in service)

Article 10 Workers must be aware of their responsibilities for their work, fulfil their duties, obey the company's directions and orders, endeavor to improve their efficiency and to maintain the order of the workplace.

[Article 11 Compliance Provisions]

Workers must comply with the following matters:

1 Workers must not use the company's facilities or articles for purposes outside the course of their employment without permission.

2 Workers must not engage in any unlawful activities, such as pursuing their own profit/soliciting in the relevant field of their duties, borrowing money or goods or receiving gifts from others in an unjust manner.

3 Workers must devote themselves to their work, and must not leave their workplace without good reason.

4 Workers must not engage in any activities that damage the company's reputation and trust.

5 Workers must not disclose confidential information concerning the companies or clients they became acquainted with in the course of duties during their employment or after their retirement.

6 Workers must not work under the influence of alcohol.

7 Workers must not engage in work for other companies without permission.

(Prohibition of Power Harassment in Workplace)

Article 12 Workers are prohibited from any activities which take advantage of their positions of authority with regard to their employment or relationships in the work environment, which go beyond the reasonable scope of duties, that cause other workers mental or physical suffering or that are damaging to the work environment.

(Prohibition of Sexual Harassment)

Article 13 Workers are prohibited from any activities that cause disadvantage or discomfort to other workers or that are damaging to the work environment by way of speech or behaviour of a sexual nature.

(Protection of Personal Information)

Article 14 A worker shall pay careful attention to the management of the information concerning the company and clients, etc., and must not unlawfully obtain information that is irrelevant to their duties.

2. In the event that a worker is transferred to a different workplace or position or he/she retires, he/she must immediately return data or documents which he/she was handling, that contain information concerning the company and clients.

(Recording the start and end times of work)

Article 15 Workers must record the daily times of starting and ending of their work by stamping time cards.

(Late Arrival, Leaving Early and Absence)

Article 16 A worker must notify the direct supervisor in advance and obtain approval when he/she will be arriving late, leaving early, absent for a full day, absent for a part day for personal reasons during the working hours. However, in the case where he/she could not notify prior to such event for unforeseeable reasons, he/she must notify immediately after the event and obtain approval.

2. In the case of the preceding paragraph, on principle, the wage corresponding to the hours of absence will be deducted pursuant to Article 41.

3. A worker must submit a physician's certificate in the case where he/she will be absent for 3 consecutive day (s) or more due to injury or illness.

Chapter 4 Working hours, Rest Periods and Days Off

(Working Hours and Rest Periods)

Article 17 The total working hours shall be 40 hours per week and 8 hours per day.

2. The start and end times of work and rest periods shall be as follows. However, A company is entitled to shift such times to an earlier or later time for certain business circumstances or other unavoidable events. In such case, A company shall notify workers of the change a minimum of one day ahead of time.

Start and End times of work	Duration of Break
Start: 9:00 am	From _12:00_ to 1_:_00
End: 6:00 pm	

(Days Off)

Article 18 The days off shall be established as follows:

① Saturdays and Sundays

② National Holidays (when the actual holiday falls on a Sunday, it shall be observed on the following day.)

③ The end and the beginning of the year (December _29_ to January _3_)

④ Summer Break (from _August 14__(month/day) to _August 16_ (month/day))

2. A company may switch the days off established in the preceding paragraph with another work day if necessary, under certain business circumstances.

(Overtime and working on Days Off)

Article 19 A company may have a worker work beyond the working hours prescribed in Article 17 or on days off prescribed in Article 18 due to certain business circumstances.

2. In such case of the preceding paragraph, the employer shall conclude the written labor-management agreement ahead of time with a representative of a majority of the workers concerning working beyond the working hours or on days off stipulated in the law and submit such agreement to the director of the relevant local Labor Standards Inspection Office.

3. A company shall not have a female workers who is pregnant or gave birth within one year (hereinafter referred to as "expectant or nursing mothers") who requests not to work, and a worker who is under 18 years of age work overtime, days off which are in paragraph 2 or late night or early morning (from 10 pm to 5 am).

4. A company may have a worker work overtime beyond the limits prescribed in paragraphs 1 to 3, the scheduled working hours or on days off in the case of an emergency, such as a certain unavoidable incident or a natural disaster. However, even in such case, A company shall not have new and expectant or nursing mothers who request not to work, work overtime or on days off.

Chapter 5 Leaves

(Annual paid leave)

Article 20 A company shall provide a worker who has worked for 6 consecutive months since the first day of his/her employment and whose attendance exceeds 80 percent of the scheduled work days during such period of time with 10 days of annual paid leave. A company shall provide a worker who continues his/her service beyond 6 months, with the specified number of days of annual paid leave for every year of service at a minimum of 80 % of the attendance during the year. The annual paid leave corresponding to the length of service granted is as shown in the following table:

Length of service	6 months	1 year and 6 months	2 years and 6 months	3 years and 6 months	4 years and 6 months	5 years and 6 months	6 years and 6 months
Days given	10 days	11 days	12 days	14 days	16 days	18 days	20 days

2. A company shall provide a worker, notwithstanding the preceding provision, whose scheduled working hours per week are less than 30 hours and whose scheduled work days are 4 days or fewer per week, and in the case where workers whose scheduled work days are based on other than weekly basis, if his/her annual scheduled work days are 216 days or fewer, with the specified number of days of annual paid leave corresponding to the the length of service as shown in the table below:

Specified work days per week	Specified work days per year	The length of service						
		6 months	1 year and 6 month	2 years and 6 months	3 years and 6 months	4 years and 6 months	5 years and 6 months	6 years and 6 months
4 days	169~216 days	7 days	8 days	9 days	10 days	12 days	13 days	15 days
3 days	121~168 days	5 days	6 days	6 days	8 days	9 days	10 days	11 days
2 days	73~120 days	3 days	4 days	4 days	5 days	6 days	6 days	7 days
1 day	4~72 days	1 day	2 days	2 days	2 days	3 days	3 days	3 days

3. A company shall allow a worker to take the annual paid leave established in the preceding paragraph 1 or 2, at the specified times requested in advance. However, in the case where having a worker take the annual paid leave at such times requested will impede the regular business operation, A company may have the workers take the annual paid leave at other times than he/she requested.

4. A company may assign the time in advance for a worker to take his/her annual paid leave for the portion beyond 5 days of his/her annual paid leave, notwithstanding the preceding paragraph, pursuant to the written labor-management agreement with a representative of the workers.

5. When calculating attendance rate set forth in the preceding paragraphs 1 and 2, the following periods shall be considered time worked:

① the period for the annual paid leave;

② the period for maternity leave;

③ the period for parental leave, child Care and Family Care Leave Act pursuant to the Act on the welfare of workers who take care of children and other family members including child care and family care leave

④ the period for leave of absence for recovery from injury or illnesses caused in the ordinary course of duties.

6. A worker is entitled to carry over the unused portion of his/her annual paid leave from the preceding year up to 2 years from the day such paid leave was granted.

7. In the case of the preceding paragraph, A company shall have a worker take the portion of annual paid leave which was carried over before taking the annual paid leave granted for the current year.
8. A company shall notify each workers of their leave balance of annual paid leave as of the last day of every pay period by stating it in their pay statement.

(Granting Annual Paid Leave by the hour)

Article 21 Conforming to the written agreement with a representative of workers, A company shall grant annual paid leave by the hour (hereinafter referred to as "annual leave by the hour") to a maximum of 5 days out of the annual paid leave per year prescribed in the preceding article in accordance with the following stipulations:

(1) The annual leave by the hour shall be applicable to all workers;
(2) When taking the annual paid leave by the hour, the equivalent number of hours to one day of annual paid leave shall be as follows:
① a worker whose scheduled working hours is between 5 and 6 hours: 6 hours;
② a worker whose scheduled working hours is between 6 and 7 hours: 7 hours;
③ a worker whose scheduled working hours is between 7 and 8 hours: 8 hours;
(3) The annual leave by the hour will be granted in one-hour blocks;
(4) The sum paid for the annual leave by the hour taken shall be calculated by multiplying the hourly regular wage which would be paid for the scheduled working hours by the number of hours of annual paid leave taken.
(5) Other matters not set forth in this article shall be governed by the clauses concerning the annual paid leave prescribed in the preceding article.

(Maternity Leave)

Article 22 A company shall grant maternity leave when a request is received from a female worker who is expecting to give birth within 6 weeks (or 14 weeks in the case of multiple births.)
2. A company shall not allow a female worker to work within 8 weeks of giving birth.
3. If a female worker after 6 weeks of giving birth requests to return to work, A company may allow such female workers to work on duties that a physician approves as safe for her to work, notwithstanding the preceding paragraph.

(Measures to maintain mothers' health)

Article 23 In the case where a female worker who is pregnant or within one year of giving birth requests, a company shall approve her visits to the hospital during the scheduled working hours for health guidance or medical examinations in compliance with the Maternal and Child Health Act (Act No.141 of 1965) with the following limits:

① Before giving birth:

up to 23 weeks---------------------------------once over 4 weeks

from 24 weeks to 35 weeks-------------once over 2 weeks

from 36 weeks to birth--------------------once a week

In the case where a physician or midwife (hereinafter referred to as a "physician or other medical professional") gives instructions otherwise, the required time shall be approved according to such instructions.

② After giving birth (within one year):

The time required according to physician's instructions

2. In the case where a female worker who is pregnant or within one year of giving birth requests adjustment in her work conditions or hours based on physician's instructions given at the health guidance or medical examinations, the company shall take measures as follows:

① In the case where the workers who is instructed to avoid commuting in a crowded condition during their pregnancy as a measure to alleviate their commuting stress, the company shall approve on principle to reduce their working hours by one hour or to shift her start and end times of work by up to a maximum of one hour.

② In the case where a worker who is so instructed with regard to rest periods during her pregnancy, A company shall increase the frequency or extend the duration of her rest periods as required.

③ In the case where a female worker who is pregnant or has given birth is given an instruction to alleviate her symptoms, A company shall take measures, such as to reduce their work load or her working hours or to grant leave of absence to comply with such physicians' instructions.

(Hours for Child Care and Menstrual Leave)

Article 24 In the case where a female worker who is raising a child (or children) under the age of one, so requests, the company shall provide such workers with the hours for child care 2 times per day, 30 minutes each time aside from their regular rest periods.

2. In the case a company receives a request from a female worker who has significant difficulties managing her work during her menstrual period, the company shall provide a leave of absence required.

(Care Leave for Children and Other Family Members)

Article 25 A worker who requires it is eligible to receive benefits, such as parental leave, child care leave, care leave for other family members, exemption from overtime for child care, limits on overtime and limits on late night/early morning shifts for care for children and other family members and reduction of regular working hours (hereinafter referred to as "Child Care and Family Care Leave Act") based on the Act on Child Care and Family Care Leave Act .

2. Policy for child Care and Family Care Leave Act are stipulated in the "rules concerning Child Care and Family Care Leave Act".

(Congratulatory and Condolence Leave)

Article 26 A company shall grant congratulatory or condolence leave to a worker if requested for any of the following events for the number of days as indicated:

① the worker's marriage: _7__ days
② the worker's wife giving a birth: _5 __ days
③ death of the worker's spouse, children or parents: _5 __ days
④ death of the worker's siblings, grandparents, spouse's parents or siblings: _3 __ days

(Sick Leave)

Article 27 In the case where a worker requires treatment for personal injury or illness and the company finds such worker's absence is inevitable, the company shall grant such workers sick leave of _3__ days.

(Leave for Jury Duty)

Article 28 A company shall grant leave for a worker who is chosen to serve as a juror, a supplemental juror or a juror candidate as follows:

① In the case of a juror or a supplemental juror: the number of days required
② In the case of a juror candidate: the number of hours required

Chapter 6 Wages

(Components of Wages)

Article 29 The components of wages are as follows:

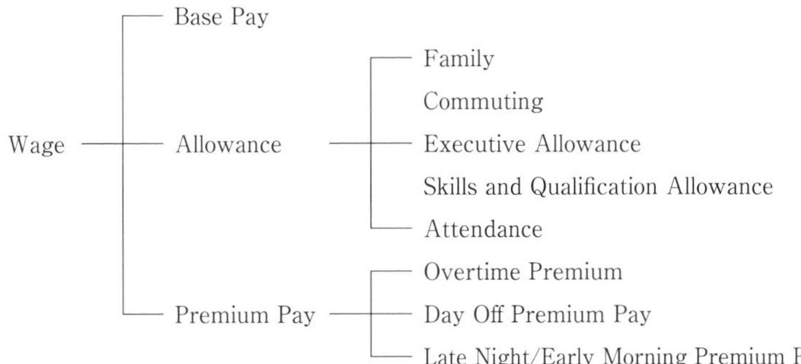

(Base Pay)

Article 30 A company shall determine the base pay for each worker taking into consideration their regulations in service, skills and abilities, achievement, and age.

(Family Allowance)

Article 31 Family Allowance shall be paid to a worker who supports his/her family members as follows:

① Children under the age of 18: __________ yen per child per month

② Parents who are 65 years of age or older: __________ yen per person per month

(Commuting Allowance)

Article 32 Commuting Allowance shall be paid in the amount equivalent to the actual cost required for commuting to and from work up to the maximum amount of __________ yen per month.

(Executive Allowance)

Article 33 Executive Allowance shall be paid to a worker who is in one of the following positions at the rate of:

Director (Head of department): __________ yen per month

Manager (Head of section): __________ yen per month

Supervisor (Head of unit): __________ yen per month

2. In the case of promotion to a position to which the executive allowance applies, such payment shall start from the pay period (month) in which such promotion takes effect. In such event, the executive allowance for the previous position he/she was in shall not be paid in that pay period (month).

3. In the case of demotion to a position to which the executive allowance applies, such payment shall start from the pay period (month) following the pay period (month) in which such demotion takes effect.

(Premium Pay)

Article 34 The premium pay for overtime shall be paid based on the premium pay rate indicated below using the calculation method in the following paragraph.

(1) The premium pay rates for the total number of overtime hours over a period of one month are as follows. In this case, the starting day of the one month pay period is the ____ (day) of each month.

1. 45 hours or less of overtime: 25%
2. more than 45 hours up to 60 hours of overtime: 35%
3. more than 60 hours of overtime: 50%
4. the hours of 3. less time off in lieu of overtime pay: 35%

(the rest of the premium rate of 15% shall be allotted to such time off in lieu of overtime pay).

(2) In the case where the total number of hours of overtime over a

period of one year exceeds 360 hours, the premium pay rate for such portion beyond 360 hours shall be 40% . In such case, the starting day of the one year pay period is ______(month/day) of each year.

(3) In calculating the premium pay for overtime, in the case where the number of hours of overtime meets both criteria(1)and(2), the higher rate shall apply.

2. The premium pay shall be calculated using the following equations.

① premium pay for overtime

(for the portion of 45 hours or less overtime over a period of one month)

$$\frac{\text{Base Pay} + \text{Executive Allowance} + \text{Skills/Qualification Allowance} + \text{Attendance Allowance}}{\text{Average number of scheduled working hours per month}} \times 1.25 \times \text{total number of hours of overtime worked}$$

(for the portion beyond 45 hours and up to 60 hours of overtime over a period of one month)

$$\frac{\text{Base Pay} + \text{Executive Allowance} + \text{Skills/Qualification Allowance} + \text{Attendance Allowance}}{\text{Average number of scheduled working hours per month}} \times 1.35 \times \text{total number of hours of overtime worked}$$

(for the portion beyond 60 hours of overtime over a period of one month)

$$\frac{\text{Base Pay} + \text{Executive Allowance} + \text{Skills/Qualification Allowance} + \text{Attendance Allowance}}{\text{Average number of scheduled working hours per month}} \times 1.50 \times \text{total number of hours of overtime worked}$$

(for the portion beyond 360 hours of overtime for a period of one year)

$$\frac{\text{Base Pay} + \text{Executive Allowance} + \text{Skills/Qualification Allowance} + \text{Attendance Allowance}}{\text{Average number of scheduled working hours per month}} \times 1.40 \times \text{total number of hours of overtime worked}$$

② premium pay for working on days off (in the case of working on legal days off)

$$\frac{\text{Base Pay} + \text{Executive Allowance} + \text{Skills/Qualification Allowance} + \text{Attendance Allowance}}{\text{Average number of scheduled working hours per month}} \times 1.35 \times \text{total number of hours of overtime worked}$$

③ premium pay for working late night/early morning (in the case of working between 10 pm and 5 am)

$$\frac{\text{Base Pay} + \text{Executive Allowance} + \text{Skills/Qualification Allowance} + \text{Attendance Allowance}}{\text{Average number of scheduled working hours per month}} \times 1.25 \times \text{total number of hours of overtime worked}$$

(Wages during leaves)

Article 35 An employer shall pay the regular wage which is paid for working the scheduled working hours for the period of annual paid leave if taken.

2. An employer shall (not pay / pay the regular wage) for the period of maternity/parental leave, hours for child care, menstrual leave, leave for mothers' health management, child care/parental leave and child Care and Family Care Leave Act based on the Act on Care Leave for Children and Other Family Members and leave for jury duty.
3. An employer shall not pay for the period of leave set forth in Article 9 on principle (__% will be paid for _____ months).

(Wages during Involuntary Leave)

Article 36 In the case where an employer has an employee take leave on a scheduled work day due to business circumstances, an employer shall pay 60 % of the average (daily) wage per day off pursuant to Article 12 of the Labor Standards Act. However, in the case where such leave is for a part day, the employer shall guarantee the equivalent of 60 % of the average wage for that day pursuant to Article 26 of the Labor Standards Act.

(Policy for different types of Absences)

Article 37 A company shall deduct the wage equivalent to the days or hours of absence from the base pay in the case of full-day absence, arriving late, leaving early and part-day leave for personal reasons.
2. in the case of the preceding paragraph, the calculation for the wage equivalent to one hour of work is as follows:
(1) In the case of monthly salary
Base pay ÷ the number of average scheduled working hours over a period of one month
(calculate the average scheduled working hours over one month using the equation set out in the paragraph 3 of Article 36)
(2) In the case of hourly wage
Base pay ÷ the number of scheduled working hours per day.

(Pay Period and Payday)

Article 38 Wages will be paid according to the pay period ending on the ______(day) of each month, and the payday will be on the ____(day) of the following month. However, in the case where the payday falls on a day off, wages would be paid on the preceding day.
2. In the case where a worker is hired or retires during the pay period described in the preceding paragraph, A company shall pay for the days worked based on the daily wage calculated by monthly wage divided by the number of scheduled work days.

(Payment and Deductions of Wages)

Article 39 A company shall pay wages directly to workerss in currency in full.
2. With regard to the preceding paragraph, A company may pay wages by transferring to the chequing, saving or consolidated trading account

at a financial institution specified by the workers upon agreement.

3. The following items shall be deducted from wages:

① Withholding income tax

② Residents' tax

③ The worker's (the insured person's) portion of the premium payments for health Insurance, worker's welfare pension insurance and employment insurance

④ Other deductions set forth in the written agreement with a representative of workers, such as fees for the company's residential properties (if used), contributions for payroll saving plans and union dues.

(Emergency Payment of Wages)

Article 40 A company may pay for the hours which a worker has already worked prior to the regular payday, upon such worker's request, in the case where the workers or those who maintain their livelihood on the income of such workers, are experiencing one of the following situations.

① In the case where a person is required to go back to their hometown for one week or longer under unavoidable circumstances.

② In the case of marriage or death.

③ In the case of birth, infectious disease or disaster.

④ In the case where a worker leaves the company due to retirement or dismissal.

(Wage Increase)

Article 41 A company shall increase wages which takes effect as of ____________(month/day) of each year for workers whose work performance was satisfactory. However, in the case where the employer experiences significant decline in their business performance or other unavoidable circumstances, the employer may not increase wages.

2. A company may increase wages of the workers whose outstanding achievement was acknowledged by the employer notwithstanding the stipulation in the preceding paragraph.

3. A company shall determine the amount of wage increase for each worker taking into account the achievement of each workers.

(Bonus)

Article 42 A company shall award bonus on principle to those workers who are on record as workers during the applicable period taking into consideration the business performance of the company. Such bonus will be paid on the days specified below. However, in the case where the company experiences significant decline in their business performance or is under other unavoidable circumstances, the employer may postpone or cancel bonus.

Applicable Period	Days for payment
From _____(month/day) to _____(month/day)	_______(month/day)
From _____(month/day) to _____(month/day)	_______(month/day)

2. A company shall determine the amount of bonus prescribed in the preceding paragraph for each worker taking into consideration the business performance of the company and the achievement of each worker's performance.

Chapter 7 Fixed retirement age, Retirement and Dismissal

(Fixed Retirement Age)

Article 43 The fixed retirement age shall be 60 years of age and a worker shall retire on the last day of the month in which the workers reaches such age.

2. A company shall continue a worker's employment if he/she wishes to continue to work after his/her retirement until he/she reaches age 65, notwithstanding the preceding paragraph, if the causes or reasons for dismissal or retirement do not apply to the workers.

(Retirement)

Article 44 Additional to the preceding article, a worker under one of the following circumstances shall retire.

① In the case where a worker submits the request for retirement and the company approves, or 14 days after such submission;

② In the case where a fixed term employment contract expires;

③ In the case where the period of leave of absence stipulated in Article 9 expires but the cause of the leave has not been resolved;

④ In the case of death;

2. In the case where a worker retires or is dismissed, the employer must immediately issue the letter of verification which states the period of service, type of work, position, wages and the reasons for retirement.

(Dismissal)

Article 45 A company may dismiss a worker if that workers falls under one of the following categories.

① a worker who cannot fulfil his/her regulations in service as a worker due to his/her significantly poor attendance/unacceptable behaviour towards work and where there is no prospect for improvement;

② a worker who is not able to perform their duties and cannot be transferred to a different position due to his/her significantly poor performance, productivity or efficiency and where there is no prospect for improvement;

③ a worker, who after 3 years of treatment, does not recover from injury or illness caused in the course of duties, and where the workers is receiving or is going to receive the compensation pension for injury or illness, including the case where the company pays the discontinuance compensation;

④ a worker who cannot endure the work due to his/her mental or physical disability;

⑤ a company ascertains that a worker is incompetent as a worker due to his/her poor efficiency or unacceptable behaviour during his/her probationary term;

⑥ a company confirms that a worker is under conditions for disciplinary dismissal in paragraph 2 of Article 56.

⑦ a company is required to curtail their business operation or to close down part of their business operations due to business circumstances, natural disasters or other unavoidable reasons, and transferring workers to different positions is difficult.

⑧ other unavoidable reasons comparable to the above items.

2. In the case where A company dismisses a worker in accordance with the clauses in the preceding paragraph, the employer must notify the workers a minimum of 30 days in advance. In the case where A company does not notify the workers, the employer must pay a dismissal allowance equivalent to a minimum of 30 days average wage. However, the number of days required prior to such notice can be compensated for by the corresponding amount of dismissal allowance.

3. The stipulation in the preceding paragraph does not apply to the case where A company dismisses a worker pursuant to stipulations concerning disciplinary dismissal in Article 60 with the authorization of the director of the Labor Standards Inspection Office or the case where such workers meets one of the following criteria.

① Workers who are hired by the day (excluding those who have been hired continuously for one month or longer.)

② Workers who are employed with a fixed term of 2 months or less (excluding those who have been employed beyond such term.)

③ Workers who are under the probationary term (excluding those who have been employed for 14 days or longer.)

4. In the case where a worker is dismissed in the cases as prescribed in paragraph 1 and he/she requests a letter of verification which states reasons for such dismissal, A company shall issue such letter.

Chapter 8 Severance Pay

(Terms for Severance Pay)

Article 46 A company shall pay severance pay to a worker whose years of service is ____ years or longer when retiring or being dismissed pursuant to the clauses under this chapter. However, A company shall not pay severance pay to a worker whose years of service is less than ____ years when retiring for his/her personal reasons. In addition, A company may not pay all or part of the severance pay to a worker who is dismissed as a disciplinary action conforming to paragraph 2 of Article 61.

2. A company shall pay severance pay to a worker who is eligible for the continued employment system at the time of retirement but shall not pay severance pay for the employment after such retirement.

(The Amount of Severance Pay)

Article 47 The amount of severance pay shall be calculated by multiplying the base pay at the time of retirement or dismissal by the pay rate which is established according to the number of years of service as follows:

Years of service	Pay rate
Less than 5 years	1.0
From 5 to 10 years	3.0
From 10 to 15 years	5.0
From 15 to 20 years	7.0
From 20 to 25 years	10.0
From 25 to 30 years	15.0
From 30 to 40 years	20.0
40 years or longer	25.0

2. The period of leave of absence taken pursuant to Article 9 shall not be included in the years of service established in the preceding paragraph except such leave occurred due to reasons attributed to the company.

(Method and Time of Payment for Severance Pay)

Article 48 A company shall pay severance pay to the workers who retires, or to the family of the workers in the case of retirement due to his/her death, within ______ month (s) from the day that the reason for paying (severance pay) occurred.

Chapter 9 Safety, Health and Accident Compensation

(Health Examinations)

Article 49 A company shall provide regular medical examinations for workerss at the time of hiring and once a year, or once every 6 months for those who engage in late night/early morning shifts.

2. A company shall conduct medical examinations for special issues for workerss who engage in hazardous duties specified by the laws in addition to those medical examinations set out in the preceding

paragraph.

3. As a result of the medical examinations set out in paragraph 1 and 2 and the meetings prescribed in paragraph 3, if required, A company may order necessary measures, such as prohibition from work for a certain length of time, reduced working hours, transferring positions in order to maintain the health of a worker.

(Policy for Personal Information concerning Health Management)

Article 50 A company shall utilize the information concerning the health management of workers.

(Education on Safety and Health)

Article 51 In the case where A company hires a new worker or transfers a worker resulting in changes to his/her duties, a worker shall provide training with respect to the safety and health necessary for the work which the workers is to be engaged in.

2. Workers must comply with the knowledge gained through the training on safety and health.

(Accident Compensation)

Article 52 In the case where a worker injures himself/herself, becomes ill or deceased in the course of duties or while commuting, A company must provide compensation pursuant to the Labor Standards Act and the Industrial Accident Compensation Insurance Act (Act No.50 of 1947).

Chapter 10 Vocational Training

(Educational Training)

Article 53 A company shall provide educational training necessary for the workers to gain the necessary knowledge, improve their skills, abilities and endowments.

2. Workers must take the educational training provided by the company if so instructed, unless they have justifiable reasons to be excluded from such training.

3. A company shall provide a written notice of such instruction specified in the preceding paragraph to the applicable workers a minimum of ____ week (s) prior to the day of the educational training.

Chapter 11 Commendations and Sanctions

(Presentation of Commendations)

Article 54 A company may present commendations to workers who meet one of the following criteria:

① a worker who makes profitable inventions or designs for the business operation;

② a worker who works faithfully for a long period of time and whose

第2章 株式会社

achievement serves as an excellent model for other workers;

③ a worker who works for a long period of time continuously without accident;

④ a worker who has a social achievement that honours the company or other workerss;

⑤ a worker who practices good deeds or renders distinguished service that is comparable to the above;

2. The presentations of the commendations shall be held on the anniversary of the foundation of the company on principle. The monetary awards shall be presented with commendations.

(Types of Disciplinary Actions)

Article 55 A company shall take disciplinary actions, classified as follows, against workerss corresponding to the actual circumstances in the case where a worker falls under the categories in the following article. :

① Reprimand

Have the workers submit a letter of apology and reprimand the workers for his/her future conduct.

② Wage reduction

Have the workers submit a letter of apology and reduce his/her wage. However, the amount of wage reduction at a time shall not exceed 50% the daily average wage, and the total reduction shall not exceed 10% of the total wage for a single pay period.

③ Suspension

Have the workers submit a letter of apology and suspend him/her from working for a maximum of ____ work day (s) without pay.

④ Disciplinary Dismissal

Dismiss the workers immediately without providing the notification period. In such event, the employer shall not provide a dismissal allowance (equivalent to the average daily wage for 30 days) provided that the company obtains the authorization from the director of the relevant local Labor Standards Inspection Office.

(Grounds for Disciplinary Actions)

Article 56 In the case where a worker falls under one of the following categories, the company shall take disciplinary actions according to the circumstances, such as reprimand, wage reduction or suspension.

① a worker who is absent for ____ days or longer without notice or justifiable reasons.

② a worker who is absent, arriving late or leaving early frequently without justifiable reasons.

③ a worker who causes loss to the company by his/her error or negligence.

④ a worker who causes damage to the order or public morale within the company by his/her unacceptable behaviours.

⑤ a worker who violates Article 11, 12, and 13.

⑥ a worker who contravenes the rules of employment or engages in activities comparable to the above paragraphs.

2. In the case where a worker falls under one of the following categories, the employer shall render disciplinary dismissal against such workers. However, the employer may render regular dismissal set out in Article 45, wage reduction or suspension prescribed in the preceding article taking into consideration his/her usual behaviour at work and other circumstances.

① a worker who is hired by presenting a false career history which is essential.

② a worker who is absent for ______ day (s) or longer without notice or justifiable reasons and does not respond to the demand to attend work.

③ a worker who arrives late, leaves early or is absent repeatedly without notice or justifiable reasons, and still does not improve after receiving admonishment ______ times.

④ a worker who frequently does not follow directions or orders concerning business operations without justifiable reasons.

⑤ a worker who causes significant loss to the company intentionally or by crucial error/negligence.

⑥ a worker who engages in an activity which is a violation of the Penal Code or other punitive laws within the company and such violation becomes known (excluding the case where such violation is insignificant).

⑦ a worker who causes significant damage to the order or public morale within the company by his/her unacceptable behaviours.

⑧ a worker who shows no sign of improvement in his/her behaviour or other issues despite the multiple disciplinary actions taken.

⑨ a worker who violates Article 12, 13, 14 , 15 and his/her intention is acknowledged as malicious.

⑩ a worker who uses facilities or articles which belong to the company without permission for purposes outside the course of business.

⑪ a worker who seeks personal profit taking advantage of his/her position in the company or receives illicit money or goods from clients or others, or demands money or goods, or receives any gifts.

⑫ a worker who engages in activities, such as personal illegal activities or expresses slanderous defamation against the company without justifiable reasons, that cause serious damage to the business due to the loss of integrity and trust in the company.

⑬ a worker who causes damage to the company or disrupts regular business operation by disclosing classified information critical to business operations of the company to the outside without justifiable reason.

⑭ a worker who engages in any other inappropriate activities comparable to the above items.

Chapter 12 Protection of Whistleblowers

(Protection of Whistleblowers)

Article 57 A company shall follow the procedures stipulated separately in the case where a worker submits a report or consultation to a public office with respect to organizational or personal activity which violates laws.

Chapter 13 Protection of Whistleblowers

(Side Business / Side Jobs)

Article 58 Workers may engage in the work of other companies, etc., outside of working hours.

2. Workers shall submit the prescribed notification to the company in advance before engaging in the work set forth in the preceding paragraph.

3. By engaging in the work of paragraph 1, the company may prohibit or limit any of the following items if they fall under any of the following items.

① there is a problem in labor provision

② a company secret is leaked

③ there is an act that damages the honor and credibility of the company, or an act that destroys trust.

④ the competition harms the profits of the company

Appendix

(date of enforcement)

Article 1 These rules of employment shall be enforced from____(month/day/year).

(出典：厚生労働省ホームページ「The Model Rules of Employment (March 2013)」を著者一部加筆)

2　定時株主総会開催までの一連の手続

会社は，定款で決算期を定めており，取締役は，毎事業年度の終了後一定の時期に定時株主総会を招集しなければならず（会社296条），計算書類及び事業報告を定時株主総会に提出し，又は提供しなければならない（会社438条）としている。

例９は，定時株主総会招集の取締役会決議，株主に対する招集通知，定時株主総会決議，定時総会後の代表取締役の選任のための取締役会議事録（抄）を掲載している。

定時株主総会開催のための取締役会において開催日時，提案事項を決議する。

〈例９　定時株主総会開催のための取締役会議事録〉

■■■■株式会社
取締役会議事録
MINUTES OF MEETING OF BOARD OF DIRECTORS
OF ■■■■ KK

第１号議案　第10期（自平成■年１月１日至平成■年12月31日）計算書類等の承認の件
Item No. 1 on Agenda: Approval of financial statements, etc. of the 10th Fiscal Year (from January 1st, ■■ to December 31st, ■■)

議長は，第10期（自平成■年１月１日至平成■年12月31日）における当会社の営業状況を詳細に報告し，下記計算書類等を提出して，その承認を求めた。
The Chairperson gave the meeting a detailed explanation of the business results of the Company for the 10th Fiscal Year (from January 1st, ■■ to December 31st, ■■), in connection with which she submitted the following financial statements, etc.:

１．貸借対照表
１．Balance sheet;
２．損益計算書
２．Profit and loss statement;
３．株主資本等変動計算書および個別注記表
３．Statement of changes in shareholders' equity and individual explanatory notes
４．事業報告

4．Business report; and
5．上記の附属明細書
5．Annex specifications.

慎重審議の結果，出席取締役は上記を全員一致で異議なく承認した。
After a full deliberation, all the Directors present approved the same without objection.

第2号議案　第10回定時株主総会招集の件
Item No. 2 on Agenda: Convocation of the 10th Ordinary General Meeting of Shareholders
議長は，当会社の第10回定時株主総会を次の通り開催したい旨を提案した。
The Chairperson proposed to the meeting that the 10th Ordinary General Meeting of Shareholders would be convened as stated below:

開催日時　■■■年3月23日　午後6時00分（東京時間）
Date and time: 6:00 p.m. on March 23rd, ■■■ (Tokyo Time)
開催場所　ドイツ連邦共和国における■■■■H本店
Place: The head office of ■■■■ in Germany
招集目的
Purpose of the meeting:
報告事項　第10期（自■■■年1月1日至■■■年12月31日）事業報告の内容報告の件
Matters to be reported: Reporting of the business report for the 10th Fiscal Year (from January 1st, ■■■ to December 31st, ■■■)
決議事項　第1号議案　第10期（自■■■年1月1日至■■■年12月31日）計算書類等の承認の件
Matters to resolution: Item No. 1 on Agenda: Approval of the financial statements, etc. for the 10th Fiscal Year (from January 1st, ■■■ to December 31st, ■■■)
第2号議案　取締役選任の件
Item No. 2 on Agenda: Appointment of Directors

慎重審議の結果，出席取締役は上記を全員一致で異議なく承認した。
After a full deliberation, all the Directors present approved the same without objection.

〈例10　監査役の会社に対する監査報告書の提出〉

■■年３月16日
March 16, ■■

東京都■■区■町■番■号
■■株式会社
代表取締役社長 ■■ 殿
■-■, ■■-cho, ■■-ku, Tokyo
■■ K.K.
Representative Director ■■

監査役 ＿＿＿＿＿＿＿＿
Statutory Auditor ■■
(■■)

監査報告書の提出について
Submission of the Audit Report

私監査役は，会社法第381条第１項の規定に基づき監査報告書を作成しましたので，別紙のとおり提出いたします。

I have prepared this audit report in accordance with the provisions of Article 381, paragraph 1 of the Companies Act of Japan, and submit the report as per enclosure.

以上
End

〈例11　監査報告書〉

監　査　報　告　書
Audit　Report

私監査役は，■■年１月１日から■■年12月31日までの第■期事業年度の取締役の職務の執行を監査いたしました。その方法及び結果につき以下のとおり報告いたします。

With respect to the directors' performance of their duties during the

■th business year (from January 1, ■ to December 31, ■), I have prepared this audit report, and hereby report as follows:

1．監査の方法及びその内容

監査役は，当会社の取締役および労働者等と意思疎通を図り，情報の収集および監査の環境の整備に努めるとともに，取締役会その他重要な会議に出席し，取締役および労働者等からその職務執行状況について報告を受け，必要に応じて説明を求め，重要な決議書類等を閲覧し，当会社の本社および主要な事業所において業務および財産の状況を調査いたしました。以上の方法に基づき，当会社の当該事業年度に係る事業報告およびその附属明細書について検討いたしました。

さらに，会計帳簿またはこれに関する資料の調査を行い，当該事業年度に係る計算書類（貸借対照表，損益計算書，株主資本等変動等計算書および個別注記表）およびその附属明細書について検討いたしました。

1．Method and Contents of Audit

Statutory auditor has communicated with directors and workers, etc. and tried to collect information and improve the auditing environment, as well as attended the board and any other important meetings, received reports from directors and workers, etc. on the status of performance of their duties, requested an explanation as appropriate, inspected material documents of settlement, etc., and examined the status of business and property at the head office and principal business places. Based on the above method, we have reviewed the business report relating to the relevant business year and the detailed schedules attached thereto.

In addition, conducting the examination with respect to the account books or materials relating thereto, Statutory auditor examined the accounting documents (balance sheets, profit and loss statement, shareholders' equity variation statement, and schedule of individual notes) and the annexed specifications thereto for the business year under consideration.

2．監査の結果

(1)　事業報告等の監査結果

一　事業報告及びその付属明細書は，法令及び定款に従い，会社の状況を正しく示しているものと認めます。

二　取締役の職務執行に関する不正の行為又は法令もしくは定款に違反する重大な事実は認められません。

(2)　計算書類及びその附属明細書の監査結果

計算書類およびその附属書類は，会社の財産および損益の状況をすべての重要な点において適正に表示しているものと認めます。

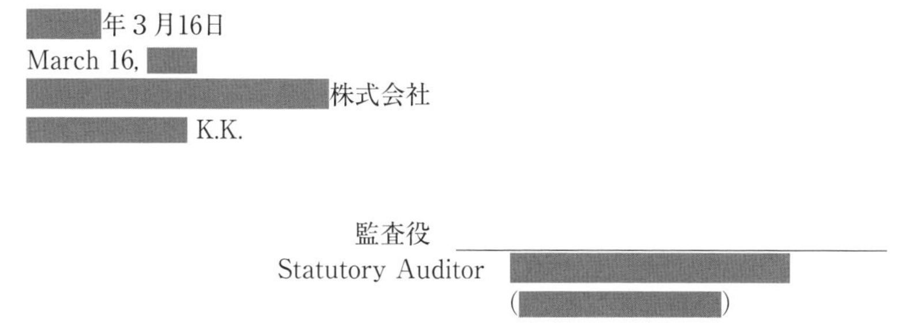

2．Result of Audit

(1) Result of Audit of Business Report, etc.

(i) I acknowledge that the business report and the annexed specifications thereto fairly present the status of the Company in conformity with the applicable laws and regulations and the articles of incorporation of the company.

(ii) I acknowledge that no misconduct or material fact constituting a violation of any law ore regulation or the articles of incorporation of the company was found with respect to the directors' performance of their duties.

(2) Results of Audit of Accounting Documents and their Annexed Specifications

I acknowledge that the Accounting Documents and their Annexed Specifications accurately indicate the status of the assets and profits and losses of the Company in all material respects.

年３月16日
March 16,
株式会社
K.K.

監査役 ＿＿＿＿＿＿＿＿
Statutory Auditor
( )

例12は取締役会の決議に従って株主に対して，開催日より定款で定められた日までに招集通知をする文例である。

〈例12　株主総会招集通知書〉

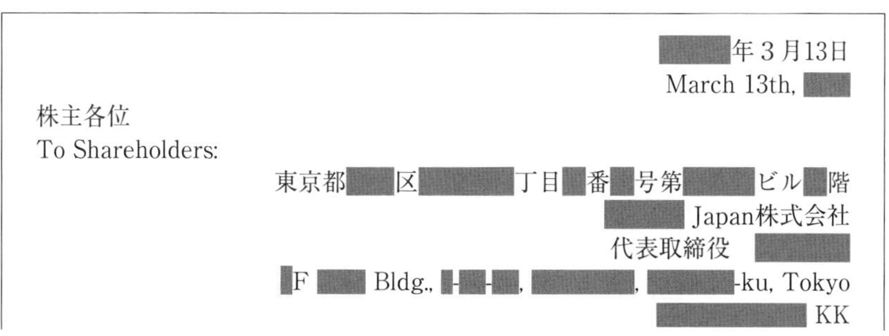

年３月13日
March 13th,

株主各位
To Shareholders:

東京都　区　丁目　番　号第　ビル　階
Japan株式会社
代表取締役
F　Bldg., - - , , -ku, Tokyo
KK

Representative Director: ■■■■

第10回定時株主総会招集ご通知
NOTICE OF THE 10TH ORDINARY GENERAL MEETING OF SHAREHOLDERS

拝啓,
時下ますますご清栄のこととお喜び申し上げます。
さて，今般当社第10回定時株主総会を下記のとおり開催いたしますので，ご出席くださいますようご通知申し上げます。

敬具

You are requested to attend the 10th Ordinary General Meeting of Shareholders, the details of which are as set forth below:

記
Particulars

開催日時　■■■年３月23日　午後６時00分（東京時間）
Date and time: 6:00 p.m. on March 23rd, ■■■（Tokyo Time）
開催場所　ドイツ連邦共和国における■■■■H本店
Place: The head office of ■■■■ in Germany
招集目的
Purpose of the meeting:
報告事項　第10期（自■■■年１月１日至■■■年12月31日）事業報告の内容報告の件
Matters to be reported: Reporting of the business report for the 10th Fiscal Year（from January 1st, ■■■ to December 31st, ■■■）
決議事項　第１号議案　第10期（自■■■年■月■日至■■■年■月■日）計算書類等の承認の件
Matters to resolution: Item No.1 on Agenda: Approval of the financial statements, etc. for the 10th Fiscal Year（from January 1st, ■■■ to December 31st, ■■■）
第２号議案　取締役選任の件
Item No.2 on Agenda: Appointment of Directors

以上
End

〈例13　招集通知書に添付する株主総会参考書類〉

株主総会参考書類
Reference documents for Shareholders meeting

議案及び参考事項
Proposal and Reference matters

報告事項　Matters to be reported
第20期（自　[redacted]年１月１日　至　[redacted]年12月31日）事業報告の報告の件
Reporting of Business report for the 20th fiscal term（January 1, [redacted] to December 31, [redacted]）

決議事項　Matters to resolution
第１号議案　第20期（自　[redacted]年１月１日　至　[redacted]年12月31日）計算書類等の承認の件
Item No.1 on the Agenda: Approval of Financial statement for 20th fiscal term（January 1, [redacted] to December 31, [redacted]）
第２号議案　取締役選任の件
Item No.2 on the Agenda: Appointment of Directors
取締役の全員が本総会終了をもって任期が満了いたしますので，その後任の取締役の選任をお願いします。　その候補者は次のとおりであります。
I would like to elect successor Directors as the term of office of all directors of the Company would expire at the conclusion of shareholders meeting. The candidates are as follows ;

候補者 番　号 No.	氏　名　Name （生年月日） Date of birth	常勤・非常勤/社外・否 Full time or Part-time Outside or not	所有する当社株式の数 Number of shares
1	[redacted] （年月日生）	常勤　/　取締役	０株
2	[redacted] （年　月　日生）	常勤　/　取締役	０株
3	[redacted] （年月日生）	常勤　/　取締役	０株

4	████ ████ （年月日生）	常勤　／　取締役	0株
5	████ ████ （　年　月　日生）	常勤　／　取締役	0株

議案の内容は，添付書類に記載のとおりです。
Proposal is as described in the attachment documents.

以上
Period

〈例14　招集通知書に添付する議決権行使書〉

議決権行使書
VOTING CARD

████株式会社　御中
To ████ K.K.

私は，████年３月31日に開催の貴社定時株主総会の各議案につき，下記（賛否を○印で表示）のとおり議決権を行使致します。
なお，賛否の表示をしない場合は，賛としてお取扱いください。
I exercise my voting rights as follows（please circle “Aye” or “Nay”）on the proposal of the Ordinay General Meeting of Shareholders on March 31, ████.
Please treat as “Aye” if there is no indication.

議決権行使株式数　　　　　　株
Number of voting righs:　　　　shares

議　案	原案に対する賛否
第１号議案（第20期計算書類等の承認の件）	賛　・　否
第２号議案（取締役選任の件）	賛　・　否

Proposal	Approval or Opposition
Proposal 1 Approval of Financial statement for 20th fiscal term	Aye　・　Nay
Proposal 2 Appointment of Directors	Aye　・　Nay

株主
Shareholder's name ....

〈例15-1　招集通知書に添付する議決権の委任状〉

委　任　状

[黒塗り]株式会社の株主である私は，＿＿＿＿＿＿＿＿
を代理人と定め下記の権限を委任致します。

記

1．[黒塗り]年10月16日開催の[黒塗り]株式会社の臨時株主総会（その継続会又は延会を含む。）に出席し，次の決議につき，私の指示（下記に○で表示）に従って議決権を行使すること。但し，賛否いずれとも表示していない議案に関する賛否及び原案に対する修正案又は議事進行等に関する動議が提出された場合の議決権行使については，白紙委任致します。

第１号議案　　原案に対し　　賛　・　否

2．復代理人選任の件。

平成　　年　　月　　日

株　主

住所：

氏名：　　　　　　　　　　印

〈例15－２　招集通知書に添付する議決権の委任状（英文）〉

Power of Attorney

KNOW ALL MEN BY THESE PRESENTS:
That I, a shareholder of ████████ KK, do hereby make, constitute and appoint________________________, as my true and lawful attorney in fact and delegate the following authority.

(Matter)

1. To attend the Extraordinary General Meeting of Shareholders of ████ ████ KK on October 16, ███ including such continue meeting or adjourn and exercise my vote rights according to my instruction as follows; however, I give the mandatary carte blanche for the execution of vote in case of the pros and cons for the proposal not stated the pros and cons and the alternative suggestions for the original proposal or where someone submits a motion relevant to the proceedings and etc.

Item No.1 on the Agenda　　Aye　　Nay　　on the original proposal

2. To appoint sub-agent

Date:

Shareholder:

Address:

Name:

〈例16　定時株主総会議事録〉

████株式会社
第10回定時株主総会議事録
MINUTES OF THE 10TH ORDINARY GENERAL MEETING OF SHAREHOLDERS OF ████ KK

████年３月23日午後６時00分（東京時間），ドイツ連邦共和国における████本店会議室において，当社第10回定時株主総会を開催した。

The 10rd Ordinary General Meeting of Shareholders of the company was held at the head office of the ██████ in Germany from 6:00 p.m. on March 23rd, ███ （Tokyo Time）.

発行済株式の総数　1,000,000株
All of issued shares:　1,000,000
議決権を行使することができる株主の総数　1名
Total number of shareholders entitled to exercise the right to vote:　1
議決権を行使することができる株主の議決権の数　1,000,000個
Number of votes of shareholders entitled to exercise the right to vote:　1,000,000
出席した当該株主の数（委任状による出席を含む。）　1名
Number of shareholders who are present at this shareholders meeting including by proxy:　1
出席した当該株主の有する議決権の数　1,000,000個
Number of votes which shareholders who are present at this shareholders meeting hold:　1,000,000

出席取締役　████, ██████████, ██████
Director present: ████, ██████████, ██████
出席監査役　██████
Statutory Auditor present：██████
議事録の作成に係る職務を行った取締役　代表取締役社長　████
Director who has performed the duty concerning preparation of these minutes: ██████ Representative Director and President

上記のとおり株主が出席したので，本総会は適法に成立した。よって，定刻に定款第15条の規定により代表取締役社長████は議長となり，開会を宣して議事の審議に入った。
The shareholders being present as described above, this general meeting was duly convened. Therfore, ██████ Representative Director and President, took the chair at the fixed time pursuant to the Article 15 of the Articles of Incorporation of the Company, announced the opening of the meeting, and commenced the deliberation of the item on the agenda.

第1号議案　第10期（自███年1月1日至███年12月31日）計算書類等の承認及び事業報告の内容報告の件
Item No. 1 on the Agenda: Approval of financial statements, etc. and Reporting of the business report for the 10th Fiscal Year（from January

1st, ████ to December 31st, ████)

議長は，第10期（自█████年１月１日至█████年12月31日）における事業状況を事業報告書により詳細に説明報告し，下記計算書類等を提出してその承認を求めた。
The Chairperson explained the contents of the business report for the 10th Fiscal Year (from January 1st, ████ to December 31st, ████) in detail and submitted following financial statements, etc. to the shareholders and asked for the approval thereof:

１．貸借対照表
１．Balance sheet;
２．損益計算書
２．Profit and loss statement;
３．株主資本等変動計算書
３．Statement of changes in shareholders' equity; and
４．個別注記表
４．Individual explanatory notes.

ついで，監査役が上記の書類を綿密に調査したところ，いずれも正確妥当であることを認めた旨を報告した。
Then, the Statutory Auditor reported that all documents shown above had been audited closely and, as a result, concluded to be correct and lawful.

慎重審議の結果，総会は別段の異議なく承認可決した。
After a full deliberation, the general meeting approved the proposal without opposition.

第２号議案　取締役選任の件
Item No. 2 on Agenda: Appointment of Directors

議長は，取締役の全員が本総会終了をもって任期が満了する旨を報告し，その後任の取締役を選任する必要があることを説明した。ついで議長が本議案について賛否を議場に諮ったところ，以下の各氏が全員一致をもって取締役に選任され，可決確定した。
The chairperson reported the attention of the meeting to the fact that the term of office of all Directors of the Company would expire at the close of this general meeting, and explained that it was accordingly necessary to elect their successors. On motion duly made and seconded, the persons stated below were unanimously elected serve as Directors:

取締役　██████，████████████████████，█████
██████

Directors: ████, ████, ████ ████

なお，選任された取締役は，その場で就任を承諾する旨を表明した。
The above Dirctors appointed accepted their election to office respectively.
以上をもって本総会の議事を終了したので，議長は，午後６時30分閉会を宣した。
Having completed the subject for this general meeting, the Chairperson declared the meeting adjourned at 6:30 p.m.

上記議事の経過の要領及びその結果を明確にするため本議事録を作成し，議長及び出席取締役全員が以下に記名・捺印又は署名する。
In order to preserve clear records of the substance of proceeding of the meeting as well as the results thereof, these minutes have been prepared, the seals were affixed or the signatures were appended by the Chairperson and all the Directors who were present at the meeting and whose names appear below.

████年３月23日
March 23rd, ████

████株式会社　第10回定時株主総会
The 10rd Ordinary General Meeting of Shareholders of ████ KK

議長・代表取締役 ████
Chairperson &
Representative Director ████

代表取締役 ████
Representative Director ████

取締役 ████
Director ████

第2章　株式会社

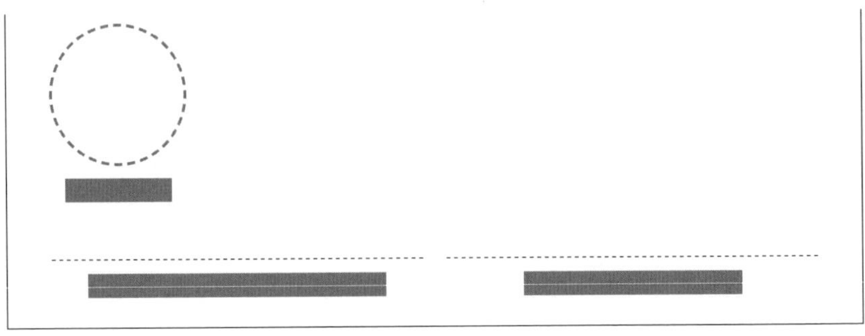

例17は商業登記規則が改正され，平成28年10月１日より登記の申請に当たり，添付書面として株主リストが必要になった（商業登記規則61条３項）。

〈**例17－１　株主リスト証明書**〉

証　明　書

[redacted]年３月24日付け臨時株主総会の全議案につき，総議決権数（当該議案につき，議決権を行使することができる全ての株主の有する議決権の数の合計をいう。以下同じ。）に対する株主の有する議決権（当該議案につき議決権を行使できるものに限る。以下同じ。）の数の割合が高いことにおいて上位となる株主であって，次の①と②の人数のうち少ない方の人数の株主の氏名又は名称及び住所，当該株主のそれぞれが有する株式の数（種類株主総会の決議を要する場合にあっては，その種類の株式の数）及び議決権の数並びに当該株主のそれぞれが有する議決権の数に係る当該割合は，次のとおりであることを証明します。

①　10名

②　その有する議決権の数の割合をその割合の多い順に順次加算し，その加算した割合が３分の２に達するまでの人数

	名　前	住　所	株式数	議決権の数	割　合
1	[redacted]	埼玉県川口市[redacted]	13,000	13,000	50.0%
2	[redacted]	埼玉県川口市[redacted]	13,000	13,000	50.0%

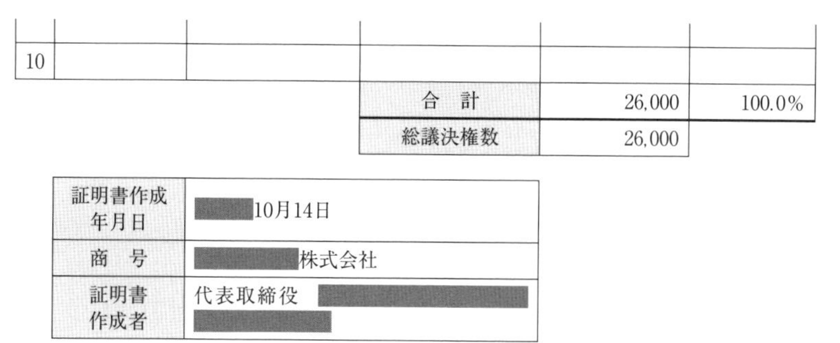

10					
			合　計	26,000	100.0%
			総議決権数	26,000	

証明書作成年月日	■■■■10月14日
商　号	■■■■■■■■株式会社
証明書作成者	代表取締役　■■■■■■■■■■■■■■■■ ■■■■■■■■■■

〈例17－2　株主リスト証明書（英文）〉

Certification for Shareholders

In comparison of the below ① and ② with respect to the total number of exercisable voting rights, this document is to certify the smaller amount. Regarding all agendas of the general meeting of Shareholders of ■■■■■■■■ K.K. dated on October 14, ■■■, it is hereby certified the name, address, number of shares, and number of voting rights of the shareholder as follows.

① 10 top shareholders

② Accumulated number of top shareholders that reach two-thirds of the total number of voting rights

	Name	Address	Number of Shares	Number of Voting Rights	Percentage
1	■■■■■ ■■■■■■ ■■■■	■■-■, ■■■■, Kawaguchishi, Saitama	13,000	13,000	50.0%
2	■■■■■■ ■■■■■■■	■■-■, ■■■■, Kawaguchishi, Saitama	13,000	13,000	50.0%
10					
			Total	26,000	100.0%
			Total Number of Voting Rights	26,000	

October 14, ■■■

■■■■■■■■■■■■■■■■■■, Representative Director　　　SEAL

例18は，招集通知に記載された提案に従って，議事並びに議決内容を簡明に記述されることになる。

〈例18　株主総会終結後の取締役会議事録（代表取締役選任）〉

株式会社
取締役会議事録
MINUTES OF MEETING OF BOARD OF DIRECTORS
OF KK

第１号議案　代表取締役選定の件
Item No.1 on Agenda: Election of Representative Directors

議長は，代表取締役を選定したい旨を述べ，議場に諮ったところ，全員一致により下記のものが選定された。
The Chairperson proposed to elect Representative Directors of the Company, and on motion duly made and seconded the following persons were unanimously elected to the office indicated below:

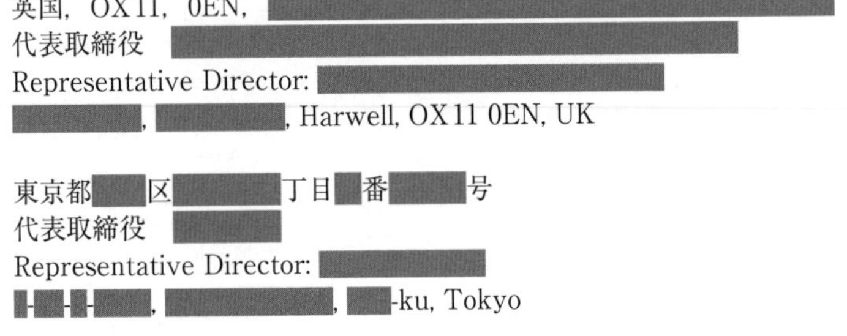

英国，OX11，0EN，
代表取締役
Representative Director:
, , Harwell, OX11 0EN, UK

東京都　区　丁目　番　号
代表取締役
Representative Director:
, , -ku, Tokyo

なお，被選定者は直ちにその就任を承諾した。
The above Representative Directors appointed accepted their election to office respectively.

例19は，取締役会設置会社でない場合で，定款の定めに基づく取締役の互選によって取締役の中から代表取締役を定めたときの互選書である。登記申請の際は各取締役の印鑑証明書を添付することになる。

〈例19　代表取締役選任の互選書〉

互　選　書

Written Appointment of Representative Director

年２月12日午前　　時　　分当会社本店会議室において，取締役全員の一致をもって，次の事項につき可決確定した。

At　　　　　　am on February 12,　　in the conference room of the head office of the Company, the following matter was unanimously approved by all Directors.

代表取締役選定の件

Concerning the Election of Representative Director

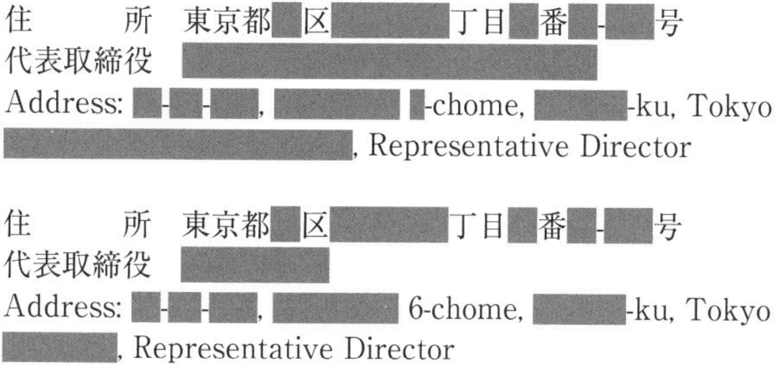

住　　所　東京都　区　　丁目　番　-　号
代表取締役
Address:　-　-　,　　-chome,　　-ku, Tokyo
, Representative Director

住　　所　東京都　区　　丁目　番　-　号
代表取締役
Address:　-　-　,　　6-chome,　　-ku, Tokyo
, Representative Director

尚，被選定者は，席上，就任承諾した。

The persons selected have accepted the offered position.

上記の決議を明確にするため，本議事録を作り，出席取締役全員がこれに記名押印する。

These minutes have been prepared in evidence of the above resolution, with the names and seals or signatures of each of the directors present affixed below.

年２月12日

February 12,

個人の実印

株式会社

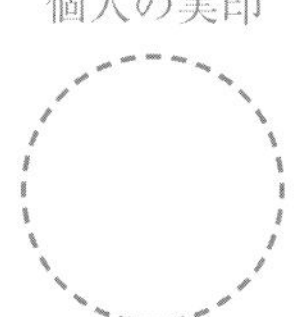

取締役

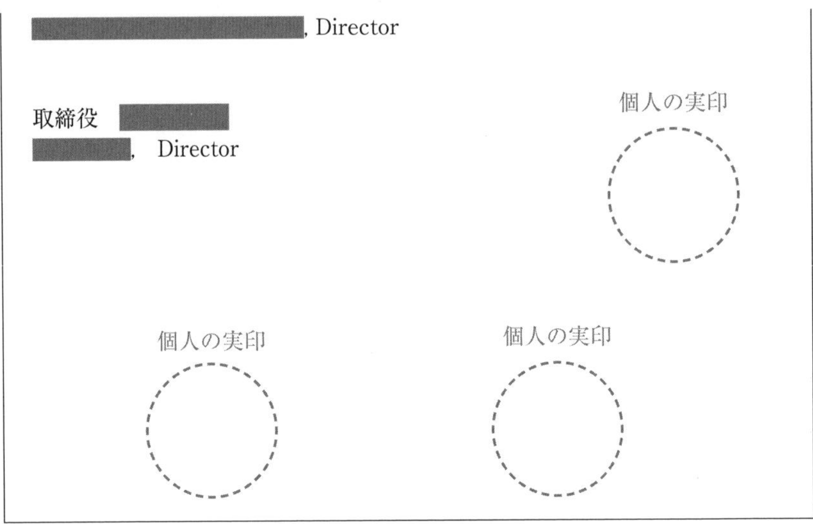

, Director

取締役
, Director

個人の実印

個人の実印

個人の実印

〈例20　取締役就任承諾書〉

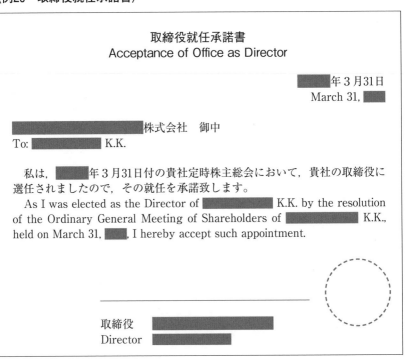

取締役就任承諾書
Acceptance of Office as Director

年３月31日
March 31,

株式会社　御中
To: K.K.

私は，年３月31日付の貴社定時株主総会において，貴社の取締役に選任されましたので，その就任を承諾致します。

As I was elected as the Director of K.K. by the resolution of the Ordinary General Meeting of Shareholders of K.K., held on March 31, , I hereby accept such appointment.

取締役
Director

〈例21　代表取締役承認承諾書〉

代表取締役就任承諾書
Acceptance of Office as Representative Director

年３月31日
March 31,

株式会社 御中
To:

私は，　年３月31日付の貴社取締役会において，貴社の代表取締役に選定されましたので，その就任を承諾致します。

As I was elected as the Representative director of　K.K. by the resolution of the Meeting of Board of Directors of　K.K., held on March 31,　, I hereby accept such appointment.

代表取締役
Representative　Director

〈例22　就任承諾書（監査役）〉

監査役就任承諾書
Acceptance of Office as Statutory Auditor

私は，　年10月16日付の貴社臨時株主総会において，貴社の監査役に選任されましたので，その就任を承諾致します。

As I was elected as the Statutory Auditor of　K.K. by the resolution of the Extraordinary General Meeting of Shareholders of　K.K., held on October 16,　, I hereby accept such appointment.

3　定款変更のための議事録等

(1)　本店移転

ア　定款変更（他管轄への本店移転）

定款の規定上，第○条（本店所在地）「当会社は，本店を東京都○○区に置く。」と規定している。そこで，当該区を管轄している登記所より，他管轄登記所管内に本店を移転するときは，定款変更事由となる。そこで，定款変更のためには，株主総会を招集し，その旨の決議が必要になる。その株主総会招集のために取締役会を開催しなければならない。

例23は，海外に居住する外国人取締役のため，電話会議システムを利用しての取締役会を開催し，その議事経過をまとめた議事録である。

〈例23　取締役会議事録（株主総会召集のための取締役会開催）〉

■■■■Japan株式会社
取締役会議事録

MINUTES OF MEETING OF BOARD OF DIRECTORS
OF ■■■■ JAPAN KK

■■■■年２月22日午後４時30分（東京時間），当会社本店会議室において取締役会が開催され，電話回線及び電話会議装置からなる電話会議システムを用いて，以下の取締役が出席した。当会社定款第24条の規定により，代表取締役社長■■■■氏が議長となり開会を告げ，電話会議システムにより，出席者の音声が他の出席者に伝わり，出席者が一堂に会するのと同等に適時的確な意思表明が互いにできる状態になっていることが確認されて，議事の審議に入った。
The Meeting of the Board of Directors was held in the meeting room at the head office of the Company from 4:30 p.m. on February 22, ■■■■ (Tokyo Time) and attended by the following Directors, using a telephone meeting system with telephone line and telephone meeting equipments. Ms. ■■■■, Representative Director and President, took the chair pursuant to the Article 24 of the Articles of Incorporation of the Company, announced the opening of the meeting, and commenced the deliberation of the item on the agenda, after confirmation that attendance can listen speech of other attendances and attendances can express their opinions promptly in session using a telephone meeting system.

本店出席取締役
Director present at the head office
電話会議による出席取締役

Director present through conference call:

（取締役総数３名，出席取締役数３名）
（Total number of Directors: 3, Number of Directors present at the meeting: 3）

第１号議案　臨時株主総会招集の件
Item No. 1 on Agenda: Convocation of the Extraordinary General Meeting of Shareholders
議長は，当会社の臨時株主総会を次の通り開催したい旨を提案した。
The Chairperson proposed to the meeting that the Extraordinary General Meeting of Shareholders would be convened as stated below:

開催日時　　年３月１日　午後４時00分（東京時間）
Date and time: 4:00 p.m. on March 1, （Tokyo Time）
開催場所　当会社本店
Place: The head office of the Company
招集目的
Purpose of the meeting:
決議事項　第１号議案　定款変更の件
Matters to resolution: Item No. 1 on the Agenda: Amendments to the Articles of Incorporation of the Company
　当社の本店を移転することに伴い，　年３月14日付で当会社の定款を下記のとおり変更する。

現　行	変更後
第３条（本店所在地） 当会社は，本店を東京都渋谷区に置く。	第３条（本店所在地） 当会社は，本店を東京都中央区に置く。

　The Articles of Incorporation of the Company shall be amended as follows as of March 14, , subject to the transfer of the Company's headquarters.

Current Provision	Proposed Provision
Article 3（Main Office Location） The Company's headquarter shall	Article 3（Main Office Location） The Company's headquarter shall

be located in Shibuya-ku, Tokyo.	be located in Chuo-ku, Tokyo.

慎重審議の結果，出席取締役は上記を全員一致で異議なく承認した。
After a full deliberation, all the Directors present approved the same without objection.

以上をもって電話会議システムを用いた本取締役会は，終始異常なく議事を終了したので，議長は，午後４時45分閉会を宣した。
Having completed the subject for this Meeting of Board of Directors using a telephone meeting system without any difficulties in transmission from start to finish, the Chairperson declared the meeting adjourned at 4:45 p.m.

上記議事の経過の要領及びその結果を明確にするため本議事録を作成し，議長及び出席取締役全員が以下に記名・捺印又は署名する。
In order to preserve clear records of the substance of proceeding of the meeting as well as the results thereof, these minutes have been prepared, the seals were affixed or the signatures were appended by the Chairperson and all the Directors who were present at the meeting and whose names appear below.

年２月22日
February 22,

株式会社　取締役会
Meeting of Board of Directors of KK

議長・代表取締役
Chairperson & Representative Director

代表取締役
Representative Director

取締役
Director

例24は，**例23**の取締役会決議に従い，株主に対して臨時株主総会の招集を通知する文書となる。株主総会の会日は，定款の規定に従い，定められた日以前に株主に招集通知を発することに注意しなければならない。

〈例24　臨時株主総会招集通知書〉

■年２月22日
February 22, ■

株主各位
To Shareholders:

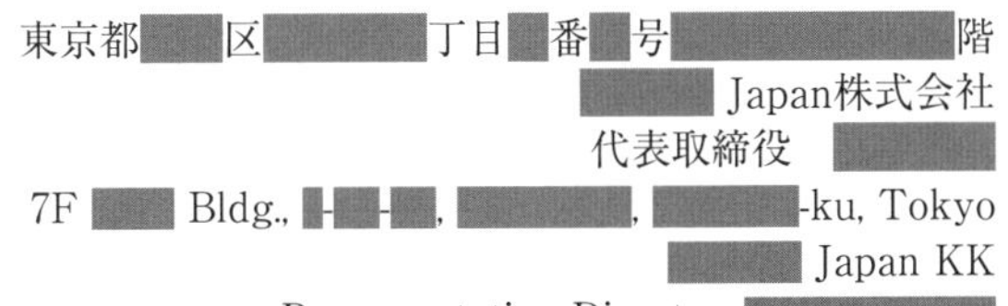
東京都■区■丁目■番■号■階
■Japan株式会社
代表取締役　■
7F ■ Bldg., ■-■-■, ■, ■-ku, Tokyo
■ Japan KK
Representative Director: ■

臨時株主総会招集ご通知
NOTICE OF THE EXTRAORDINARY GENERAL MEETING OF SHAREHOLDERS

拝啓，
時下ますますご清栄のこととお喜び申し上げます。
さて，今般当社臨時株主総会を下記のとおり開催いたしますので，ご出席くださいますようご通知申し上げます。

敬具

You are requested to attend the Extraordinary General Meeting of Shareholders, the details of which are as set forth below:

記
Particulars

開催日時　■年３月１日　午後４時00分（東京時間）
Date and time: 4:00 p.m. on March 1, ■ (Tokyo Time)
開催場所　当会社本店
Place: The head office of the Company
招集目的
Purpose of the meeting:
決議事項　第１号議案　定款変更の件
Matters to resolution: Item No. 1 on the Agenda: Amendments to the Articles of Incorporation of the Company

当社の本店を移転することに伴い，████年３月14日付で当会社の定款を下記のとおり変更する。

現　行	変更後
第３条（本店所在地） 当会社は，本店を東京都渋谷区に置く。	第３条（本店所在地） 当会社は，本店を東京都中央区に置く。

The Articles of Incorporation of the Company shall be amended as follows as of March 14, ████, subject to the transfer of the Company's headquarters.

Current Provision	Proposed Provision
Article 3（Main Office Location） The Company's headquarter shall be located in Shibuya-ku, Tokyo.	Article 3（Main Office Location） The Company's headquarter shall be located in Chuo-ku, Tokyo.

以上
End

〈例25　臨時株主総会議事録の本店所在地変更決議事項（抄）〉

第１号議案　定款変更の件
Item No. 1 on the Agenda: Amendments to the Articles of Incorporation of the Company

議長は，当社の本店を移転することに伴い，████年３月14日付で当会社の定款を下記のとおり変更したい旨を提案した。

現　行	変更後
第３条（本店所在地） 当会社は，本店を東京都渋谷区に置く。	第３条（本店所在地） 当会社は，本店を東京都中央区に置く。

The Chairperson proposed to the meeting that the Articles of Incorporation of the Company shall be amended as follows as of March 14, ████, subject to the transfer of the Company's headquarters.

Current Provision	Proposed Provision
Article 3（Main Office Location） The Company's headquarter shall be located in Shibuya-ku, Tokyo.	Article 3（Main Office Location） The Company's headquarter shall be located in Chuo-ku, Tokyo.

> 次いで議長が本件を議場に諮ったところ，審議の後議長の提案は満場一致で承認可決された。
> Then the Chairperson referred the matter to the meeting, at which after deliberation, the proposal by the Chairperson was unanimously approved.

イ　定款変更（同一管轄登記所内での本店移転）

定款の規定上，第○条（本店所在地）「当会社は，本店を東京都中央区区に置く。」としているときに，その本店が中央区銀座にあり，本店を中央区日本橋に移転するのであれば，同一管轄登記所内での本店移転であり，定款変更事由が発生しない。この場合は，取締役会において決議すればよいことになる。

〈例26　取締役会議事録（抄）〉

> 第１号議案　本店移転の件
> Item No. 1 on Agenda: Relocation of Headquarters
>
> 議長は，業務の都合上本店を下記の場所に移転したい旨を提案した。
> The Chairperson proposed to the meeting to relocate the headquarters of the Company for its commercial benefit, as detailed below.
>
> 本店　　東京都■区■丁目■番■号　■ビル７階
> Headquarters:　■ Bldg 7th floor, ■-■, ■ ■-chome, ■-ku, Tokyo
> 移転日　■年３月14日
> Relocation Date:　March 14, ■
>
> 慎重審議の結果，出席取締役は上記を全員一致で異議なく承認した。
> After a full deliberation, all the Directors present approved the same without objection.

(2)　商号変更

商号変更は定款変更事由に該当するので株主総会決議事項である。株主総会招集のための取締役会については，前記(1)の書式を参考にしていただきたい。

株主総会の目的となる事項について取締役会又は株主からの提案につ

き，当該事項について議決権を有する全ての株主が書面又は電磁的記録をもって当該提案に同意したときは，当該提案を可決する旨の株主総会の決議があったものとみなされる（会社319条１項）。

この書面又は電磁的記録には，①取締役，株主又は社員の提案の内容，②株主又は社員がこの提案に対しての同意の２点が書面又は電磁的記録に記載されていなければならない。

この書面又は電磁的記録が全ての株主又は社員から会社に到達時点で決議があったものと見なされる。

〈例27　株主同意書〉

同　意　書
Certificate of Consent

■■株式会社（「当会社」という）御中
To: ■■ K.K.（the "Company"）

弊社は，会社法第319条第１項の規定に基づき，下記の株主総会決議事項についての取締役提案の内容に同意します。
I hereby agree to the proposal by the Directors of the Company with respect to the following matter which is the purpose of the shareholders meeting pursuant to Paragraph 1 of Article 319 of the Companies Act, Japan.

取締役提案の内容 The proposal by the Directors of the Company
１．定款の一部変更　Amendment to the Articles of Incorporation of the Company
当会社の定款を，■■年10月１日をもって以下のとおり変更する。
Articles of Incorporation of the Company shall be amended as of October 1, ■■ as follow:

現定款　Current Articles	変更案　Proposed Amendment
第１条（商号） 当会社は，■■株式会社と称し，英語では■■ K.K.と表示する。 Article 1.（Corporate Name） This company shall be called	第１条（商号） 当会社は，■■・M株式会社と称し，英語では■■ M K.K.と表示する。 Article 1.（Corporate Name） This company shall be called

" Kabushiki-Kaisha", which shall be expressed in English as "・K.K."	" M Kabushiki-Kaisha", which shall be expressed in English as " M K.K."

2．取締役の選任　Election of Directors

当会社は，下記の者を，年10月1日をもって当会社の取締役に選任する。

The Company shall elect the following persons as Directors of the Company as of October 1, :

取締役候補者: ,

Candidates for Directors: ,

年9月28日 / September 28,

B.V.

By: ＿＿＿＿＿＿＿＿＿＿＿＿
Name:
Title:

例28は，全株主の同意書によって株主総会の議決があったものと見なされるとしても，当然議事録は作成されなければならない（会社法施行規則72条4項1号）。

〈例28　臨時株主総会議事録（決議省略，商号変更）〉

臨時株主総会議事録
Minutes of the Extraordinary General Meeting of Shareholders

年9月28日，下記の事項について，株主全員の同意が書面によりなされたため，会社法第319条第1項に基づき，当該提案を可決する旨の株主総会の決議があったものとみなされた。

Regarding the following matter, it should be deemed that the resolution to approve such proposal at the shareholders meeting has been made as the Company received their intention to agree to such proposal in writing pursuant to the provisions of Article 319 (1) of Companies Act on September 28, .

1．みなし決議事項の内容 Content of the matter deemed to be resolved

会社法第319条第１項に基づき，株主総会決議があったものとみなされた事項の内容

Contents of the matter that the Resolution of the Shareholders Meeting was deemed to have been made under the provision of Article 319（1）of Companies Act

(a)　定款の一部変更 Amendment to the Articles of Incorporation of the Company

当会社の定款を，█████年10月１日をもって以下のとおり変更する。

Articles of Incorporation of the Company shall be amended as of October 1, ████ as follow:

現定款　Current Articles	変更案　Proposed Amendment
第１条（商号） 当会社は，█████株式会社と称し，英語では█████ K.K.と表示する。 Article 1.（Corporate Name） This company shall be called "█████ Kabushiki-Kaisha", which shall be expressed in English as "█████ K.K."	第１条（商号） 当会社は，█████ M株式会社と称し，英語では█████ M K.K.と表示する。 Article 1.（Corporate Name） This company shall be called "█████ M Kabushiki-Kaisha", which shall be expressed in English as "█████ M K.K."

(b)　取締役の選任　Election of Directors

当会社は，下記の者を，█████年10月１日をもって当会社の取締役に選任する。

The Company shall elect the following persons as Directors of the Company as of October 1, ████:

取締役候補者: ████████, ██████

Candidates for Directors: ████████████, ████████████

2．株主総会決議があったものとみなされた事項の提案者

Proposer of the matter that the Resolution of the Shareholders Meeting was deemed to have been made

代表取締役　████████████

Representative Director ████████

3．株主総会の決議があったものとみなされた日

The date when the Resolution of the Shareholders Meeting was deemed to have been made

█████年９月28日 / September 28, ████

4．議事録の作成に係る職務を行った取締役　Director who prepared Minutes
　代表取締役
　Representative Director

5．同意した株主 Shareholders who agreed to the proposal
　議決権を行使することができる株主の総数　1名
　Number of shareholders who may exercise their vote
　議決権を行使することができる株主の議決権の数　3,000個
　Number of voting rights which may be exercised their rights
　同意した株主の総数　1名
　Number of shareholders who agreed to the proposal
　同意した株主の議決権の数　3,000個
　Number of voting rights which was agreed to the proposal

上記のとおり，株主総会の決議の省略を行ったので，会社法第319条第1項に基づき，株主総会の決議があったものとみなされた事項を明確にするため，本議事録を作成し，議事録作成者は次に記名押印する。

These minutes have been prepared as an evidence of the matter that the Resolution of the Shareholders Meeting was deemed to have been made by the Omission of Resolution of it as the above pursuant to the provision of Articles 319(1)and the minutes preparer affixed below.

年9月28日 / September 28,

・・・株式会社　臨時株主総会
The Extraordinary General Meeting of K.K.

代表取締役
Representative Director

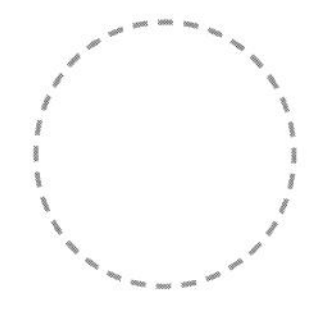

Company Seal

(3) 事業目的・発行可能株式総数の変更

通常の定款の形式上第2条は目的が掲載されている。その目的に変更があるときは，定款変更事由に該当し，株主総会決議事項となる。外国

会社の場合には，その事業目的変更は外国為替及び外国貿易法上，対内直接投資等に該当し，目的によっては，事前届出又は事後報告に該当することがあるので注意しなければならない。日本銀行国際局・国際収支課，外為法手続グループが発刊している「外為法Q&A（対内直接投資・特定取引編）」（令和２年６月改訂，日本銀行ホームページ）を参照されることを推奨する。

例29は，事業目的変更と発行可能株式総数の変更であり，いずれも定款変更事由のため株主総会決議事項である。

〈例29　臨時株主総会議事録（抄，事業目的・発行可能株式総数変更決議事項）〉

臨時株主総会議事録
Minutes of General Meeting of Shareholders

■■年４月25日午前10時00分，■■県■■市■区■■■■丁目■番■■号にある■株式会社 本社会議室において，臨時株主総会を開催した。

A general meeting of Shareholders of ■ Inc. was convened on April 25, ■■ at 10:00 a.m. in the conference room of the head office of ■ Inc. located at Unit #■■, ■-■, ■■■■ ■-chome, ■■■-ku, ■■■■-shi, ■■■■.

発行済株式の総数	500株
株主総数	１名
議決権の総数	500個
本日の出席株主数	１名
この有する議決権数	500個
出席取締役 ■■■■■■（議長兼議事録作成者）	
Total number of issued shares:	500
Total number of shareholders:	1
Total number of voting rights:	500
Number of shareholders present in:	1
Number of voting rights held by the above:	500
Director Present: ■■■■■■ (Chairperson and minutes preparer)	

上記のとおり株主が出席したので，本臨時株主総会は適法に成立した。
定刻に，定款の規定により代表取締役■■■■■■は議長席に着き，開会を宣し，議事の審議に入った。
As the shareholder is participating, the general meeting of Shareholders was duly convened.

At the appointed time, ██████, Representative Director, assumed the chair in accordance with the provision of the articles of incorporation of the company, declared the meeting open, and commenced deliberations of the items on the agenda.

第１号議案　定款一部変更の件
Agenda 1: Amendment of a part of the Articles of Incorporation

議長から，██年５月25日付けで次のとおりの定款一部変更を行いたい旨及びその理由の説明があった。
そして議場にその可否を諮ったところ，満場一致をもって，異議なく承認可決された。
The Chairperson states that it is necessary to amend a part of the Articles of Incorporation effective from May 25, ██, as follows and explained the reason, then caused those present to take a vote of pros and cons with respect to this matter. The proposal was unanimously approved.

現行定款 Current Articles of Incorporation	変更案 Proposal to revise
（目的） 第２条　当会社は，次の事業を営むことを目的とする。 １．ネット販売の検索エンジンの運営 ２．ホームページの作成 ３．オンライン，オフライン商品カタログの制作等 ４．上記各号に付随する一切の業務 (Purposes) Article 2 Purposes of the Company are to engage in the following businesses: 1. To run search engines for internet commerce; 2. Homepage building service; 3. Creating merchandise catalog for off-line and on-line commerce; and 4. Any and all business incidental to the business listed in the preceding items.	（目的） 第２条　当会社は，次の事業を営むことを目的とする。 １．ネット販売の検索エンジンの運営 ２．ホームページの作成 ３．オンライン，オフライン商品カタログの制作等 ４．不動産の売買，賃貸及び管理 ５．上記各号に付随する一切の業務 (Purposes) Article 2 Purposes of the Company are to engage in the following businesses: 1. To run search engines for internet commerce; 2. Homepage building service; 3. Creating merchandise catalog for off-line and on-line commerce; 4. To purchase, sell, lease, and manage real estate; and 5. Any and all business incidental to the business listed in the preceding items.

第2章　株式会社

(発行可能株式総数) 第6条　当会社の発行可能株式総数は, 5000株とする。 (Total Number of Shares the Company is Authorized to Issue) Article 6 The total number of shares the Company is authorized to issue shall be 5,000 shares.	(発行可能株式総数) 第6条　当会社の発行可能株式総数は, 10,000株とする。 (Total Number of Shares the Company is Authorized to Issue) Article 6 The total number of shares the Company is authorized to issue shall be 10,000 shares.

(4)　決算期変更

決算期の変更についても定款変更事由に該当し，株主総会決議事項となる。

例30については，会社法370条「取締役会設置会社は，取締役が取締役会の決議の目的である事項について提案をした場合において，当該提案につき取締役（当該事項について議決に加わることができるものに限る。）の全員が書面又は電磁的記録により同意の意思表示をしたとき（監査役設置会社にあっては，監査役が当該提案について異議を述べたときを除く。）は，当該提案を可決する旨の取締役会の決議があったものとみなす旨を定款で定めることができる。」と規定し，これを当該会社が定款上に定めている場合で，取締役の提案から取締役会決議，株主に対する同意手続並びに取締役会議事録，総会総会議事録を作成する一連の手続の書式を掲載したものである。

〈例30　取締役会決議事項に関する取締役の提案及びその同意のお願い〉

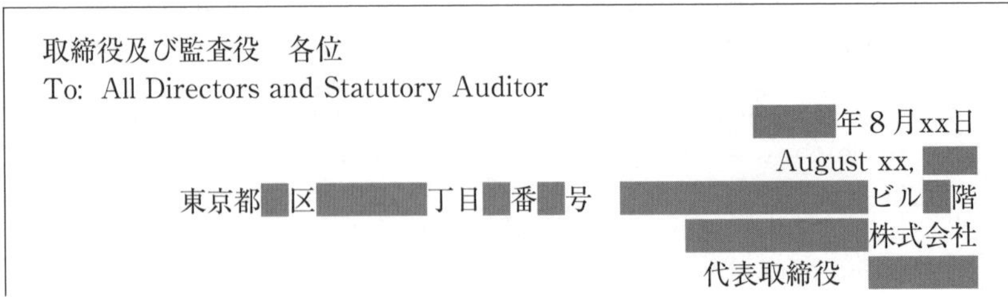
取締役及び監査役　各位
To: All Directors and Statutory Auditor

年8月xx日
August xx,
東京都　区　丁目　番　号　ビル　階
株式会社
代表取締役

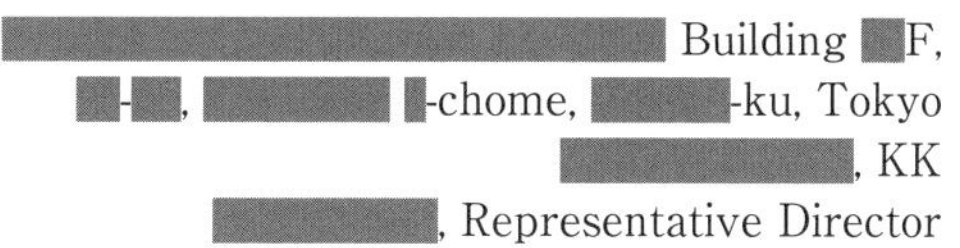

取締役会決議事項に関する取締役の提案及びその同意のお願い
Director's Proposal concerning
Matters to be Resolved at Meeting of Board of Directors
and Request for Consent

この度，会社法第370条及び当会社定款第30条の規定に基づき，取締役会の目的である事項について別紙記載のとおりご提案致します。

つきましては，かかる取締役の提案の内容につき異議なくご同意いただける場合には，同封の同意書にご署名又はご捺印の上，ご返送下さいますようお願い申し上げます

In accordance with the provisions of Article 370 of the Companies Act and Article 30 of the Articles of Incorporation of the Company, I hereby propose the matters to be resolved at the meeting of the Board of Directors as described in the Annex attached hereto.

If you consent without any objection to the particulars of such proposal by the Director, please sign or affix your seal to the Letter of Consent enclosed herewith and return it to us.

以上
End

〈例31　取締役の提案の内容（決算期変更）〉

Japan株式会社　御中
To: Japan, KK

取締役会決議事項の取締役の提案の内容に対する同意書
Written Consent to Director's Proposal concerning
Matters to be Resolved at Meeting of Board of Directors

Japan株式会社（以下「当会社」という。）の取締役である私は，会社法第370条及び当会社定款第30条の規定に基づき，取締役会の決議事項に関する別紙記載の取締役の提案の内容につき，これに異議を述べず同意します。

I, Director of Japan, KK (hereinafter the "Company"), hereby consent to, and do not raise any objection to, the proposal by the Director concerning the matters to be resolved at the meeting of the Board of Directors as described in the Annex attached hereto, in accordance with the provisions of Article 370 of the Companies Act and Article 30 of the Articles of Incorporation of the Company.

以上
End

年８月xx日
August xx,

取締役
Director

〈例32　取締役決議事項の取締役の提案の内容に対する同意書〉

Japan株式会社　御中
To: Japan, KK

取締役会決議事項の取締役の提案の内容に対する同意書
Written Consent to Director's Proposal concerning
Matters to be Resolved at Meeting of Board of Directors

株式会社（以下「当会社」という。）の取締役である私は，会社法第370条及び当会社定款第30条の規定に基づき，取締役会の決議事項に関する別紙記載の取締役の提案の内容につき，これに異議を述べず同意します。

I, Director of , KK (hereinafter the "Company"), hereby consent to, and do not raise any objection to, the proposal by the Director concerning the matters to be resolved at the meeting of the Board of Directors as described in the Annex attached hereto, in accordance with the provisions of Article 370 of the Companies Act and Article 30 of the Articles of Incorporation of the Company.

以上
End

年８月xx日
August xx,

取締役
Director

〈例33　取締役会議事録（決算期変更）〉

株式会社
取締役会議事録
MINUTES OF MEETING OF BOARD OF DIRECTORS
OF KK

株式会社（以下「当会社」という。）は，令和元年８月　日付をもって，取締役会決議事項につき取締役の提案を行い，同日付をもって当該事項につき議決に加わることができる取締役の全員より，かかる提案に同意する旨の同意書の提出を受けたので，会社法第370条及び当会社定款第30条の規定に基づき，次のとおり取締役会の決議があったものとみなされた。なお，監査役からの異議はなかった。

In accordance with the provisions of Article 370 of the Companies Act and Article 30 of the Articles of Incorporation of KK (hereinafter the "Company"), a Director of the Company proposed the matters to be resolved at the meeting of the Board of Directors and obtained the written consents from all Directors entitled to vote as of August , . Accordingly, the resolution of the Board of Directors was deemed to have been adopted as follows. The Statutory Auditor raised no objection to the proposal.

Ⅰ．取締役会の決議があったものとみなされた事項の内容
Matters passed by resolution of the meeting of the Board of Directors

別紙記載のとおり
As described in the Annex attached hereto

Ⅱ．Ⅰ．の事項の提案をした取締役の氏名
Name of the Director who proposed the matters described in I above

代表取締役
, Representative Director

Ⅲ．取締役会の決議があったものとみなされた日
Date of resolution of the meeting of the Board of Directors

年８月xx日
August xx,

Ⅳ．議事録の作成に係る職務を行った取締役の氏名

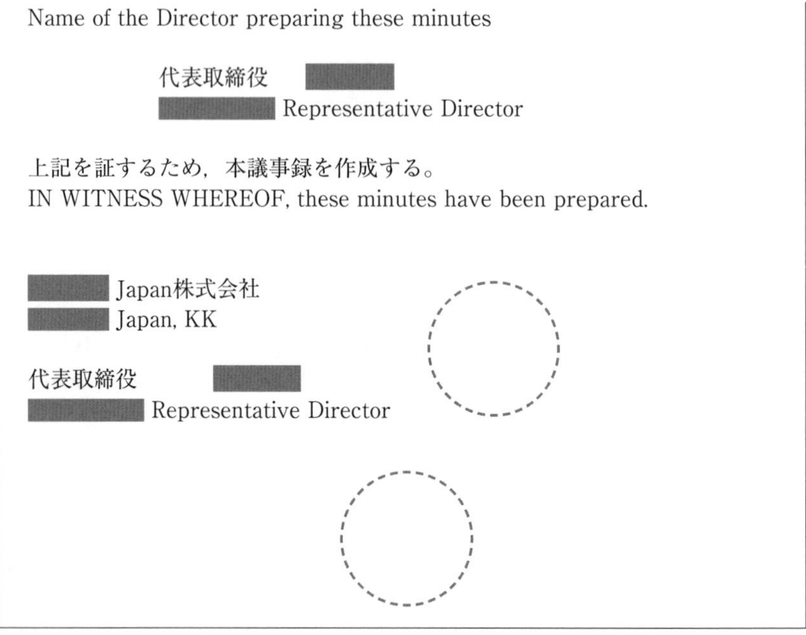

Name of the Director preparing these minutes

代表取締役 [redacted]
[redacted] Representative Director

上記を証するため，本議事録を作成する。
IN WITNESS WHEREOF, these minutes have been prepared.

[redacted] Japan株式会社
[redacted] Japan, KK

代表取締役 [redacted]
[redacted] Representative Director

〈例34　株主に対する株主総会決議に関する取締役の提案及びその同意のお願い〉

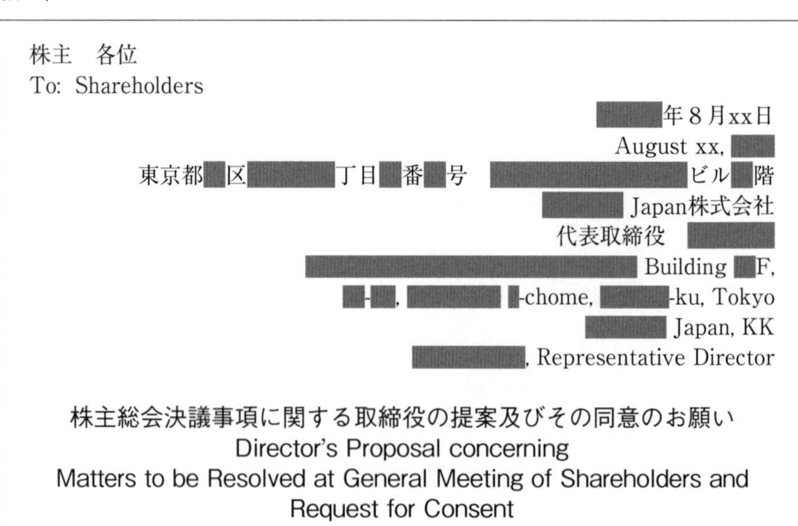

株主　各位
To: Shareholders

[redacted]年８月xx日
August xx, [redacted]

東京都[redacted]区[redacted]丁目[redacted]番[redacted]号　[redacted]ビル[redacted]階
[redacted] Japan株式会社
代表取締役 [redacted]
[redacted] Building [redacted]F,
[redacted]-[redacted], [redacted] [redacted]-chome, [redacted]-ku, Tokyo
[redacted] Japan, KK
[redacted], Representative Director

株主総会決議事項に関する取締役の提案及びその同意のお願い
Director's Proposal concerning
Matters to be Resolved at General Meeting of Shareholders and
Request for Consent

この度，会社法第319条の規定に基づき，株主総会の目的である事項について別紙記載のとおりご提案致します。

つきましては，かかる取締役の提案の内容につき異議なくご同意いただける場合には，同封の同意書にご署名又はご捺印の上，ご返送下さいますようお願い申し上げます

In accordance with the provisions of Article 319 of the Companies Act, I hereby propose the matters to be resolved at the meeting of the General Meeting of Shareholders as described in the Annex attached hereto.

If you consent without any objection to the particulars of such proposal by the Director, please sign or affix your seal to the Letter of Consent enclosed herewith and return it to us.

以上
End

〈例35　株主から会社に対する同意書〉

■■■■ Japan株式会社　御中
To: ■■■■ Japan, KK

株主総会決議事項の取締役の提案の内容に対する同意書
Consent to the Proposals by the Director on the Matters to be resolved by the General Meeting of Shareholders

私は、会社法第319条に基づき、別紙の取締役の提案の内容につき、これに異議を述べず同意します。

Pursuant to the provisions of Article 319 of the Companies Act, the undersigned hereby consent, without any objection, to the proposals submitted by the director stated in the Annex attached hereto.

■■■■年８月xx日
August xx, ■■■

普通株式（6,500,000株）
A種優先株式（3,496,503株）
Common Stock (6,500,000 shares)
Series A Preferred Stock (3,496,503 shares)

株主　■■■■.
Shareholder: ■■■■.

██████, Inc.

____
██████████
Chief Executive Officer

＊別紙省略

〈例36　臨時株主総会議事録〉

██████ Japan株式会社
臨時株主総会議事録
MINUTES OF THE EXTRAORDINARY GENERAL MEETING OF SHAREHOLDERS OF ████████ JAPAN, KK

私は，██████ Japan株式会社（以下「当会社」という。）が，会社法第319条の定めに基づき，下記のとおり株主総会を開催することなく当会社株主に対する提案を行い，当会社株主が取締役の提案を可決したことをここに証明いたします。

I hereby certify that the matters below were proposed to the shareholder of ██████ Japan, KK (the “Company”), and that such resolutions were adopted by the shareholders as proposed by the director, without holding a general meeting of the shareholders in accordance with the provisions of Article 319 of the Companies Act.

記
Note

決議事項
Matters to be resolved

Ⅰ．株主総会の決議があったものとみなされた事項の内容
Matters deemed to have been resolved at a general meeting of shareholders

別紙のとおり
As described in the Annex attached hereto

Ⅱ．Ⅰ．の事項の提案をした者の氏名または名称
Name of the person who proposed the matters described in Note I above

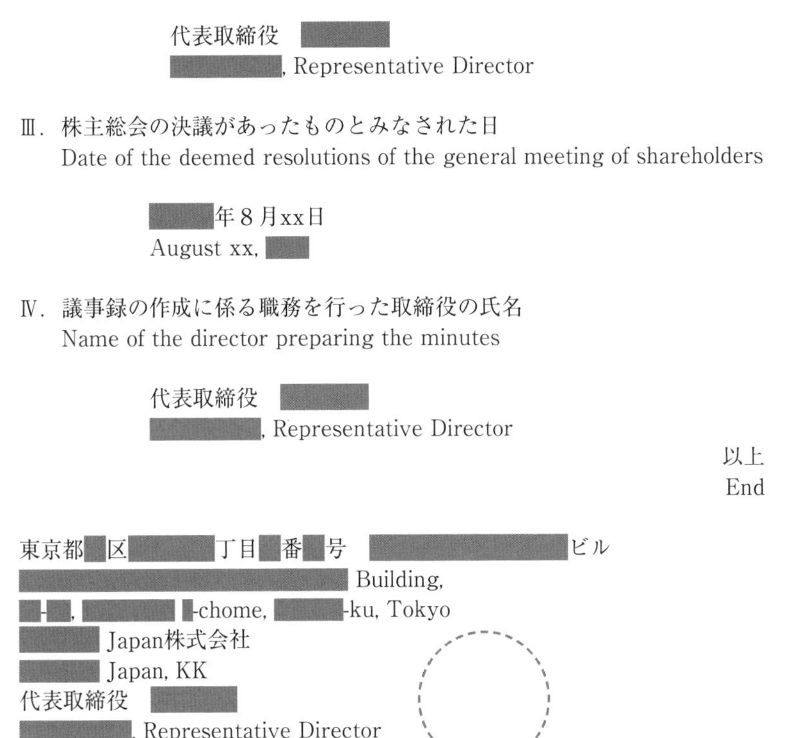
代表取締役 ■■■■
■■■■, Representative Director

Ⅲ．株主総会の決議があったものとみなされた日
Date of the deemed resolutions of the general meeting of shareholders

■■■■年８月xx日
August xx, ■■■■

Ⅳ．議事録の作成に係る職務を行った取締役の氏名
Name of the director preparing the minutes

代表取締役 ■■■■
■■■■, Representative Director

以上
End

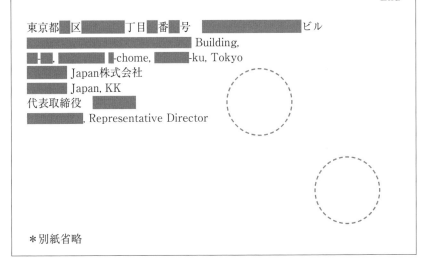

東京都■区■■■丁目■番■号 ■■■■ビル
■■■■ Building,
■-■, ■■■■ ■-chome, ■■■■-ku, Tokyo
■■■■ Japan株式会社
■■■■ Japan, KK
代表取締役 ■■■■
■■■■, Representative Director

＊別紙省略

(5)　取締役会，監査役会廃止

取締役会，監査役会設置会社が，会社規模縮小に伴い，その取締役会，監査役会を廃止することも実務上多く見かけられる。この取締役会，監査役会設置を廃止するのも定款変更事由に該当し，株主総会決議事項である。

例37は，臨時株主総会を開催の上，廃止決議事項部分についての臨時株主総会議事録の一部を掲載したものである。

〈例37　臨時株主総会議事録（抄，取締役会・監査役会廃止）〉

臨時株主総会議事録
MINUTES OF THE EXTRAORDINARY GENERAL MEETING OF SHAREHOLDERS

第１号議案　取締役会設置会社及び監査役設置会社の定めの廃止に関する件
Proposal 1: Abolishment of the Stipulation Regarding Company with a Board of Directors and Statutory Auditor based Corporate Governance Structure

議長は，当会社の定款を変更し，取締役会設置会社及び監査役設置会社の定めを廃止する必要がある旨を述べその可否を議場に諮ったところ，満場一致をもってこれを承認可決した。

As the Chairman stated that it was necessary to amend the Articles of Incorporation of the Company to abolish the stipulation regarding company with a board of Directors and Statutory Auditor based corporate governance structure and then caused those present to take a vote of pros and cons in respect to the partial amendment of Articles of Incorporation, the proposal has been approved unanimously.

(6)　その他の定款変更事項

ア　会計監査人の交代

株式会社における機関の一つで，会社の計算書類などを会計監査することを主な職務，権限とし，公認会計士又は監査法人のみが就任できる（会社337条）。

〈例38　臨時株主総会議事録（抄，監査法人交代）〉

臨時株主総会議事録
Minutes of the Extraordinary General Meeting of Shareholders

会計監査人の選任　Election of an Accounting Auditor
当会社は，下記の法人を，■■■■年11月15日をもって当会社の会計監査人に選任する。

The Company shall elect the following entity as an Accounting Auditor of the Company as of November 15, :
有限責任監査法人
Deloitte Touche LLC

イ　役員報酬

取締役の報酬，賞与その他の職務執行の対価として株式会社から受ける財産上の利益についての①額が確定しているものについては，その額，②額が確定していないものについては，その具体的な算定方法，③金銭でないものについては，その具体的内容に関する事項が，定款に定めていないときは，株主総会の決議によって定める（会社361条）としている。

〈例39　株主総会における役員報酬等の決議〉

株式会社
臨時株主総会議事録
MINUTES OF THE EXTRAORDINARY GENERAL MEETING OF SHAREHOLDERS OF KK

第１号議案　取締役の月額報酬の件
Item No.1 on the Agenda: Amount of Director's monthly remuneration
議長は，当期の各取締役の月額報酬について，昨期から変更せずに下記のとおりとしたい旨を提案した。
：　月額金1,500,000円
他の取締役には支給しない。
The Chairperson proposed to the meeting that the amount of monthly remuneration payable to each Director for this fiscal year be as follows, without changing from the last fiscal year.
Ms. : 1,500,000 JPY per month
No remuneration shall be payable to the other Directors.

次いで議長が本件を議場に諮ったところ，審議の後議長の提案は満場一致で承認可決された。
Then the Chairperson referred the matter to the meeting, at which after deliberation, the proposal by the Chairperson was unanimously

approved.

第２号議案　取締役に対する賞与支給の追認の件
Item No.2 on the Agenda: Subsequent Approval of Payment of Bonus to Directors

議長は，第10期の当社の業績を考慮して，各取締役に対して下記の金額を第10期の賞与として支給したことに対する追認を得たい旨を提案した。
　支給日：　■■■年４月10日
　■■■■：　金787,500円
　他の取締役には支給しない。
The Chairperson proposed to seek the subsequent approval to the meeting that in consideration of the business results of the Company for the 10th fiscal year, the following amount was paid to each Director for the said fiscal year;
　Payment date: April 10, ■■■
　Ms. ■■■■■■: 787,500 JPY
　No bonus shall be payable to the other Directors.

次いで議長が本件を議場に諮ったところ，審議の後議長の提案は満場一致で承認可決された。
Then the Chairperson referred the matter to the meeting, at which after deliberation, the proposal by the Chairperson was unanimously approved.

〈例40　臨時株主総会における退職慰労金支給の決議〉

退職慰労金支給に関する臨時株主総会決議

議案　退職慰労金支給の件
　議長は，■■■年８月31日をもって取締役を辞任する取締役■■■氏に対し，当社の役員退職慰労金規定に基づき，退職慰労金を支給したい旨，及び，その詳細手続等については，取締役会に一任したき旨を述べた。ついで議長が本議案について賛否を議場に諮ったところ，全員異議なくこれを承認可決した。

Agenda: Payment of Retirement allowance
The chairman stated and explained that the Retirement allowance should be paid to ■■■■■■ who would resign the director as of August 31, ■■■ pursuant to the provision concerning the Officers' retirement allowance of the company and the procedures would be entrusted with

the board of Directors. Then the chairman put the proposal to a vote and the proposal was unanimously approved as in the original.

〈例41　株主総会決議を受け取締役会で具体的慰労金支給額の決定〉

株主総会決議を受け取締役会において具体的支給額の決定

議案　退職慰労金支給の件

議長は，■■■年８月29日開催の当社臨時株主総会にて，■■■年８月31日付にて退任される取締役■■■氏の退職慰労金について，その詳細等は当社の役員退職慰労金規定に基づき取締役会に一任する旨の決議がなされたので，これを決定したい旨を述べ，その審議を行った。慎重審議の結果，当社役員退職慰労金規定に基づき，相当額の範囲内で次のように支給する旨を出席取締役全員異議なくこれに承認可決した。

　支払金額　金　　　　　　　　円
　支払時期　平成　　年　　月　　日
　支払方法

Agenda Payment of Retirement allowance

The Chairman stated that as the Extraordinary General Meeting of Shareholders on August 29, ■■■ left to us regarding the retirement allowance of Mr. ■■■ who would resign the Director as of August 31, ■■■, we should decide the details pursuant to the provision concerning the Officers' retirement allowance of the company and after a full deliberation, the board of directors resolved and approved unanimously that his retirement allowance should be paid as follows within the reasonable amount pursuant to the provision concerning the Officers' retirement allowance of the company.

Amount payable: JPY
Time of payment:
Payment method:

(7) 株券不発行

〈例42　取締役会議事録（株券不発行）〉

■■■ジャパン株式会社 取締役会議事録
Minutes of Meeting of Board of Directors of ■■■ Japan K.K.

■■■年９月26日午後４時30分（日本時間），当会社本店おいて取締役会が開催され，電話回線並びに電話会議装置からなる電話会議システムを用いて，取締役および監査役全員が出席した。代表取締役■■■が選ばれて議長となり，議長席につき開会を告げ，電話会議システムにより，出席者の音声が他の出席者に伝わり，出席者が一堂に会するのと同等に適時的確な意思表明が互いにできる状態になっていることが確認されて，議事の審議に入った。

The Meeting of the Board of Directors of the Company was held at the head office of the Company from 4:30 p.m. on September 26, ■■■ (Japan time) and attended by all Directors and all Statutory Auditors, using a telephone meeting system with telephone line and telephone meeting equipment. Mr. ■■■, the representative director of the Company, was duly elected as Chairman and took the chair at the fixed time, announced the opening of the meeting, and commenced the deliberation of the item on the agenda, after confirmation that attendance can listen to the speech of other attendance and attendance can express their opinions promptly in session using a telephone meeting system.

当社本店出席取締役：■■■
電話回線を通じて出席した取締役：■■■，■■■
当社本店出席監査役：■■■
電話回線を通じて出席した監査役：■■■，■■■
議長：代表取締役■■■
議事録の作成に係る職務を行った取締役：代表取締役■■■
Directors present at the head office of the Company: ■■■, ■■■
Director present through telephone line: ■■■, ■■■
Statutory Auditor present at the head office of the Company: ■■■
Statutory Auditors present through telephone line : ■■■, ■■■
Chairman : ■■■, Representative director
Director preparing minutes : ■■■, Representative director

第１号議案　株主総会の招集通知の電子化に関する件

議長は，株主総会において，会社法299条第３項の規定に基づき，下記の要領により株主総会の招集通知を電磁的方法により通知することとしたい旨を提案した。

① 招集通知の電子化について事前に株主の承諾手続を行い，その承諾を得て，所定の電子メールアドレス等の届出のあった株主に対してのみ電磁的方法により招集通知を送信する。

② 招集通知を電子メールにより届出のあった電子メールアドレス宛に送信し，法定の添付書類及び参考書類は当社のウェブサイトに掲載する。

③ 招集通知の電子化について承諾のあった株主からの電磁的方法による通知または請求は，当社所定の電子メールアドレス宛に行う。

慎重審議の結果，出席取締役は上記提案を全員一致で異議なく承認した。

Item No. 1 on Agenda　Matters concerning the digitization of notices of general meeting of shareholders

The Chairman proposed that based on Article 299(3)of the Companies Act, notice of convocation of the General Meeting of Shareholders shall be given by electromagnetic means as follows;

1. The notice of convocation shall be sent by electromagnetic means only to the shareholders who have notified their Electronic Mail Address, etc. after obtaining the approval of the shareholders in advance through the approval procedure.
2. The notice of convocation shall be sent by e-mail to the notified e-mail address and legal attachments and reference documents regarding the general meeting of shareholders shall be posted on the company website.
3. Any notices or requests by electromagnetic means from shareholders who consent to the electronic notice of convocation shall be addressed to the e-mail address specified by the company.

After careful deliberation, the directors present unanimously approved the above proposal without objection.

第２号議案　会社法319条に基づく株主への提案及び株主の同意に関する通知の電子化に関する件

議長は，下記の要領により会社法319条に基づく株主への提案及び株主の電磁的記録による同意の意思表示の通知を電磁的方法により通知することとしたい旨を提案した。

① 会社法319条に基づく株主への提案及び株主からの電磁的記録による同意の意思表示の通知の電子化について事前に株主の承諾手続を行い，その承諾を得て，所定の電子メールアドレス等の届出のあった株主に対して電磁的方法により通知を送信する。

② 上記通知の電子化について承諾のあった株主からの会社法319条に基づく電磁的方法による同意の通知は，当社所定の電子メールアドレス宛

に行う。

慎重審議の結果，出席取締役は上記提案を全員一致で異議なく承認した。

Item No. 2 on Agenda　Matters related to the digitization of notices concerning proposals to shareholders and consent of shareholders under Article 319 of the Companies Act

The Chairman proposed to notify by electromagnetic means of a proposal to the shareholders under Article 319 of the Companies Act and of the shareholders' manifestation of intention to consent by electromagnetic record as follows:.

1．The approval procedure of shareholders shall be carried out in advance for the digitization of notice of intent to give consent by means of proposals to shareholders and electromagnetic records from shareholders under Article 319 of the Companies Act, and after obtaining their approval, the notice shall be transmitted by electromagnetic means to shareholders who have notified their Electronic Mail Address, etc..
2．A notice of consent by electromagnetic means pursuant to Article 319 of the Companies Act from a shareholder who has consented to the electronic filing of the notice shall be sent to an e-mail address specified by the company.

After careful deliberation, the directors present unanimously approved the above proposal without objection.

第３号議案　株券を発行する旨の定めの廃止の件

議長は，株券を発行する旨の定めの廃止をしたい旨提案した。

慎重審議の結果，出席取締役は上記提案を全員一致で異議なく承認した。

Item No. 3 on Agenda　Abolition of Provisions on Issuance of Share Certificates

The Chairman proposed to abolish Provisions on Issuance of Share Certificates.

After careful deliberation, the directors present unanimously approved the above proposal without objection.

第４号議案　営業結果の報告

議長より，[illegible]年度第二四半期の営業結果についての報告があった。

Item No.4 on Agenda　Chairman reported business result of the second quarter of year [illegible].

以上をもって本日の電話会議システムを用いた本取締役会は，終始異常なく議事を終了したので，議長は，午後５時00分閉会を宣した。

Having completed the agenda for this meeting of board of directors using a telephone meeting system without any difficulties in transmission from start to finish, the Chairman declared the meeting closed, and dissolved at 5:00 p.m.

上記決議を明確にする為この議事録を作成し，議長および出席取締役，監査役全員が以下に記名・捺印または署名する。

In order to confirm the above resolution, these minutes have been prepared, and the seals were affixed or the signatures were appended by all the directors who were present at the meeting and whose names appear below.

年９月26日
September 26, 2019
ジャパン株式会社・取締役会
Board of Directors of Japan K.K.

議長・代表取締役
Chairman
Representative Director

年９月26日
September 26, 2019
ジャパン株式会社・取締役会
Board of Directors of Japan K.K.

取締役
, Director

年９月26日
September 26, 2019
ジャパン株式会社・取締役会
Board of Directors of Japan K.K.

取締役
, Director

年９月26日
September 26, 2019
ジャパン株式会社・取締役会
Board of Directors of Japan K.K.

取締役

, Director

年９月26日

September 26, 2019

ジャパン株式会社・取締役会

Board of Directors of Japan K.K.

監査役

, Statutory Auditor

年９月26日

September 26, 2019

ジャパン株式会社・取締役会

Board of Directors of Japan K.K.

監査役

, Statutory Auditor

年９月26日

September 26, 2019

ジャパン株式会社・取締役会

Board of Directors of Japan K.K.

監査役

, Statutory Auditor

〈例43　株主総会の通知の電子化に関する案内及び承諾書〉

株主総会に関する通知の電子化に関するご案内

Notice Concerning the Computerization of Notices of General Meeting of Shareholders

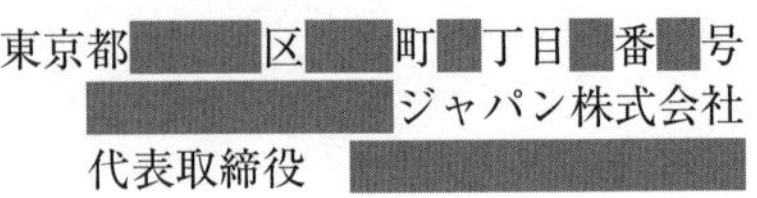

東京都区町丁目番号

ジャパン株式会社

代表取締役

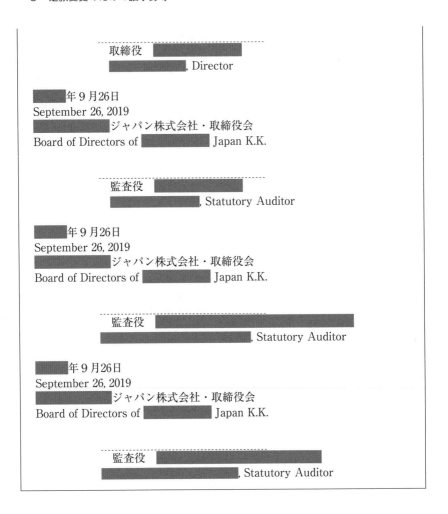

█████, Representative Director
█████ Japan K.K.
█-█ █████-cho █-chome, █████-ku, Tokyo

拝啓　平素は格別のご高配を賜り，有り難く厚くお礼申しあげます。

当会社は，████年　　月　　日付け取締役会において，株主総会の招集通知及び会社法319条に基づく株主様へのご提案及び株主様の同意に関する通知（以下，「株主総会に関する通知」といいます。）について，下記電磁的方法により行う旨決議致しました。

At the meeting of the Board of Directors held on　　　　　, ███, the Company resolved that the notice of convocation of the general meeting of shareholders and the notice regarding the proposal to the shareholders and the consent of the shareholders under Article 319 of the Companies Act (Hereinafter referred to as "Notice of Shareholders Meeting".) shall be given by the following electromagnetic means.

①　電子メール　　　　　当会社メールアドレス（xxxxxxxx@xxx.xx）を使用致します。
②　ウェブサイトへの掲載　ウェブサイトは電子メールにて通知致します。
①　Email: We use our email address (xxxxxxxx@xxx.xx).
②　Posting on the website: The website will be notified by email.

つきましては，株主総会に関する通知について，当該電磁的方法をご希望される場合には，下記ご承諾書にご捺印及びご連絡先となるメールアドレスのご記入をいただき，当会社までご返送の程お願い申し上げます。

Therefore, if you wish to use the electromagnetic method for notification regarding the General Meeting of Shareholders, please fill in the following consent form with the seal and the email address to contact you, and return it to the Company.

敬具

株　主　各　位

█████ジャパン株式会社　宛
To █████ Japan K.K.

承　諾　書
Written Consent

上記電磁的方法による株主総会に関する通知について承諾致します。なお，当該通知の際には下記メールアドレスを使用し，本人確認等の際には下記パスワードを使用致します。

I accept above notice regarding the general meeting of shareholders by the above electromagnetic method. The following email address will be used for the notification and the following password will be used for identification etc..

メールアドレス	
パスワード	

Email address	
Pass word	

令和　　年　　月　　日

株主

プレジデント

Shareholder　　K.K.

Representative Director

〈例44　臨時株主総会・書面決議（株券不発行の決議）〉

ジャパン株式会社
臨時株主総会議事録
MINUTES OF THE EXTRAORDINARY MEETING OF
SHAREHOLDERS OF　　Japan K.K.

ジャパン株式会社（以下「当会社」という）は，会社法第319条の規定に基づき，下記のとおり株主総会を開催することなく当会社株主に対する提案を行い，全ての株主から同意書の提出を受けたので，次のとおり株主総会の決議があったとみなす。

Based on the provisions of Article 319 of Companies Act, Japan K.K. (hereinafter referred to as "the Company")made propose to shareholders of the Company without holding a shareholders meeting as follows, and received written consent from all shareholders. Therefore, it shall be deemed that a resolution of the shareholders meeting were made as follows:

1．株主総会の決議があったものとみなされた事項の内容
　決議事項
　第１号議案 定款の一部変更の件
　　当会社は，株券を発行する旨の定めを廃止し，それに伴い，別紙のとおり定款の一部を変更する。なお，当該効力発生日は，■■■■年５月１日とする。
1．Matters deemed to have been resolved at the shareholders meeting
　Matters to be resolved:
　　Proposal 1: Amendment of a part of the Articles of Incorporation
　The Company will abolish the provision to issue share certificates, and accordingly, part of the Articles of Incorporation will be changed as shown in the attachment. The effective date shall be May 1, ■■■.

2．上記事項を提案した者
　代表取締役 ■■■■■■
2．Person who proposed the above item
　■■■■■■, Representative Director

3．株主総会の決議があったものとみなされた日
　■■■■年３月２６日
3．Date when the resolution of the shareholders meeting are deemed to have been Made
　　March 26, ■■■

4．議事録の作成に係る職務を行った取締役の氏名
　代表取締役 ■■■■■■
4．Name of director who performed duties regarding the preparation of minutes
　■■■■■■, Representative Director

上記を証するためこの議事録を作成し，議事録の作成に係る職務を行った取締役がこれに署名する。
In order to certify the above, director who prepared minutes and performed duties pertaining to the preparation of minutes hereby signs and seals on thereof.

■■■■年３月26日
March 26, ■■■

■■■■■■ジャパン株式会社
代表取締役 ■■■■■■

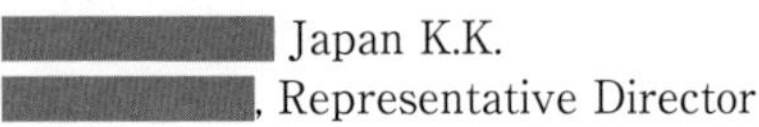

Japan K.K.
, Representative Director

【別紙】【Attachment】

現行定款 Current Articles of Incorporation	変更案 Proposal to revise
(株式および株券の種類) 第７条　当会社の株式はすべて普通株式とし，その株券は１株券，10株券，100株券，1,000株券及び10,000株券の５種とする。 (Classes of Shares and Share Certificates) Article 7: All shares of the Company shall be common shares and the share certificates shall be classified into 5 types: 1 share certificate, 10 share certificate, 100 share certificate, 1,000 share certificate and 10,000 share certificate.	(株式の種類) 第７条　当会社の株式はすべて普通株式とする。 (Classes of Shares) Article 7 All shares of the Company shall be common stock.
(名義書換) 第10条　株式の名義書換を請求するときは，当会社所定の請求書に株券を添えて提出するものとする。 (Name transfer) Article 10 When requesting a name transfer of shares, it shall be submitted with a stock certificate in addition to the company's prescribed invoice.	(名義書換) 第10条　株式の名義書換を請求するときは，当会社所定の請求書を提出するものとする。 (Name transfer) Article 10 When requesting a name transfer of shares, it shall be submitted with the company's prescribed invoice.
(質権の登録及び信託財産の表示) 第11条　質権の登録，信託財産の表示，又はこれらの抹消を請求しようとするときは，当会社所定の請求書に株券を添えて提出するものとする。 (Registration of Pledges and Indication of Trust Property) Article 11 When requesting registration of pledge, display of trust property, or cancellation of these, it shall be submitted along with a stock certificate with the company's prescribed invoice.	(質権の登録及び信託財産の表示) 第11条　質権の登録，信託財産の表示，又はこれらの抹消を請求しようとするときは，当会社所定の請求書を提出するものとする。 (Registration of Pledges and Indication of Trust Property) Article 11 When requesting the registration of a pledge, indication of trust property or cancellation thereof, the applicant shall submit a written request prescribed by the Company.
(株券の再発行) 第12条　株券の毀損，汚損又は株式の分割併合により株券再発行を請求するときは，当会社所定の請求書に株券を添	(削 除) (Deleted)

えて提出するものとする。 2．株券の毀損若くは汚損の程度が著しくてその真偽を判別し難い場合又は株券喪失により株券の再発行を請求するときは，当会社所定の請求書に除権判決の正本若くは謄本を添えて提出するものとする。 (Reissuance of Share Certificates) Article 12 When requesting reissuance of share certificates due to damage, defacement or consolidation of shares, share certificates shall be submitted together with share certificates in a written request prescribed by the Company. 2. Damage to Share Certificates: When it is difficult to determine the truth or falsity of a share certificate due to a significant degree of damage, or when a request for reissuance of share certificates due to loss of share certificates is filed, an authenticated copy or a transcript of a judgment of nullification of a right shall be attached to a written request prescribed by the Company.	(第12条以下，条数繰り上げ) (Article 12 and below, advance of the number of articles)

〈例45　株券不発行会社への移行に関する通知書〉

株券不発行会社への移行に関する通知書
Notice of Transfer to Company Not Issuing Share Certificates

令和■年　月　日
Date: 　　　, ■■

■■■■ 御中
To: ■■■■

東京都■■区■■町■丁目■番■号
■■■■ジャパン株式会社
代表取締役 ■■■■
■■■■, Representative Director
■■■■ K.K.
■-■ ■■■■-cho ■cho-me, ■■■■-ku, Tokyo

当会社は，■■年　月　日開催の株主総会において，同日付けで株券を発行する旨の定款の定めを廃止することにいたしましたので，会社法第218条１項の規定により通知いたします。

The Company has decided that it will abolish the provisions of the Articles of Incorporation that Share Certificates are issued on the same day at the General Meeting of Shareholders held on , ■■. So, will give notice in accordance with Article 218, Paragraph 1 of the Companies Act.

〈例46　株主に対する案内及び同意書（通知の電子化に関する案内と同意書）〉

株主総会に関する通知の電子化に関するご案内
Notice Concerning the Computerization of Notices of General Meeting of Shareholders

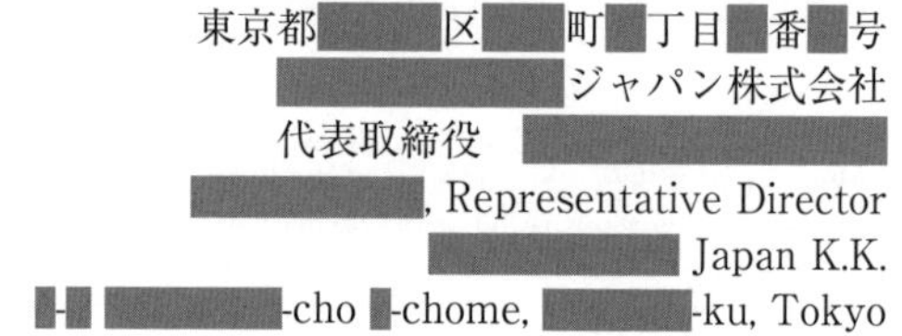
東京都■■区■■町■丁目■番■号
■■ジャパン株式会社
代表取締役　■■
■■, Representative Director
■■ Japan K.K.
■-■ ■■-cho ■-chome, ■■-ku, Tokyo

拝啓　平素は格別のご高配を賜り，有り難く厚くお礼申しあげます。

当会社は，■■年　月　日付け取締役会において，株主総会の招集通知及び会社法319条に基づく株主様へのご提案及び株主様の同意に関する通知（以下，「株主総会に関する通知」といいます。）について，下記電磁的方法により行う旨決議致しました。

At the meeting of the Board of Directors held on , ■■, the Company resolved that the notice of convocation of the general meeting of shareholders and the notice regarding the proposal to the shareholders and the consent of the shareholders under Article 319 of the Companies Act (Hereinafter referred to as "Notice of Shareholders Meeting".) shall be given by the following electromagnetic means.

①　電子メール　当会社メールアドレス（xxxxxxxx@xxx.xx）を使用致します。
②　ウェブサイトへの掲載　ウェブサイトは電子メールにて通知致します。
①　Email: We use our email address（xxxxxxxx@xxx.xx）.
②　Posting on the website: The website will be notified by email.

つきましては，株主総会に関する通知について，当該電磁的方法をご希望される場合には，下記ご承諾書にご捺印及びご連絡先となるメールアドレスのご記入をいただき，当会社までご返送の程お願い申し上げます。

Therefore, if you wish to use the electromagnetic method for notification regarding the General Meeting of Shareholders, please fill in the following consent form with the seal and the email address to contact you, and return it to the Company.

敬具

〈例47　株主に対する承諾書（通知の電子化に関する承諾書）〉

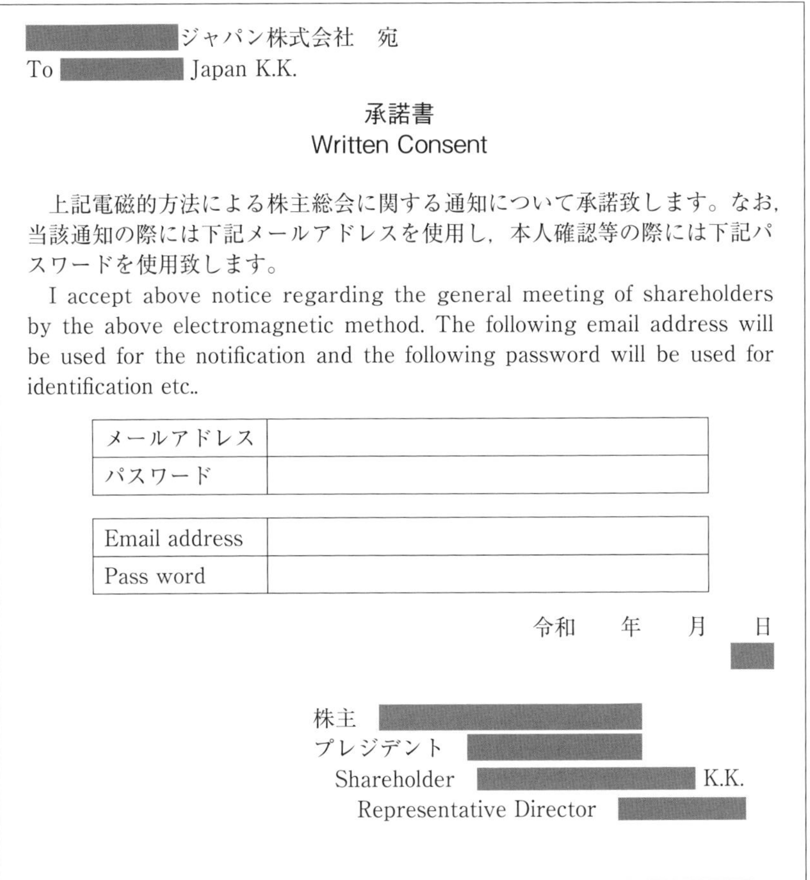

ジャパン株式会社　宛
To Japan K.K.

承諾書
Written Consent

上記電磁的方法による株主総会に関する通知について承諾致します。なお，当該通知の際には下記メールアドレスを使用し，本人確認等の際には下記パスワードを使用致します。

I accept above notice regarding the general meeting of shareholders by the above electromagnetic method. The following email address will be used for the notification and the following password will be used for identification etc..

メールアドレス	
パスワード	

Email address	
Pass word	

令和　　年　　月　　日

株主
プレジデント
Shareholder K.K.
Representative Director

4　増資手続

(1)　株主割当増資

募集株式の発行の態様については，①株主に株式の割当を受ける権利を付与する募集株式の発行（株主割当）と，②株主割当以外の募集株式の発行（第三者割当），③公募（一般募集，縁故募集）がある。

①　株主割当方法による募集株式の発行手続（会社202条）

i　募集事項の決定

募集株式数，払込金額，払込期日，金銭以外の財産を出資の目的とするときは，その旨，その財産の内容，価額，増加資本金又は資本準備金等の事項を定める。

ii　募集事項の決定機関

・非公開会社の場合は，株主総会の特別決議又は定款の定めにより取締役会の決議（又は取締役の決定。会社202条３項）で決定する。

・公開会社の場合は，原則として取締役会の決議によることとされている（会社202条３項３号）。

②　株主割当以外（第三者割当）による募集株式の発行手続

i　募集方法の決定

募集株式数，払込金額，払込期日，金銭以外の財産を出資の目的とするときは，その旨，その財産の内容，価額，増加資本金又は資本準備金等の事項を定める。

ii　募集事項の決定機関

・非公開会社の場合は，株主総会の特別決議（会社199条２項），ただし，株主総会の特別決議により募集事項の決定を取締役会の決議（又は取締役の決定）に委任することができる（会社200条１項）。この場合，募集株式の数の上限及び払込金額の下限を定めなければならない。払込期日又は期間の場合はその末日がその決定日から１年内の日である募集でなければならない（会社200条３項）。

・公開会社の場合は，有利発行以外は取締役会の決議による（会社201条１項）。

③　**公募（不特定多数，縁故募集）による募集株式の発行手続**

第三者割当同様の手続となる。

④　**株主に対する通知又は公告**

公開会社は，払込期日又は払込期間の初日の２週間前までに，株主に対して募集事項を通知又は公告をし（会社201条３項），非公開会社は，引受申込者に対して，会社商号，募集事項，払込取扱い場所，その他法務省令で定める事項を通知する（会社302条１項）。

⑤　**株式の申込み・割当**

ⅰ　株主の場合（会社203条）

株主は，申込事項の通知に対して，引受申込みをすれば，当然引受人になる。

ⅱ　第三者割当の場合（会社204条）

・申込人は，申込事項の通知に対し，引受申込みをする。

・会社（公開会社の場合は取締役会，非公開会社の場合は原則は株主総会の特別決議，例外は，取締役会設置会社は取締役会，定款の別段の定めがあるときはその定めに従う。）は，株式の割当を決定する。

・株主は，株式引受人になる。

・総数引受契約の特則―株式譲渡制限株式を除き，上記申込み，割当の手続は不要である（会社205条２項）。

⑥　**株式引受人の出資**

株式引受人は，払込期日又は払込期間内に銀行等の払込取扱い場所に，払込金額全額を払い込む（会社208条１項）。現物出資の場合には，給付期日又は給付期間内に払込金額の全額に相当する現物出資財産を給付する。

⑦　**資本金の額**

増加した払込又は給付の額の２分の１を超えない額を資本金として計上しなくてよく，計上しない額を資本準備金とすることができる（会社445条1項・2項)。増加した資本金は登記事項である。

例48は，定款の定めにより取締役会の決議（又は取締役の決定。会社202条3項）で決定する募集株式の増資手続である。

〈例48　取締役会議事録（抄，株主割当による新株発行)〉

取締役会議事録
MINUTES OF MEETING OF BOARD OF DIRECTORS

第2号議案　株主割当による新株発行の件
Proposal 2: Approval of the Issuance of New Shares through Shareholder Allotment

議長は，下記の発行要領にて株主割当の方法による新株発行を行いたい旨述べ，詳細な説明を行った後，これを議場に諮ったところ，全員一致をもってこれを承認可決した。

The Chairperson explained in detail that the following issuance of new shares through shareholder allotment was necessary pursuant to the terms described below. This proposal was unanimously approved without opposition.

記
Particulars:

1．発行新株式数　　普通株式　400株
Number of new shares to be issued:　Ordinary shares: 400 shares
2．発行価額　　1株につき金50,000円
Issue price:　50,000 yen per share
3．発行価額中資本に組み入れない額　　全額資本に組み入れる
Issue price and the amount that is not allocated to the stated capital:
The whole amount will be allocated to the stated capital
4．発行価額の総額　　金2,000万円
Total amount of Issue price　20,000,000 yen
5．申込期間　　■■年　月　日から
■■年　月　日
Subscription term　From:　, ■■
To:　, ■■
6．払込期日　　■■年　月　日
Payment date　, ■■

7．申込取扱場所　当会社本店
Place of subscription:　The Head Office of the Company

8．申込証拠金　1株について金50,000円とし，払込期日に新株式払込金に振替充当する。但し，申込証拠金には利息を付さない。
Deposit upon subscription: 50,000 yen per share, which is to be applied toward payment for new shares on the payment for new shares on the payment date; provided, however, that interest shall not accrue on such deposit money.

9．払込取扱銀行及びその場所　東京都■■区■■町一丁目■番■号 ■■銀行　東京支店
Bank handling payment　■-■, ■■-cho ■-chome, ■■-ku, Tokyo ■■ Bank, ■■ Tokyo Branch

10．割当方法　株主割当によるものとし，全て■■年　月　日午後7時現在の株主名簿記載の株主に対し，その所有株式1株につき新株式2株の割合で割り当てる。
Allocation of new shares: All new shares shall be allocated to shareholders who are registered in the shareholders list of the Company as of 　, ■■ at 7:00 p.m. The shareholders may be allocated two (2) newly issued shares per one share owned by said shareholders.

以上をもって議案の審議を終え，午前11時30分散会した。
Whereupon, all business presently before the board having been completed, the Chairperson declared the meeting closed at 11:30 a.m.

〈例49　株式申込証〉

株式申込証
APPLICATION FOR SUBSCRIPTION

（商号）　株式会社■■　普通株式　400株
(Trade Name)　■■ Co., Ltd.　Ordinary shares: 400 shares

この申込証拠金　金20,000,000円（1株につき金50,000円）
Application deposit for the above shares: ¥20,000,000 (¥50,000 per share)

⑴　申込証拠金は払込金に充当すること。
The application deposit is to be applied to the purchase price for the shares.

⑵　申込証拠金には利息をつけないこと。
No interest shall accrue to the application deposit.

貴社の定款および本申込証記載事項を承認のうえ上記の株式を引き受けたく，証拠金を添えて申し込みます。

In accordance with the Articles of Incorporation and the matters contained in this Application for Shares of your company, I hereby apply to purchase the above shares, accompanied by the application deposit as entered above.

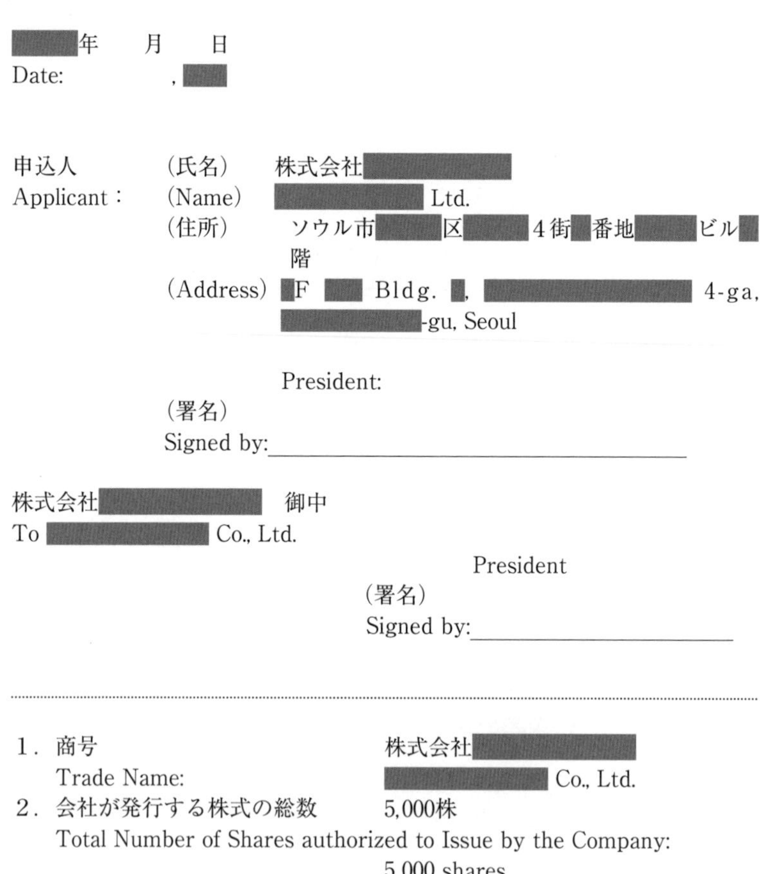

年　月　日
Date: ,

申込人　（氏名）　株式会社
Applicant：　(Name)　Ltd.
（住所）　ソウル市　区　4街　番地　ビル　階
(Address)　F　Bldg.　,　4-ga,　-gu, Seoul

President:
（署名）
Signed by:______________________

株式会社　御中
To　Co., Ltd.

President
（署名）
Signed by:______________________

1．商号　株式会社
Trade Name:　Co., Ltd.

2．会社が発行する株式の総数　5,000株
Total Number of Shares authorized to Issue by the Company: 5,000 shares

3．発行済株式の総数　　普通株式　　200株
Total Number of Issued Shares:　Ordinary shares: 200 shares
4．資本の額　　金1,000万円
Amount of Capital:　¥10,000,000
5．新株の種類及び数　　普通株式　　400株
The class and the number of new shares to be issued:
Ordinary shares: 400 shares
6．新株の発行価額　　1株につき金50,000円
Issue price of new shares to be issued: 50,000 yen per share
7．払込期日　　■■年　月　日
Payment date:　,2006
8．発行価額中資本に組み入れない額
全額資本に組み入れる
Issue price and the amount that is not allocated to the stated capital:
The whole amount will be allocated to the stated capital
9．払込取扱銀行及びその場所　　東京都■■区■■町■丁目■番■号
■■銀行　東京支店
Bank handling payment:　■-■, ■■-cho ■-chome, ■■-ku, Tokyo
■■ Bank, Korea Tokyo Branch
10．株式の譲渡制限に関する規定
当会社の株式を譲渡するには，取締役会の承認を受けなければならない。
Restriction on Transfer of Shares:
Transfers of shares of the Company shall be subject to approval by the Board of Directors.

以　上
End

〈例50　会計帳簿証明書　会社に対する貸付債権を現物出資した会計帳簿上の証明〉

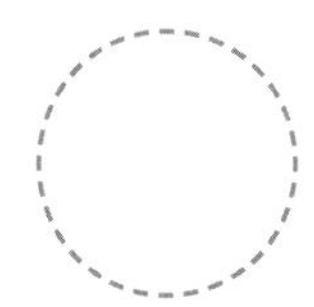

Company Seal

金銭債権について記載された会計帳簿であることを証する書面
Certificate of the accounting book contained in monetary claims

別紙会計帳簿は，現物出資財産である金銭債権について記載された当会社の会計帳簿に相違ありません。
なお，当会社は，■■■年１月17日当該債権に係る期限の利益を放棄しました。
The attached accounting book must be the accounting book of the Company that describes monetary claims that are in-kind contributions.
Furthermore, the Company abandoned the profit on the due date of the said claims on January 17, ■■■.

■■■年１月17日
January 17, ■■■.

■■■株式会社
代表取締役　■■■
■■■ K.K.
Representative ■■■

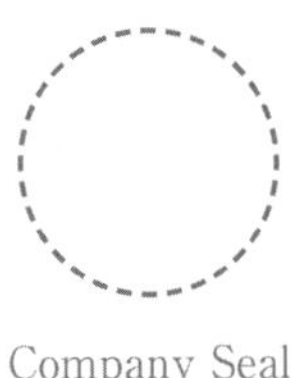
Company Seal

〈例51　日本銀行への株式の取得に関する報告書〉

別紙様式第十一

根拠法規：対内直接投資等に関する命令

株式 ~~持分~~ の取得に関する報告書

■■■年４月　日

財務大臣　殿
経済産業大臣　殿

（日本銀行経由）

	氏名又は名称及び代表者の氏名	株式会社■■■ 代表者　■■■		
	住所又は主たる事務所の所在地	■■■市■■■ ■４街■番地 ■■■ビル■階	国籍	韓国

<table>
<tr><td rowspan="6">報告者</td><td colspan="2">職業又は営んでいる事業の内容</td><td>コンピュータハードウエア及びコンピュータソフトウエアの製造，開発等</td><td>資本金</td><td>25億ウォン</td></tr>
<tr><td colspan="2">報告者となる法的根拠
（該当分に○）</td><td colspan="3">イ　非居住者個人　(ロ)　外国法人等　ハ　イ及びロが直接，間接に議決権の50％以上を保有している会社　ニ　イが役員の過半数を占める本邦法人等　ホ　イ～ニのために取得するもの</td></tr>
<tr><td rowspan="2">代理人</td><td>氏名又は名称及び代表者の氏名</td><td colspan="3">司法書士 ■■■</td></tr>
<tr><td>住所又は主たる事務所の所在地</td><td colspan="3">東京都■区■■丁目■番■号■ビル</td></tr>
<tr><td colspan="2">事務上の連絡先
（担当者電話）</td><td>合同事務所 ■■■
■■■
（担当：■■）</td><td>ＴＥＬ</td><td>03-■■-■■</td></tr>
</table>

下記のとおり報告します。

<table>
<tr><td rowspan="5">1
発行会社</td><td>(1)</td><td>名称</td><td>株式会社■■■</td></tr>
<tr><td>(2)</td><td>本店の所在地</td><td>東京都■区■■町■丁目■番■号</td></tr>
<tr><td>(3)</td><td>定款上の事業目的</td><td>1．コンピューターソフトウェア及びハードウェアの輸出入及び販売
2．コンピューターシステムの企画，開発，販売及びコンサルティング
3．上記に附帯関連する一切の業務</td></tr>
<tr><td>(4)</td><td>資本金
（払込資本）</td><td>取得前　1,000万円（200株）
取得後　3,000万円（600株）</td></tr>
<tr><td>(5)</td><td>外資比率</td><td>取得後の外資比率　100％（取得前 100％）</td></tr>
<tr><td rowspan="3">2
取得又は一任運用をした株式（持分）</td><td>(1)</td><td>上場，非上場等の区分
（該当分に○）</td><td>イ　上場銘柄　ロ　店頭売買銘柄　(ハ)　その他</td></tr>
<tr><td>(2)</td><td>取得の態様</td><td>増資新株の取得</td></tr>
<tr><td>(3)</td><td>数量，取得価額等</td><td>数　量　400株
取得価額　2,000万円（一株当たり５万円）
取得後の出資比率　100％（取得前の出資比率100％）</td></tr>
</table>

3　報告時に報告者と特別の関係にあるもの（政令第２条第４項に掲げるもの）が所有する同一発行会社の株式の数量等		なし
4 相手方	(1)　氏名又は名称	
	(2)　住所又は主たる事務所の所在地	
	(3)　譲渡数量	
5　取得年月日		■■ 3月31日
6　支払年月日		■■ 3月31日
7　その他の事項		

（日本工業規格Ａ４）

例52は，事業拡大のため事業目的の変更，発行可能株式総数を変更し，第三者割当で，金銭及び現物出資を求めての増資手続である。

〈例52　臨時株主総会議事録（目的，発行可能株式総数並び資本の額の変更）〉

臨時株主総会議事録
Minutes of General Meeting of Shareholders

■■年４月25日午前10時00分，■■県■■市■区■■■■丁目■番■■■■号にある■株式会社 本社会議室において，臨時株主総会を開催した。

A general meeting of Shareholders of ■ Inc. was convened on April 25, ■■ at 10:00 a.m. in the conference room of the head office of ■ Inc. located at Unit #■■, ■-■, ■■■■ ■-chome, ■■■-ku, ■■■■-shi, ■■■■.

発行済株式の総数	500株
株主総数	１名
議決権の総数	500個
本日の出席株主数	１名
この有する議決権数	500個
出席取締役　■■■■■■（議長兼議事録作成者）	
Total number of issued shares:	500

Total number of shareholders: 1
Total number of voting rights: 500
Number of shareholders present: 1
Number of voting rights held by the above: 500
Director Present: ████████ (Chairperson and minutes preparer)

上記のとおり株主が出席したので，本臨時株主総会は適法に成立した。
定刻に，定款の規定により代表取締役██████████は議長席に着き，開会を宣し，議事の審議に入った。

As the shareholder is participating, the general meeting of Shareholders was duly convened.

At the appointed time, ████████, Representative Director, assumed the chair in accordance with the provision of the articles of incorporation of the company, declared the meeting open, and commenced deliberations of the items on the agenda.

第１号議案　定款一部変更の件
Agenda 1: Amendment of a part of the Articles of Incorporation

議長から，██年５月25日付けで次のとおりの定款一部変更を行いたい旨及びその理由の説明があった。
そして議場にその可否を諮ったところ，満場一致をもって，異議なく承認可決された。

The Chairperson states that it is necessary to amend a part of the Articles of Incorporation effective from May 25, ██, as follows and explained the reason, then caused those present to take a vote of pros and cons with respect to this matter. The proposal was unanimously approved.

現行定款 Current Articles of Incorporation	変更案 Proposal to revise
(目的) 第２条　当会社は，次の事業を営むことを目的とする。 １．ネット販売の検索エンジンの運営 ２．ホームページの作成 ３．オンライン，オフライン商品カタログの制作等	(目的) 第２条　当会社は，次の事業を営むことを目的とする。 １．ネット販売の検索エンジンの運営 ２．ホームページの作成 ３．オンライン，オフライン商品カタログの制作等

4．上記各号に付随する一切の業務 (Purposes) Article 2 Purposes of the Company are to engage in the following businesses: 1. To run search engines for internet commerce; 2. Homepage building service; 3. Creating merchandise catalog for off-line and on-line commerce; and 4. Any and all business incidental to the business listed in the preceding items.	4．不動産の売買，賃貸及び管理 5．上記各号に付随する一切の業務 (Purposes) Article 2 Purposes of the Company are to engage in the following businesses: 1. To run search engines for internet commerce; 2. Homepage building service; 3. Creating merchandise catalog for off-line and on-line commerce; 4. To purchase, sell, lease, and manage real estate; and 5. Any and all business incidental to the business listed in the preceding items.
（発行可能株式総数） 第６条　当会社の発行可能株式総数は，5000株とする。 (Total Number of Shares the Company is Authorized to Issue) Article 6 The total number of shares the Company is authorized to issue shall be 5,000 shares.	（発行可能株式総数） 第６条　当会社の発行可能株式総数は，10,000株とする。 (Total Number of Shares the Company is Authorized to Issue) Article 6 The total number of shares the Company is authorized to issue shall be 10,000 shares.

議案２　募集株式の発行に関する件
Agenda 2: Issue of Shares for Subscription

議長は，下記要領により各募集株式の発行をしたい旨を述べ，その理由等を詳細に説明した。そして議場にその可否を諮ったところ，満場一致をもって，異議なく承認可決された。

The Chairperson stated that subscription shares should be issued as follows, explained that reason in detail, and then caused those present to take a vote of pros and cons with respect to this matter. The proposal was unanimously approved.

1，募集株式の数　　　　普通株式　1,004　株
Number of Shares for Subscription: 1,004 Ordinary Shares
募集株式の発行方法　　第三者割当とする

Method for issue of shares for subscription: Allotment to a Third Party

募集株式は申し込みを条件として以下の通り割り当てる

県　市　区　丁目　番　-　号

1,004株

Shares for subscription shall be allotted as follows upon application thereto by the applicant:

Unit #, -, -chome, -ku, -shi,

1,004 shares

募集株式の払込金額　　1株につき金10,000円

Amount to be paid-in: 10,000 yen per share

払込期日　　年5月25日

Deadline of Payment: May 25,

増加する資本金の額　　1株につき金1万円

Amount of Capital to Increase: 10,000 yen per share

増加する資本準備金の額　0円

Amount of Capital Reserve to Increase: 0 yen

払込を取扱う銀行ならびにその取扱いの場所

県　市　区　-　-

銀行　支店

Recipient Bank: --, -ku, -shi,

Banking Corporation, Branch

2, 募集株式の数　　普通株式　496　株

Number of shares for subscription: 496 Ordinary Shares

募集株式の発行方法　　第三者割当とする

Method for issue of shares for subscription: Allotment to a Third Party

募集株式は申し込みを条件として以下の通り割り当てる

県　市　区　丁目　番　-　号

496株

Shares for subscription shall be allotted as follows upon application thereto by the applicant:

Unit #, -, -chome, -ku, -shi,

496 shares

募集株式の払込金額　　1株につき金10,000円

Amount to be paid-in: 10,000 yen per share

払込期間　　年4月26日から　年5月25日

Payment Period: From April 26, to May 25,

増加する資本金の額　　1株につき金1万円

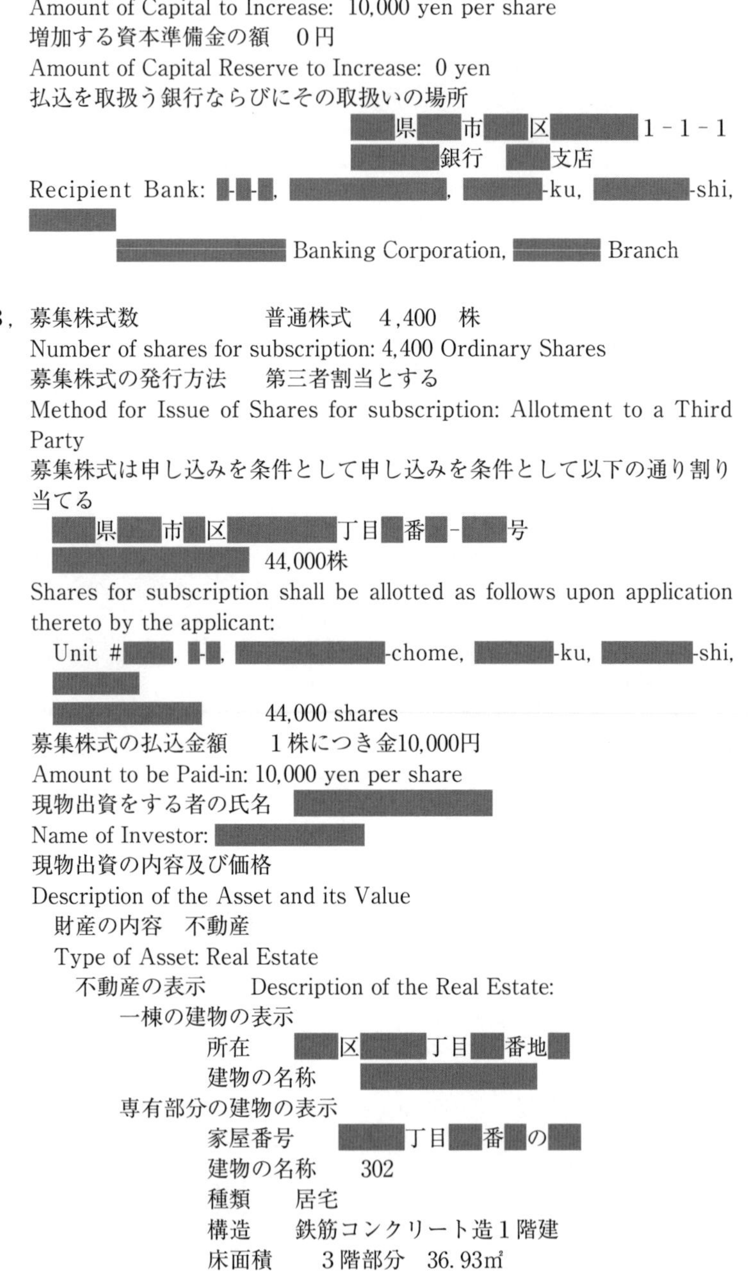

Amount of Capital to Increase: 10,000 yen per share
増加する資本準備金の額　0円
Amount of Capital Reserve to Increase: 0 yen
払込を取扱う銀行ならびにその取扱いの場所
県　市　区　1－1－1
銀行　支店
Recipient Bank: - - , , -ku, -shi,
Banking Corporation, Branch

3，募集株式数　普通株式　4,400　株
Number of shares for subscription: 4,400 Ordinary Shares
募集株式の発行方法　第三者割当とする
Method for Issue of Shares for subscription: Allotment to a Third Party
募集株式は申し込みを条件として申し込みを条件として以下の通り割り当てる
県　市　区　丁目　番　-　号
44,000株
Shares for subscription shall be allotted as follows upon application thereto by the applicant:
Unit #, -, -chome, -ku, -shi,
44,000 shares
募集株式の払込金額　1株につき金10,000円
Amount to be Paid-in: 10,000 yen per share
現物出資をする者の氏名
Name of Investor:
現物出資の内容及び価格
Description of the Asset and its Value
財産の内容　不動産
Type of Asset: Real Estate
不動産の表示　Description of the Real Estate:
一棟の建物の表示
所在　区　丁目　番地
建物の名称
専有部分の建物の表示
家屋番号　丁目　番　の
建物の名称　302
種類　居宅
構造　鉄筋コンクリート造1階建
床面積　3階部分　36.93㎡

敷地権及びその目的である土地の表示
符号　　1
所在及び地番　　■区■丁目■番■
地目　　宅地
地積　　177.96㎡
敷地権の種類　　所有権
敷地権の割合　　■分の4200
Description of Entire Building
Location: ■-■, ■-chome, ■-ku
Name of Building: ■
Description of Proprietary Part
Building Number: ■-chome ■-■-■
Name of Building: ■
Type of Building: Housing
Structure: 1 story, reinforced concrete construction
Floor Space: 36.93 square meters on the 3rd floor
Description of the Land upon which the Entire Building is built on:
Code: 1
Location and Number: ■-■, ■-chome, ■-ku
Classification: Housing Land
Area: 177.96 square meters
Type of Right: Freehold
Share of right: 4200/■
出資の目的物たる不動産の価格　金4,400万円
Value of the Real Estate: 44,000,000 yen
募集株式と引換えにする財産の給付期日　■年５月25日
Date of Providing Asset in Consideration of the Shares for Subscription: May 25, ■
増加する資本金の額　　１株につき金１万円
Amount of Capital to Increase: 10,000 yen per share
増加する資本準備金の額　０円
Amount of Capital Reserves to Increase: 0 yen

議長は，以上をもって本日の議案全部を終了した旨を述べ，午前10時30分散会した。
Whereupon, all matters before the General Meeting having been completed, the Chairperson presented closing address, and declared this meeting dissolved at 10:30 a.m.

上記の議事の経過の要領及びその結果を明確にするため，この議事録を作

り，議長及び出席取締役がこれに記名押印する。

These minutes have been prepared as a summary and evidence of the above proceedings, with the name and seal of the Chairperson present affixed below.

■■年４月25日
April 25, ■■

■■株式会社 臨時株主総会
General Meeting of Shareholders of ■■ Inc.

議長・代表取締役 ■■■■
Chairperson/Representative Director: ■■■■

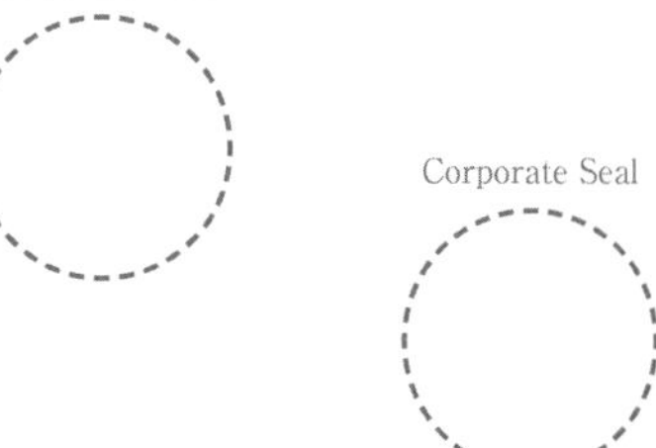

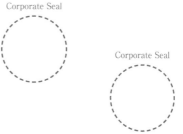

〈例53　募集株式申込証〉

募集株式申込証
Application for Share Subscription

■■■■ 普通株式　4,400株
■■■■ 4400 Ordinary shares

貴社の募集株式の発行につき，貴社の定款及び募集事項を承認の上，会社法の規定に基づき，上記のとおり株式の引受けを申し込みます。

I hereby apply to the Company for share subscription as above, under the provisions of the Companies Act of Japan, on understanding the Articles of Incorporation of the Company and the subscription requirements.

■■年４月25日

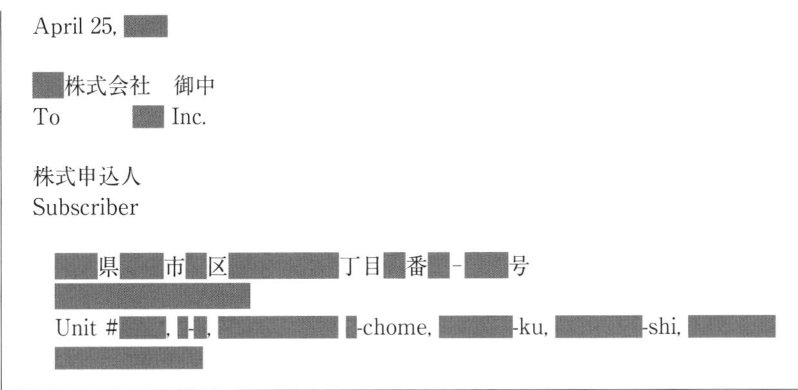
April 25,

株式会社　御中
To Inc.

株式申込人
Subscriber

県 市 区 丁目 番 - 号

Unit #, -, -chome, -ku, -shi,

〈例54 払込証明書（払込金額がユーロの場合の為替相場記載事例）〉

証　明　書
Certification

当会社の募集株式の発行については，以下のとおり，全額の払込みがあったことを証明します。
It is hereby certified that full payment was made for the issue of shares for subscription as set forth below.

発行株式数　496株
Number of Shares to Issue: 496

払込みを受けた金額については以下のとおり
Details of the paid-in amount are as follows.
【会社計算規則第14条第１項第１号イ】
〈Rules for Corporate Accounting, Article 14, Paragraph 1, Number 1, イ〉
(1) 払込金額　40,000ユーロ
Paid-in Amount: 40,000 EURO
(2) 払 込 日　年４月26日
Date of Payment: April 26,
(3) 払込日の為替相場　１ユーロにつき124円
Exchange Rate: 124 yen per EURO

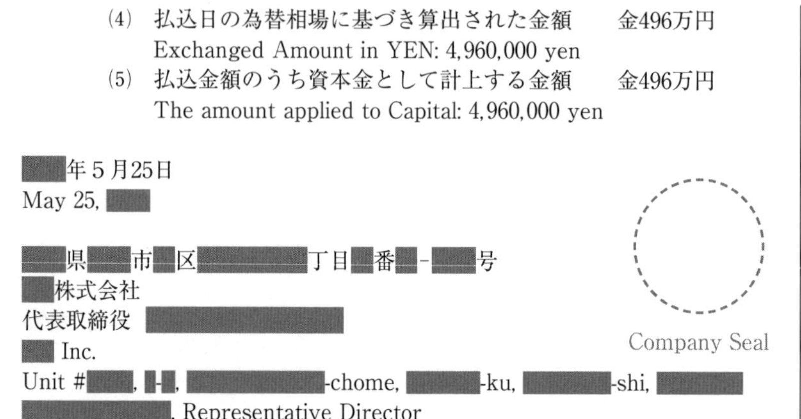

(4)　払込日の為替相場に基づき算出された金額　　金496万円
Exchanged Amount in YEN: 4,960,000 yen

(5)　払込金額のうち資本金として計上する金額　　金496万円
The amount applied to Capital: 4,960,000 yen

■■年５月25日
May 25, ■■

■■県■■市■■区■■丁目■■番■■-■■号
■■株式会社
代表取締役　■■
■■ Inc.
Unit #■■, ■-■, ■■-chome, ■■-ku, ■■-shi, ■■
■■, Representative Director

Company Seal

〈例55　資本金の額の計上に関する証明書〉

Company Seal

資本金の額の計上に関する証明書
Certification for the Amount Applied to Capital

①　払込を受けた金銭の金額
Value of the Paid-in Amount
(会社計算規則第14条第１項第１号)
(Rules for Corporate Accounting, Article 14, Paragraph 1, Number 1)
金1,500万円
15,000,000 yen

②　給付を受けた金銭以外の財産の給付があった日における当該財産の価額
(会社計算規則第14条第１項第２号)
Value of Assets other than Cash
(Rules for Corporate Accounting, Article 14, Paragraph 1, Number 2)
金4,400万円
44,000,000 yen

③　資本金等増加限度額（①+②）

Maximum Amount of Capital to Increase（①+②）
金5,900万円
59,000,000 yen

④　資本準備金計上額　金0円
Amount Applied to Capital Reserve: 0
差引き資本金計上額　金5,900万円
Amount Applied to Capital: 59,000,000 yen

募集株式の発行により増加する資本金の額5,900万円は会社法第445条及び会社計算規則第14条の規定に従って計上されたことに相違ないことを証明する。

It is hereby certified that the increased capital amount of 59,000,000 yen due to the issue of shares for subscription, was duly accounted pursuant to the provisions of the Companies Act, Article 445 and Rules for Corporate Accounting, Article 14.

なお，本募集株式の発行においては，自己株式の処分を伴わない。

For the issue of shares for subscription, sale or disposal of treasury shares of the Company was not carried out.

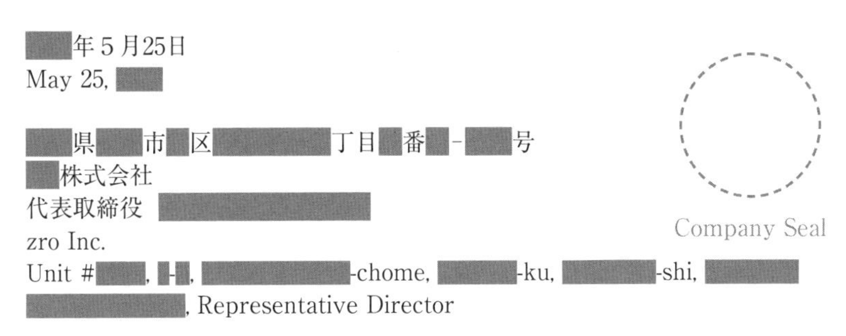

■年5月25日
May 25, ■

■県■市■区■丁目■番■-■号
■株式会社
代表取締役　■
zro Inc.
Unit #■, ■-■, ■-chome, ■-ku, ■-shi, ■
■, Representative Director

〈例56－1　現物出資についての証明書〉

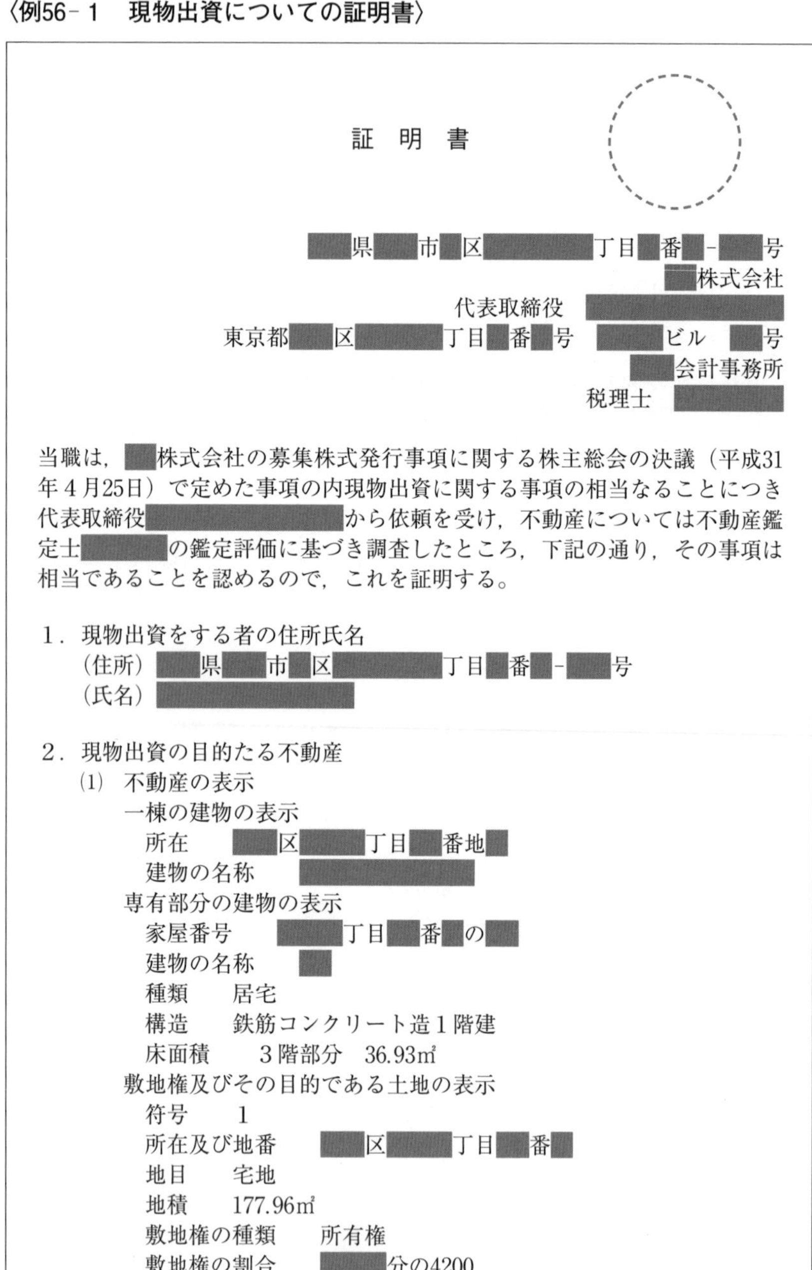

証　明　書

■県■市■区■丁目■番■-■号
■株式会社
代表取締役　■
東京都■区■丁目■番■号　■ビル　■号
■会計事務所
税理士　■

当職は，■株式会社の募集株式発行事項に関する株主総会の決議（平成31年４月25日）で定めた事項の内現物出資に関する事項の相当なることにつき代表取締役■から依頼を受け，不動産については不動産鑑定士■の鑑定評価に基づき調査したところ，下記の通り，その事項は相当であることを認めるので，これを証明する。

１．現物出資をする者の住所氏名
　（住所）■県■市■区■丁目■番■-■号
　（氏名）■

２．現物出資の目的たる不動産
　⑴　不動産の表示
　　一棟の建物の表示
　　　所在　■区■丁目■番地■
　　　建物の名称　■
　　専有部分の建物の表示
　　　家屋番号　■丁目■番■の■
　　　建物の名称　■
　　　種類　居宅
　　　構造　鉄筋コンクリート造１階建
　　　床面積　３階部分　36.93㎡
　　敷地権及びその目的である土地の表示
　　　符号　1
　　　所在及び地番　■区■丁目■番■
　　　地目　宅地
　　　地積　177.96㎡
　　　敷地権の種類　所有権
　　　敷地権の割合　■分の4200

(2)　出資の目的物たる不動産の価格　　　　金4,400万円
(3)　現物出資者に与える株式の種類及び数　普通株式　4,400株

3．不動産の鑑定評価
(1)　鑑定評価を行った不動産鑑定士
東京都■区■丁目■番■号
株式会社■不動産評価研究所
不動産鑑定士　■

(2)　鑑定評価の年月日　■年4月22日

(3)　鑑定評価額　　金44,000,000円

以上の記載のとおり現物出資の目的たる財産の価格が相当であることを証明する。

■年　　月　　日

東京都■区■丁目■番■号　■ビル　■号
■会計事務所
税理士　■

〈例56－2　現物出資についての証明書（英文）〉

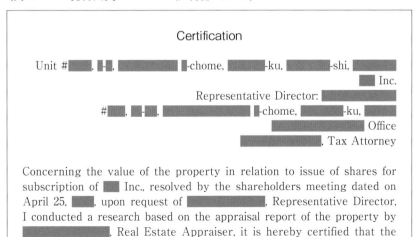

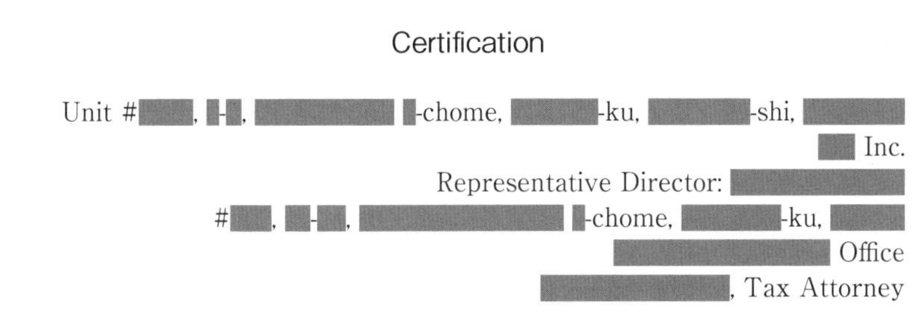
Certification

Unit #■, ■-■, ■ ■-chome, ■-ku, ■-shi, ■
■ Inc.
Representative Director: ■
#■, ■-■, ■ ■-chome, ■-ku, ■
■ Office
■, Tax Attorney

Concerning the value of the property in relation to issue of shares for subscription of ■ Inc., resolved by the shareholders meeting dated on April 25, ■, upon request of ■, Representative Director, I conducted a research based on the appraisal report of the property by ■, Real Estate Appraiser, it is hereby certified that the below matters are proper and appropriate.

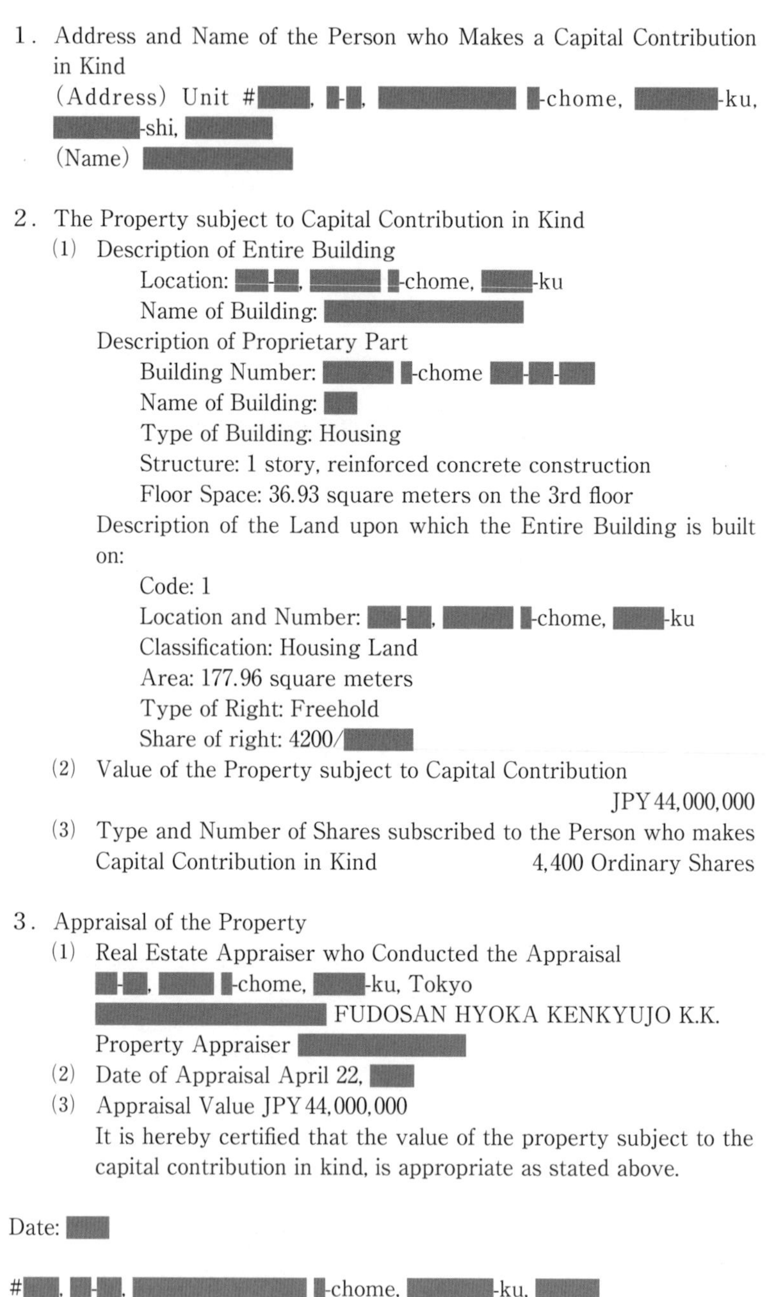

1. Address and Name of the Person who Makes a Capital Contribution in Kind
   (Address) Unit #■■, ■-■, ■■■ ■-chome, ■■■-ku, ■■■-shi, ■■■
   (Name) ■■■

2. The Property subject to Capital Contribution in Kind
   (1) Description of Entire Building
       Location: ■-■, ■■■ ■-chome, ■■■-ku
       Name of Building: ■■■
   Description of Proprietary Part
       Building Number: ■■■ ■-chome ■-■-■
       Name of Building: ■■
       Type of Building: Housing
       Structure: 1 story, reinforced concrete construction
       Floor Space: 36.93 square meters on the 3rd floor
   Description of the Land upon which the Entire Building is built on:
       Code: 1
       Location and Number: ■-■, ■■■ ■-chome, ■■■-ku
       Classification: Housing Land
       Area: 177.96 square meters
       Type of Right: Freehold
       Share of right: 4200/■■■
   (2) Value of the Property subject to Capital Contribution
       JPY 44,000,000
   (3) Type and Number of Shares subscribed to the Person who makes Capital Contribution in Kind 4,400 Ordinary Shares

3. Appraisal of the Property
   (1) Real Estate Appraiser who Conducted the Appraisal
       ■-■, ■■■ ■-chome, ■■■-ku, Tokyo
       ■■■ FUDOSAN HYOKA KENKYUJO K.K.
       Property Appraiser ■■■
   (2) Date of Appraisal April 22, ■■
   (3) Appraisal Value JPY 44,000,000
       It is hereby certified that the value of the property subject to the capital contribution in kind, is appropriate as stated above.

Date: ■■

#■■, ■-■, ■■■ ■-chome, ■■■-ku, ■■■

████ Accounting Office
████████, Tax Attorney

⑵　新株予約権

新株予約権とは，その権利を有する者が，予め定められた一定期間（行使期間）内に予め定められた一定金額（権利行使価額）をその会社に対して払込みをすることによって，その会社から一定数の株式の交付を受けることができる権利（会社2条21号）である。

この新株予約権制度には，主に次のような用途があるといわれている。

i　取締役等の職務執行に対する対価（インセンティブ報酬）

ii　転換社債型新株予約権付社債

iii　敵対的企業買収への対抗策

新株予約権は，取締役会等の決議により募集新株予約権を引き受ける者の募集によって新株予約権を発行する場合と，取得請求権付株式等の取得対価として発行する場合とがある（会社107条2項2号ハ）。

①　**募集新株予約権の発行手続の流れは，次の通りである。**

i　会社は，募集新株予約権の募集事項を決定

ii　募集新株予約権の引受申込みをしようとする者が会社へ申し込む

iii　会社は，申込者の中から割当を受ける者及び割当数決定する

iv　割当日に割当を受けた申込者は新株予約権者となる

②　**新株予約権の下記の募集事項の決定しなければならない**（会社238条1項）。

i　募集新株権の内容と数

ii　金銭の払込みを要しないことにする場合には，その旨

iii　払込金額又は算定方法

iv　割当日

v　払込期日

vi　新株予約権付社債の場合は，募集社債に関する事項

vii　新株予約権付社債の場合において，新株予約権買取請求，新株

予約権の価額決定，組織変更，吸収合併，新設合併，新設分割，株式移転の買取請求の方法に付き別段の定めをするときは，その定め

③　新株予約権の内容は下記の通りである（会社236条1項）。

i　新株予約権を目的である株式の数又はその数の算定方法

ii　新株予約権行使の際の価額又はその算定方法

iii　新株予約権行使の際の価額が現物出資のときは，その旨並びに財産の内容及び価額

iv　行使期間

v　新株予約権行使により株式発行する場合における増加する資本金及び資本準備金に関する事項

vi　新株予約権譲渡制限付の場合には，その旨

vii　条件付新株予約権の場合の条件事項

ⓐ　一定事由発生日に取得する旨及びその事由

ⓑ　別に定める日が到来することをもってⓐの事由とするときは，その旨

ⓒ　ⓐの事由発生日にⓐの新株予約権の一部を取得するときは，その旨及び取得する新株予約権の一部の決定の方法

ⓓ　ⓐの新株予約権取得と引換えに株式を交付するときは，その株式数又はその算定方法

ⓔ　ⓐの新株予約権取得と引換えに社債を交付するときは，その社債の種類及び各社債金額の合計額又はその算定方法

ⓕ　ⓐの新株予約権取得と引換えに他の新株予約権を交付するときは，その他の新株予約権の内容及び又はその算定方法

ⓖ　ⓐの新株予約権取得と引換えに新株予約権付社債を交付するときは，その新株予約権付社債についてのⓔに規定している事項及びその種類及び新株予約権付社債に付された新株予約権についてのⓕに規定する事項

ⓗ　ⓐの新株予約権取得と引換えにその株式以外の財産交付するときは，その財産の内容及び数又はその算定方法

viii　会社が，合併，吸収分割，新設分割，株式交換，株式移転の場合において，その存続又は新設会社の新株予約権を交付するときは，その旨及び条件

ix　新株予約権の端株の切捨てを定めるときは，その旨

x　新株予約権証券を発行するときは，その旨

xi　証券発行の際に，記名式と無記名式との間の転換請求の全部又は一部をすることができないとするときは，その旨

④　募集事項の決定機関

i　非公開会社　株主総会の特別決議（会社238条２項）である。

ii　公開会社　　取締役会の決議である。ただし，有利発行の場合は株主総会の特別決議（会社240条１項・238条３項各号）。この場合，募集事項を割当日の２週間前までに，株主に通知，又は公告に代替する。更に金融商品取引法上の届出をしている場合は通知，公告を不要とする（会社240条４項）。

iii　募集事項の取締役会への委任

非公開会社の場合は，株主総会の特別決議（会社238条２項），ただし，株主総会の特別決議により募集事項の決定を取締役会の決議（又は取締役の決定）に委任することができる。この場合，募集新株予約権内容及び数の上限，金銭払込を要しないとする場合は，その旨，払込金額の下限を定めなければならない（会社239条１項）。有利発行の場合には，取締役は株主総会でその理由を説明する義務がある（会社239条２項）。割当日がその決議の日から１年内で日である募集についてのみ効力を有する（会社239条３項）。

⑤　新株予約権の申込み

会社は，引受申込者宛て，商号，募集事項，金銭の場合の払込取扱場所を通知する。申込者は，会社宛て，氏名又は名称及び住所，引受新株予約権数を記載した書面の提出する（会社242条）。

⑥　新株予約権の割当

i　決定機関

非公開会社においては，定款に別段の定めない限り，株主総会

の特別決議（取締役会設置会社は，取締役会）で，割当数を決定する。

公開会社においては，定款の別段の定めない限り，取締役会で割当数を決定する。

ii　株主に新株予約権の割当を受ける権利を付与の場合は，定款の別段の定めない限り，公開会社では取締役会，非公開会社では，株主総会の決議による（会社241条３項）。

iii　総数引受契約を締結の場合には，新株予約権の申込み，割当手続は不要である（会社244条１項）。

iv　公開会社における募集新株予約権の割当の特則

平成26年法改正で，公開会社が行う支配株主の移動を伴う募集株式の割当等の特則として一定の場合に限り，株主総会の承認を要するとした（会社206条の２）。そこで，募集新株予約権の引受人が当該新株予約権の行使等の結果として公開会社の総株主の議決権の過半数を有することとなりうる場合についても同様な規定が設けられている（会社244条の２）。

⑦　新株予約権者となる時期

申込者又は総数引受者は，割当日に，新株予約権者となる（会社245条）。引受人は，払込みなしで新株予約権者となる点で募集株式について払込期日（又は期間）に払込みをすることにより株主となることとは異なる。

⑧　募集新株予約権にかかわる払込をすべき時期

新株予約権者が，予約権を行使することができる期間の初日の前日（又は払込期日）までに，払込取扱い場所へ払込金額全額の払込みをなさなくてはならない（会社246条１項）。払込みをなさないときは，新株予約権は消滅する（会社287条）。

新株予約権者は，会社の承諾を得て払込みに代えて財産の給付又は会社に対する債権をもって相殺することができる（246条２項）。現物給付については，裁判所が選任した検査役による検査制度はない（平18・３・31民商782号民事局通達）。

例57は，取締役等の職務執行に対する対価（インセンティブ報酬）型の新株予約権発行の場合である。

〈例57　新株予約権（定時株主総会における募集事項の取締役会への委任の決議）〉

株式会社
定時株主総会議事録
MINUTES OF THE ORDINARY GENERAL MEETING OF SHAREHOLDERS
OF JAPAN KK

年３月30日午前09時00分，東京都区丁目番号ビルの当会社において，第４回定時株主総会を開催した。

The 4th Ordinary General Meeting of Shareholders meeting of the of Japan, KK (hereinafter referred to as the "Company") was held on March 30, , at 9:00 a.m., at Japan, KK, Building, -, -chome, -ku, Tokyo.

出席株主数及びその議決権数
Number of Shareholders present and Number of Voting Rights represented:
議決権を行使できる総株主数　６名　その議決権数　9,996,503個
Total number of Shareholders with Voting Rights: 6
Total number of Voting Rights represented by such Shareholders: 9,996,503
出席株主数　６名　その議決権数　9,996,503個
（委任状による出席を含む）
Number of Shareholders present (including attendance by way of proxy) :6
Number of Voting Rights represented by Shareholders present: 9,996,503

出席取締役
Directors present:　全員
欠席取締役
Directors not present:
出席監査役
Statutory Auditor present:　全員
欠席監査役
Statutory Auditor not present:

定刻，定款の規定により代表取締役が議長となり，本総会を開会

する旨宣し，本総会の全ての議案の決議に必要な定足数を満たしている旨を述べて，議事に入った。

Mr. ■■■■ Representative Director, assumed the Chairperson of the meeting in accordance with the Articles of Incorporation of the Company, declared the meeting at the appointed time and further stated that the necessary quorum for all the resolutions at the meeting was in attendance, and the meeting opened for business.

報告事項

Matters to be reported

■■■■年12月31日をもって終了した事業年度に関する事業報告の内容報告の件

Report on the particulars of the Business Report for the fiscal year ended on December 31, ■■■■

議長は，■■■■年12月31日をもって終了した事業年度に関する事業報告を別添1のとおり提出し，その内容を報告した。

The Chairperson submitted the business report, as set forth in Exhibit 1 attached hereto, for the fiscal year ended on December 31, ■■■■ and reported its contents in detail.

決議事項

Matters to be resolved

第1号議案　■■■■年12月31日をもって終了した事業年度に関する計算書類承認の件

First Item of Business: Approval of the financial statements for the fiscal year ended on December 31, ■■■■

議長は，別添1のとおり当会社の第4期（■■■■年1月1日から■■■■年12月31日まで）の計算書類（貸借対照表，損益計算書，株主資本等変動計算書及び個別注記表）を提出し，それらの内容を説明した上，承認を求めたところ，出席株主の議決権の過半数の賛成をもって原案どおり承認可決された。

The Chairperson presented the financial statements (the balance sheet, the statement of profit and loss, and the statement of changes in the net assets and notes thereto) for the 4th fiscal year (from January 1, ■■■■ to December 31, ■■■■) as described in Exhibit 1.

Thereupon, the Chairperson explained the contents and put the matter to a vote of the Shareholders present. The proposal was approved by a majority of the votes of the Shareholders present and resolved as proposed.

第2号議案　取締役7名選任の件

Second Item of Business: Appointment of seven(7)Directors

議長は，当会社の取締役７名全員の任期が本定時株主総会終結時をもって満了するため，以下の取締役７名を選任することを提案し，議場に諮ったところ，出席株主の議決権の過半数の賛成をもって原案どおり承認可決された。各被選者は，その場で就任を承諾した。

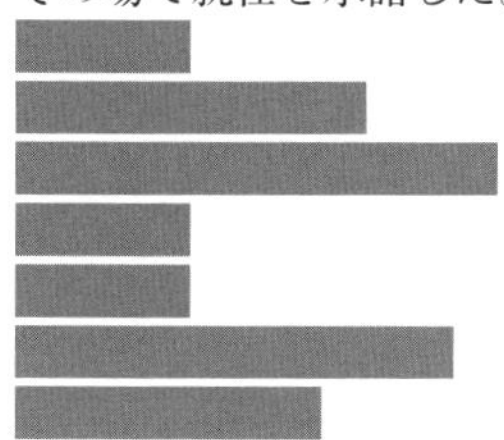

The Chairperson proposed that the following seven (7) Directors of the Company shall be appointed, in as much as the terms of office of all of seven (7) Directors will be expired at the time of the closing of this Ordinary General Meeting of Shareholders.

Thereupon the Chairperson put the matter to a vote of the Shareholders present and the proposal was approved by a majority of the votes of the Shareholders present and resolved as proposed. Each of the appointed Directors has accepted the offices.

第３号議案　　取締役に対する報酬の件
Third Item of Business: Compensation for Directors

議長は，当会社取締役に対する報酬総額を年額26,437,500円（労働者兼務取締役の労働者分の賞与を含まない）とし，その配分方法は取締役会に一任したい旨提案し，議場に諮ったところ，出席株主の議決権の３分の２以上の賛成をもって原案どおり承認可決された。

The Chairperson proposed that the total amount of the compensation for the Directors of the Company shall be up to JPY 26,437,500 per year (excluding the amount of the bonus to be paid to the worker director) and the distribution to each Director shall be entrusted to the Board of Directors.

Thereupon the Chairperson put the matter to a vote of the shareholders present and the proposal was approved by a two thirds majority or more of the votes of the Shareholders present and resolved as proposed.

第４号議案　　募集新株予約権の募集事項の決定を取締役会に委任する件
Fourth Item of Business: Authorization to the Board of Directors of the Company of Determination of the Details concerning the Issuance of the Stock Acquisition Rights

議長は，当会社新株予約権の募集事項の決定を，当会社取締役会に委任したい旨提案し，議場に諮ったところ，出席株主の議決権の３分の２以上の賛成をもって原案通り承認可決された。なお，その委任に基づいて募集事項の決定をすることができる募集新株予約権の内容及び数の上限並びに払込金額の下限は別添２のとおりとする。

The Chairperson proposed that the Company shall authorize the Board of Directors of the Company to determine the details concerning the issuance of the stock acquisition rights（the terms and conditions, the maximum number and minimum issuance price of the stock acquisition rights so authorized are set forth in Exhibit 2 attached hereto）.

Thereupon the Chairperson put the matter to a vote of the Shareholders present and the proposal was approved by a two thirds majority or more of the votes of the Shareholders present and resolved as proposed.

〈例58　新株予約権（種類株主総会議事録）〉

■■■■株式会社
普通株主による種類株主総会議事録
MINUTES OF THE CLASSIFIED GENERAL MEETING OF COMMON SHAREHOLDERS
OF ■■■■ JAPAN KK

■■年３月30日午前09時30分，東京都■区■■丁目■番■号■■■■ビルの当会社において，普通株主による種類株主総会を開催した。

The Classified General Meeting of Common Shareholders meeting of the of ■■■ Japan, KK（hereinafter referred to as the "Company"）was held on March 30, ■■, at 9:30 a.m., at ■■■ Japan, KK, ■■■■■■ Building, ■-■, ■■■ ■-chome, ■■■-ku, Tokyo.

出席普通株主数及びその議決権数
Number of Common Shareholders present and Number of Voting Rights represented:
議決権を行使できる総普通株主数　１名　その議決権数　6,500,000個

Total number of Common Shareholders with Voting Rights: 1
Total number of Voting Rights represented by such Common Shareholders: 6,500,000
出席普通株主数　　　　　　　　　1名　その議決権数　6,500,000個
（委任状による出席を含む）
Number of Shareholders present (including attendance by way of proxy) :1
Number of Voting Rights represented by Shareholders present: 6,500,000

出席取締役
Directors present: ■■■, ■■■, ■■■, ■■■, ■■■, ■■■, ■■■
欠席取締役
Directors not present:
出席監査役
Statutory Auditor present: ■■■
欠席監査役
Statutory Auditor not present:

定刻，定款の規定により代表取締役■■■が議長となり，本総会を開会する旨宣し，本総会の全ての議案の決議に必要な定足数を満たしている旨を述べて，議事に入った。

Mr. ■■■, Representative Director, assumed the Chairperson of the meeting in accordance with the Articles of Incorporation of the Company, declared the meeting at the appointed time and further stated that the necessary quorum for all the resolutions at the meeting was in attendance, and the meeting opened for business.

決議事項
Matters to be resolved
第１号議案　募集新株予約権の募集事項の決定を取締役会に委任する件
First Item of Business: Authorization to the Board of Directors of the Company of Determination of the Details concerning the Issuance of the Stock Acquisition Rights

議長は，当会社新株予約権の募集事項の決定を，当会社取締役会に委任したい旨提案し，議場に諮ったところ，出席株主の議決権の３分の２以上の賛成をもって原案通り承認可決された。なお，その委任に基づいて募集事項の決定をすることができる募集新株予約権の内容及び数の上限並びに払込金額の下限は別添２のとおりとする。

The Chairperson proposed that the Company shall authorize the Board of Directors of the Company to determine the details concerning the issuance of the stock acquisition rights (the terms and conditions, the maximum number and minimum issuance price of the stock acquisition rights so authorized are set forth in Exhibit 2 attached hereto).

Thereupon the Chairperson put the matter to a vote of the Shareholders present and the proposal was approved by a two thirds majority or more of the votes of the Shareholders present and resolved as proposed.

以上をもって本総会は，報告及び全議案の審議を終了したので，議長は午前09時45分閉会を宣した。

The Chairperson announced the completion of the report and the agenda and declared the meeting held closed at 9:45 a.m.

上記議事の経過の要領及びその結果を記載し，議長である代表取締役が記名押印又は署名する。

These minutes are prepared in evidence of the above proceedings and resolutions and bear the name and seal or signature of the Chairperson who is the Representative Director.

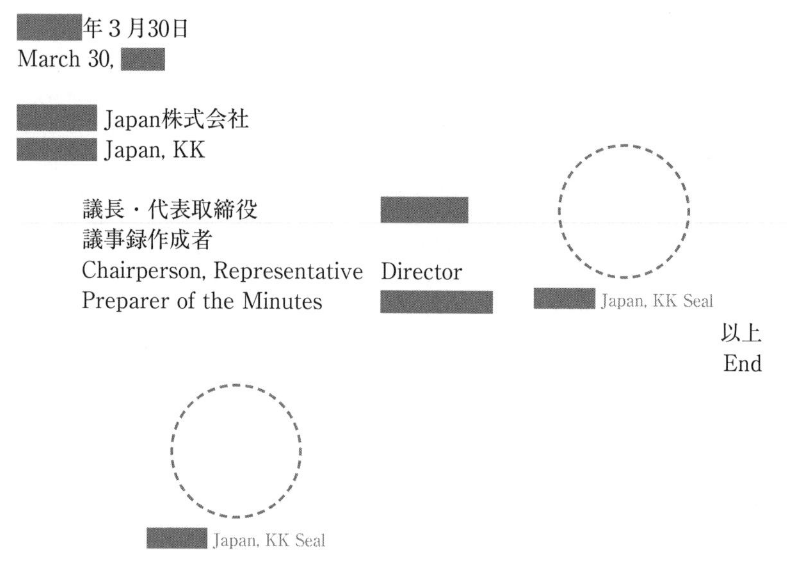

年３月30日
March 30,
Japan株式会社
Japan, KK
議長・代表取締役
議事録作成者
Chairperson, Representative Director
Preparer of the Minutes
Japan, KK Seal
以上
End
Japan, KK Seal

〈例59　新株予約権の募集事項委任につき，新株予約権の数の上限並びに払込金額の下限の決定〉

新株予約権の募集事項（株主総会決議）

[黒塗り] KK Series 2 Stock Acquisition Rights Terms and Conditions

(Subject to the resolutions at a general meeting of shareholders)

会社法第236条，第238条及び第239条の規定に基づき，以下の要領で[黒塗り]株式会社（以下「当会社」という。）又は当会社関係会社（以下[黒塗り] Inc.を含む。）の取締役，監査役，労働者及びコンサルタントに対して発行する新株予約権（以下「本新株予約権」という。）の募集事項の決定を当会社取締役会に委任する。

Pursuant to the provisions of Articles 236, 238 and 239 of the Companies Act of Japan, the determination of the terms and conditions of the stock acquisition rights to be granted to the directors, statutory auditors, workers and consultants of [黒塗り] KK (the "Company") and affiliates of the Company (including [黒塗り] Inc.) in accordance with the following particulars (the "Stock Acquisition Rights") shall be entrusted to the board of directors of the Company.

本株主総会においてその決定する事項に基づいて募集事項の決定をすることができる本新株予約権の内容及び数の上限

Details and maximum number of the Stock Acquisition Rights to be granted the terms and conditions of which may be determined, based on the resolutions to be adopted by the shareholders:

1．本新株予約権の名称

1．Name of stock options

[黒塗り]株式会社第2回ストックオプション

[黒塗り] KK Series 2 Stock Acquisition Rights

2．本新株予約権の数の上限

2．Maximum number of the Stock Acquisition Rights:

170,500個（本新株予約権1個あたりの目的となる当会社普通株式の数は1株とする。但し，下記4.(1)に定める株式の数の調整を行った場合は，同様の調整を行う。）を上限とする。

170,500 (The number of shares of common stock to be issued upon exercise of each one of the Stock Acquisition Rights shall be one (1); provided, however, that if any adjustment is made pursuant to the provisions of Paragraph 4.(1) below with respect to the number of shares to be issued, said number of shares shall be adjusted accordingly.)

3．本新株予約権の払込金額の下限

3．Minimum amount of cash payment to be required in exchange for the Stock Acquisition Rights:

本新株予約権1個あたりの払込価額の下限は，12円とする。なお，当該金額は，主観的及び客観的諸要素（当会社と利害関係のない第三者評価機関が行った算定結果を含むが，これに限られない。）を参考に当会社取締役会が算定したものである。

The minimum issuance price of each of the Stock Acquisition Rights shall be JPY12, as determined by the board of directors of the Company based on subjective and objective factors, including, but not limited to having contemporaneous valuations performed by an unrelated valuation specialist.

4．本新株予約権の内容

4．Details of the Stock Acquisition Rights:

(1)　本新株予約権の目的である株式の種類及び数

(1)　Class and number of shares to be issued upon exercise of the Stock Acquisition Rights:

本新株予約権1個あたりの目的である株式の数（以下「付与株式数」という。）は，当会社普通株式1株とする（当会社普通株式170,500株を上限とする。）。

なお，本新株予約権の割当日後，当会社が株式分割又は株式併合を行う場合，次の算式により付与株式数を調整するものとする。但し，かかる調整は本新株予約権のうち，当該時点では権利行使又は消滅していない付与株式数についてのみ行われ，調整の結果1株未満の端数が生じた場合には，これを切り捨てるものとする。但し，新株予約権者が，2個以上の本新株予約権を同時に行使する場合には，行使される本新株予約権にかかる割当株式数の合計数について，その1株未満の端数を切り捨てるものとする。

調整後付与株式数　＝　調整前付与株式数　×　分割又は併合の比率

The number of shares to be granted upon exercise of each one of the Stock Acquisition Rights (the "Number of Shares for Grant") shall be one (1) share of common stock of the Company (Up to 170,500 shares of common stock of the Company).

After the date of the grant of the Stock Acquisition Rights, in the event that the Company performs a split of shares (kabushiki-bunkatsu) or consolidation of shares (kabushiki-heigo), the Number of Shares for Grant shall be adjusted in accordance with the following formula; provided, however, that such adjustment shall be made only with respect to the Number of Shares for Grant that have not been exercised or not lapsed at the time of the relevant adjustment. Any fractional shares less than one (1) share resulting from the calculation for such adjustment shall be discarded; provided, however, that if the holder of the Stock Acquisition Rights exercises two (2) or more Stock Acquisition Rights simultaneously, the Number of Shares for Grant with respect to the Stock Acquisition Rights subject to such exercise shall be aggregated and any number of fractional shares less than one (1) share obtained as a result of such aggregation shall be disregarded:

(Number of Shares for Grant after adjustment) = (Number of Shares for Grant before adjustment) × (Ratio of split/consolidation)

また，本新株予約権を割当日以降，当会社が合併，会社分割又は資本金の額の減少を行う場合その他付与株式数の調整を必要とする事由が生じたときは，当会社は合併，会社分割又は資本金の額の減少の条件等を勘案の上，必要かつ合理的な範囲で，付与株式数の調整を適切に行うものとする。但し，かかる調整は本新株予約権のうち，当該時点では権利行使又は消滅していない付与株式数についてのみ行われ，調整の結果1株未満の端数が生じた場合には，これを切り捨てるものとする。但し，新株予約権者が，2個以上の本新株予約権を同時に行使する場合には，行使される本新株予約権にかかる割当株式数の合計数について，その1株未満の端数を切り捨てるものとする。

In addition, in the event that any adjustment of the Number of Shares for Grant shall be required due to a merger, demerger or capital decrease to be performed in respect of the Company or any other events occurring after the date of the grant of the Stock Acquisition Rights, the Company shall appropriately adjust the Number of Shares for Grant to a necessary and reasonable extent, after taking into account the conditions for the relevant merger, demerger or capital decrease, etc.; provided, however, that such adjustment shall be made only with respect to the Number of Shares for Grant that have not been exercised or not lapsed at the time of the relevant adjustment. Any fractional shares less than one (1) share resulting from the calculation for such adjustment shall be discarded; provided, however, that if the holder of the Stock Acquisition Rights exercises two (2) or more Stock Acquisition Rights simultaneously, the Number of Shares for Grant with respect to the

Stock Acquisition Rights subject to such exercise shall be aggregated and any number of fractional shares less than one (1) share obtained as a result of such aggregation shall be disregarded.

(2)　本新株予約権の行使に際して出資される財産の価額

(2)　Value of assets to be contributed upon exercise of the Stock Acquisition Rights:

①各新株予約権の行使に際して出資される財産の価額は，各新株予約権を行使することにより交付を受けることができる株式1株当たりの払込金額（以下「行使価額」という。）に付与株式数を乗じた金額とし，行使価額は103円とする。なお，当該金額は，当会社取締役会が算定したものである。

なお，本新株予約権の割当日後，当会社が当会社普通株式について株式分割又は株式併合を行う場合，次の算式により行使価額を調整し，調整により生ずる1円未満の端数は切り上げる。

$$\text{調整後行使価額} = \text{調整前行使価額} \times \frac{1}{\text{分割・併合の比率}}$$

また，本新株予約権の割当日後，当会社が時価（下記②で定義する。）を下回る価額で当会社普通株式の新規発行又は自己株式を処分する場合（新株予約権の行使により新規株式を発行する場合及び自己株式の処分並びに株式交換による自己株式の移転の場合を除く）には，次の算式により行使価額を調整し，調整により生ずる1円未満の端数は切り上げる。

$$\text{調整後行使価額} = \text{調整前行使価額} \times \frac{\text{既発行株式数} + \dfrac{\text{新規発行株式数} \times \text{1株当たり払込金額}}{\text{新規発行前の1株当たりの時価}}}{\text{既発行株式数} + \text{新規発行株式数}}$$

上記の算式において「既発行株式数」とは，当会社普通株式にかかる発行済株式総数から当会社の保有する当会社普通株式にかかる自己株式の総数を控除した数とし，当会社普通株式にかかる自己株式の処分を行う場合には「新規発行株式数」を「処分する自己株式数」に，「1株当たり払込金額」を「1株当たり処分金額」に，「新規発行前の時価」を「処分前の時価」に，それぞれ読み替えるものとする。

上記のほか，本新株予約権の割当日後，当会社が他社と合併する場合，会社分割を行う場合，資本金の額の減少を行う場合，その他これらの場合に準じ，行使価額の調整を当会社が必要と認めるときは，当会社は，必要かつ合理的な範囲で，行使価額の調整を行うことができるものとし，調整により生ずる1円未満の端数は切り上げる。

(i)　The value of assets to be contributed upon exercise of any Stock Acquisition Right shall be calculated by multiplying (x) the amount payable per share of the shares to be issued upon exercise of each of the relevant Stock Acquisition Rights (the "Exercise Price") by (y) the Number of Shares for Grant. The Exercise Price shall be JPY 103 as determined by the board of directors of the Company.

After the date of the grant of the Stock Acquisition Rights, provided that in the event that the Company performs a split of shares (kabushiki-bunkatsu) or consolidation of shares (kabushiki-heigo) for common stock of the Company, the Exercise Price shall be adjusted in accordance with the following formula. Any fraction less than one yen resulting from the calculation for such adjustment shall be rounded up to the nearest yen:

$$(\text{Exercise Price after adjustment}) = (\text{Exercise Price before adjustment}) \times \frac{1}{(\text{Ratio of split/consolidation})}$$

After the date of the grant of the Stock Acquisition Rights, if the Company issues new shares of common stock of the Company or disposes of its treasury stocks at any price less than the Fair Market Value (as defined in (ii) below) per share of the Company (except for the cases of the issuance of new shares or disposal of its treasury stock upon exercise of any Stock Acquisition Right, or transfer of its treasury stock as a result of a share-for-share exchange), the Exercise Price shall be adjusted in accordance with the following formula. Any fraction less than one yen resulting from the calculation for such adjustment shall be rounded up to the nearest yen:

$$\text{(Exercise Price after adjustment)} = \text{(Exercise Price before adjustment)} \times \frac{\text{(Number of issued and outstanding shares)} + \dfrac{\text{(Number of new shares to be issued)} \times \text{(Payment amount per share)}}{\text{(Fair Market Value per share before issuance of new shares)}}}{\text{(Number of issued and outstanding shares)} + \text{(Number of new shares to be issued)}}$$

In the foregoing formula, "Number of issued and outstanding shares" means the number calculated by reducing (x) the total number of the Company's treasury common stock held by the Company from (y) the number of the issued and outstanding shares of common stock of the Company. In the case of the disposition by the Company of any of its treasury common stock, "Number of new shares to be issued", "Payment amount per share" and "Fair Market Value per share before issuance of new shares" shall be replaced with "Number of shares of common stock to be disposed of", "Disposition price per share" and "Fair Market Value before disposition of shares", respectively.

In addition to the foregoing, after the date of the grant of the Stock Acquisition Rights, in the case of a merger with any other company, demerger or capital decrease performed in respect of the Company, or any other similar event that would require any adjustment to the Exercise Price in the Company's view, the Company may perform such adjustment to a necessary and reasonable extent. Any fraction less than one yen resulting from the calculation for such adjustment shall be rounded up to the nearest yen.

② 以下に定める用語は，それぞれ以下の意味を有するものとする。

(ii) The following terms shall have the meaning set forth below:

(a) 「時価」とは，(i)株式公開前は，取締役会がその裁量により合理的な手段として採用する，評価日時点における事実関係及び状況に基づく合理的な評価手法によって誠実に定められ，かつ確定的な当会社普通株式1株あたりの公正な市場価格をいい，(ii)株式公開時においては，かかる株式公開における当会社普通株式1株あたりの募集価格をいうものとし，(iii)株式公開後は，当会社普通株式が上場し，取引される主たる証券取引所における適用日の終値とし，当該適用日の終値がないときは，その直前日の終値とする。但し，株式公開後，当会社普通株式が登録証券取引所に上場していないときは，「時価」は，取締役会が希薄化された当会社普通株式1株あたりの公正な市場価格と誠実に定めた金額をいうものとする。

(a) the "Fair Market Value" shall mean (i) prior to an IPO, the fair market value per share of common stock, as determined in good faith by the board of directors acting in its discretion using the reasonable application of a reasonable valuation method based on the facts and circumstances existing on the valuation date, which determination will be conclusive; (ii) at the time of an IPO, the price per share of common stock offered to the public in such IPO; and (iii) after an IPO, the closing price reported as having occurred on the primary exchange with which the common stock is listed and traded on the applicable date or, if there is no such closing price reported on that date, then on the last preceding date on which such a closing price was reported; provided, however, if, after an IPO, the common stock is not listed on a national securities exchange, the Fair Market Value shall mean the amount determined in good faith by the board of directors to be the fair market value per share of common stock, on a fully diluted basis.

(b)「株式公開」とは，日本国内又は国外において，当会社の発行済株式（自己株式数を除く。）が金融商品取引所（証券取引所）に上場され又は店頭有価証券売買市場に登録されることをいう。

(b) the "IPO" shall mean the listing of the then-outstanding shares (excluding treasury shares) of the Company on any stock exchange or the registration with any over-the-counter securities transactions market in or outside Japan.

(3) 本新株予約権を行使することができる期間

(3) Exercise period for the Stock Acquisition Rights:

　[■]年５月１日から[■]年３月30日までとする。但し，行使期間の最終日が当会社の休業日にあたるときは，その前営業日を最終日とする。

From May 1st, [■] to March 30th, [■]

In the event that the last date of the exercise period is a non-business day of the Company, it shall be the business day immediately preceding such date.

(4) 本新株予約権の行使により株式を発行する場合における増加する資本金及び資本準備金に関する事項

(4) Matters pertaining to the increase of the amounts of paid-in capital and capital reserve in the case of an issuance of shares upon exercise of the Stock Acquisition Rights:

①　本新株予約権の行使により株式を発行する場合において増加する資本金の額は，会社計算規則第17条第１項に従い算出される資本金等増加限度額の２分の１の金額とし，計算の結果端数が生じたときは，その端数を切上げるものとする。

(i) In the case where shares are issued upon exercise of the Stock Acquisition Rights, the amount of paid-in capital shall increase by such amount as is equal to half of the limit for increase in capital and other items calculated in accordance with Paragraph 1 of Article 17 of the Company Calculation Rules. Any fraction less than one yen resulting from such calculation shall be rounded up to the nearest yen.

②　本新株予約権の行使により株式を発行する場合において増加する資本準備金の額は，上記①記載の資本金等増加限度額から上記①に定める増加する資本金の額を減じた額とする。

(ii) In the case where shares are issued upon exercise of the Stock Acquisition Rights, the amount of capital reserve shall increase by such amount as is equal to the difference after subscribing the increased amount of paid-in capital from the limit for increase in capital and other items prescribed in (i) above.

(5) 譲渡による本新株予約権の取得の制限

(5) Restrictions on acquisition of the Stock Acquisition Rights by means of transfer:

　譲渡による本新株予約権の取得については、当会社取締役会の決議による承認を要するものとする。

Any transfer of the Stock Acquisition Rights shall be subject to the approval resolved by the board of directors of the Company.

(6) 当会社が本新株予約権を取得することができる事由及び取得の条件

(6) Events in which the Company may acquire the Stock Acquisition Rights and the

第2章　株式会社

conditions for such acquisition:

① 新株予約権者が権利行使をする前に，行使条件に該当しなくなったため本新株予約権を行使することができない場合は，取締役会が別途定める日に当該新株予約権を無償で取得することができる。

(i) In the event that any person entitled to exercise any of the Stock Acquisition Rights becomes unable to exercise the Stock Acquisition Rights before his/her exercise thereof due to his/her disqualification from the exercise of the Stock Acquisition Rights, the Company may acquire the relevant Stock Acquisition Rights without compensation on such date as is separately determined by the board of directors.

② 当会社は，新株予約権者が新株予約権割当契約書の条項に違反した場合，取締役会が別途定める日に無償で新株予約権を取得することができる。

(ii) In the event that any holder of the Stock Acquisition Rights violates any of the provisions of the Stock Option Allotment (Grant) Agreement, the Company may acquire the relevant Stock Acquisition Rights without compensation on such date as is separately determined by the board of directors.

③ 当会社は，以下の議案につき当会社株主総会で承認された場合（株主総会決議が不要な場合は，当会社の取締役会決議がなされた場合）は，取締役会が別途定める日に，当該新株予約権を有償（本新株予約権1個あたり，当会社普通株式1株あたりの時価から行使価額を控除した価額に付与株式数を乗じた金額）で取得することができる。

(iii) In the event that any one of the proposals set forth in (a) through (f) below is approved by a general meeting of shareholders of the Company (or, by the board of directors of the Company, if the resolution at a shareholders' meeting is not required), the Company may acquire the Stock Acquisition Rights with compensation (the price of such acquisition shall be equal to the same the Fair Market Value per share of common stock of the Company multiplied by the Number of Shares for Grant less aggregate amount of the applicable Exercise Price per Stock Acquisition Right) on such date as is separately determined by the board of directors.

ア　当会社が消滅会社となる合併契約承認の議案

(a) a proposal for the approval of a merger agreement under which the Company would become a dissolved company;

イ　当会社が分割会社となる会社分割契約又は会社分割計画承認の議案

(b) a proposal for the approval of a demerger agreement or a demerger plan under which the Company would become a demerged company;

ウ　当会社が完全子会社となる株式交換契約又は株式移転計画承認の議案

(c) a proposal for the approval of a share-for-share exchange agreement or a share transfer plan under which the Company would become a wholly-owned subsidiary of any other company;

エ　当会社の発行する全部の株式の内容として譲渡による当該株式の取得について当会社の承認を要することについての定めを設ける定款の変更承認の議案

(d) a proposal for the amendment to the Articles of Incorporation of the Company by which any transfer of any shares of the Company will be subject to an approval of the Company; or

オ　本新株予約権の目的である種類の株式の内容として譲渡による当該種類の株式の取得について当会社の承認を要すること若しくは当該種類の株式について当会社が当会社株主総会の決議によってその全部を取得することについての定めを設ける定款の変更承認の議案

(e) a proposal for the amendment to the Articles of Incorporation of the Company by which (A) any transfer of the class of shares to be issued upon exercise of Stock Acquisition Rights will be subject to an approval of the Company or (B) the class of shares to be issued upon exercise of Stock Acquisition Rights will be subject to class-wide call option of the Company upon resolution of the general meeting of the shareholders of the Company.

カ　本新株予約権の目的である種類の株式の併合承認の議案

(f) a proposal for the approval of a consolidation of the class of shares to be issued upon exercise of Stock Acquisition Rights

(7) 組織再編に伴う本新株予約権の承継

(7) Takeover of the Stock Acquisition Rights upon organizational restructuring:

当会社が，合併（当会社が合併により消滅する場合に限る。），吸収分割，新設分割，株式交換又は株式移転（当会社が完全子会社となる場合に限る。以上を総称して以下，「組織再編行為」という。）をする場合において，組織再編行為の効力発生の時点において残存する本新株予約権の新株予約権者に対し，それぞれの場合につき，会社法第236条第1項第8号のイからホまでに掲げる株式会社（以下，「再編対象会社」という。）の新株予約権を以下の条件に基づきそれぞれ交付することとする。この場合においては，残存する本新株予約権は消滅し，再編対象会社は新株予約権を新たに発行するものとする。但し，以下の条件に沿って再編対象会社の新株予約権を交付する旨を，吸収合併契約，新設合併契約，吸収分割契約，新設分割計画，株式交換契約又は株式移転計画において定めた場合に限るものとする。

If the Company becomes a dissolved company as a result of a merger, if the Company becomes a demerged company as a result of an absorption-type demerger (kyushu-bunkatsu) or incorporation-type demerger (shinsetsu-bunkatsu) or if the Company becomes a wholly-owned subsidiary as a result of a share-for-share exchange or a share transfer (hereinafter collectively the "organizational restructuring"), the joint-stock company (kabushiki-kaisha) prescribed in (a) through (e) of Item 8 of Paragraph 1 of Article 236 of the Companies Act of Japan (hereinafter the "restructuring target company") shall grant stock acquisition rights to the holders of the remaining Stock Acquisition Rights of the Company at the time of the effectuation of the organizational restructuring in each event, in accordance with the following terms and conditions. In such case, the remaining Stock Acquisition Rights of the Company shall extinguish, and the restructuring target company shall grant new stock acquisition rights. Provided, however, that in order to grant such new stock acquisition rights, the absorption-type merger agreement, the incorporation-type merger agreement, the absorption-type demerger agreement, the incorporation-type demerger plan, the share-for-share exchange agreement or the share transfer plan must provide that the restructuring target company shall issue the stock acquisition rights in accordance with the following conditions:

ア　交付する再編対象会社の新株予約権の数

組織再編行為の効力発生の時点において残存する本新株予約権の新株予約権者が保有する新株予約権の数と同一の数をそれぞれ交付するものとする。

(a) Number of stock acquisition rights to be granted by the restructuring target company:

Such number as is equal to the number of the remaining Stock Acquisition Rights held by each holder of the Stock Acquisition Rights at the time of the effectuation of the organizational restructuring.

イ　新株予約権の目的である再編対象会社の株式の種類

再編対象会社の普通株式とする。

(b) Class of shares of the restructuring target company to be issued upon exercise of the stock acquisition rights:

Shares of common stock of the restructuring target company.

ウ　新株予約権の目的である再編対象会社の株式の数

組織再編行為の条件等を勘案の上，(1)に準じて決定する。

(c) Number of shares of the restructuring target company to be issued upon exercise of the stock acquisition rights:

The number shall be determined mutatis mutandis in accordance with the provisions of Sub-paragraph (1) above, after taking into account the conditions for the organizational restructuring and other factors.

エ　新株予約権の行使に際して出資される財産の価額

交付される各新株予約権の行使に際して出資される財産の価額は，組織再編行為の条件等を勘案の上，(2)①において定められた行使価額を調整して得られる再編後の行使価額に，上記ウに従って決定される当該新株予約権の目的である再編対象会社の株式の数を乗じた額とする。

(d) Value of assets to be contributed upon exercise of the stock acquisition rights:

The value of assets to be contributed upon exercise of each stock acquisition right shall be the amount calculated by multiplying (x) the Exercise Price to be applied after the organizational restructuring (which shall be determined with any necessary adjustment to be made to the Exercise Price determined at Sub-paragraph (2)(i) above after taking into account the conditions for the organizational restructuring and other factors) by (y) the number of shares of the restructuring target company to be issued upon exercise of the relevant stock acquisition rights in accordance with (c) above.

オ　新株予約権を行使することができる期間

(3)に定める新株予約権を行使することができる期間の開始日と組織再編行為の効力発生日のいずれか遅い日から，(3)に定める新株予約権を行使することができる期間の満了日までとする。

(e) Exercise period for the stock acquisition rights:

From the starting date of the exercise period set forth in Sub-paragraph (3) above or the effective date of the organizational restructuring, whichever is later, to the ending date of the exercise period described in Sub-paragraph (3) above.

カ　新株予約権の行使により株式を発行する場合における増加する資本金及び資本準備金に関する事項

(4)に準じて決定する。

(f) Matters pertaining to the increase of the amounts of paid-in capital and capital reserve in the case of the issuance of shares upon exercise of the stock acquisition rights:

To be determined mutatis mutandis in accordance with Sub-paragraph (4) above.

キ　譲渡による新株予約権の取得の制限

譲渡による新株予約権の取得については，再編対象会社の承認を要するものとする。

(g) Restrictions on acquisition of the stock acquisition rights by means of transfer:

Any transfer of the stock acquisition rights shall be subject to the approval of the restructuring target company.

ク　再編対象会社による新株予約権の取得

(6)に準じて決定する。

(h) Acquisition of the stock acquisition rights by the restructuring target company:

To be determined mutatis mutandis in accordance with Sub-paragraph (6) above.

ケ　その他新株予約権の行使の条件

(9)に準じて決定する。

(i) Other Conditions for the exercise of the Stock Acquisition Rights:

To be determined mutatis mutandis in accordance with Sub-paragraph (9) below.

(8) 本新株予約権を行使した新株予約権者に交付する株式の数に１株に満たない端数がある場合には，これを切り捨てるものとする。

(8) If any fractional shares less than one (1) share is obtained as a result of the calculation to determine the number of shares to be issued to any holder of the Stock Acquisition Rights having been exercised, such fractional shares shall be discarded.

(9)　本新株予約権の行使の条件

(9)　Conditions for the exercise of the Stock Acquisition Rights:

①　本新株予約権の割当を受けた者が当会社又は当会社関係会社（[illegible], Inc.を含む。）の取締役，監査役又は労働者である場合には，権利行使時においても，当会社又は当会社関係会社の取締役，監査役又は労働者の地位にあることを要する。但し，退任，辞職，解任，免職（懲戒免職又はそれに相当する場合を除く。），死亡又は行為無能力その他当会社取締役会が別途認めた理由がある場合は，前文の適用は無く引き続き新株予約権を行使することができる。

(i)　If any person to whom the Stock Acquisition Rights are allocated is a director, statutory auditor or worker of the Company or any of its affiliates (including [illegible], Inc.), such person must be a director, statutory auditor or worker of the Company or any of its affiliate at the time of his/her exercise of the Stock Acquisition Rights; provided, however, where such person is disqualified as a director, statutory auditor or worker due to his or her retirement or resignation, removal or dismissal (other than punitive dismissal or an equivalent thereto), death or disability, or any other due cause separately provided by the board of directors of the Company, the foregoing shall not apply and such person shall continue to be permitted to exercise all or any of the Stock Acquisition Rights.

②　新株予約権者に法令，定款もしくは社内規則に違反する行為があった場合又は新株予約権者が当会社と競業関係にある相手先の取締役，執行役員，監査役，労働者，嘱託，顧問，社外協力者又はコンサルタントとなった場合若しくは理由の如何を問わず当会社と新株予約権者の雇用その他の契約が終了してから６カ月の間に当会社と競業関係にある相手先の取締役，執行役員，監査役，労働者，嘱託，顧問，社外協力者又はコンサルタントとなった場合等，新株予約権の発行の目的上，新株予約権者に本新株予約権を行使させることが相当でないと当会社取締役会が認めた事由が生じた場合は，本新株予約権は行使することができない。

(ii)　If it is deemed by the board of directors of the Company inappropriate to permit any holder's exercise of the Stock Acquisition Rights for any reason (e.g., in the case where such holder has conducted any action in violation of any of the applicable laws and regulations or of the articles of incorporation or internal rules of the Company, or where such holder has assumed the office as director, executive officer, statutory auditor, worker, non-regular staff, advisor, outside collaborator or consultant of any competitor of the Company or during the six (6) month period following such holder's termination of employment or other service with the Company for any reason) in light of the purpose of the issuance of the stock acquisition rights, such holder may not exercise any Stock Acquisition Right.

③　本新株予約権の割当を受けた者は，当会社が株式公開をする日又は当会社関係会社以外の第三者が当会社のＡ種優先優先株式の議決権の３分の２以上を取得する日のいずれか早く到来する日（以下，総称して「支配権異動日」という。）まで新株予約権を行使することができない。

(iii)　Any person to whom the Stock Acquisition Rights are allocated shall not be permitted to exercise any Stock Acquisition Right until the date of the IPO of the Company or the acquisition of at least two third (2/3) voting rights of Series A Preferred Stock of the Company by a third party not affiliated with the Company, whichever comes earlier (collectively, the "Liquidity Event").

④　本新株予約権の割当を受けた者は，本新株予約権の割当日から行使期間の満了までにおいて次に掲げる各事由（以下「権利消滅事由」という。）が生じた場合には，権利消滅事由が生じた時点で行使されていない本新株予約権のすべてを行使することができないものとする。

(iv)　Any person to whom the Stock Acquisition Rights are allocated shall no longer be able to exercise any of his/her Stock Acquisition Rights that have not been exercised if any of the following events (the "Knockout Events") occur before the expiration of the exercise period for the Stock Acquisition Rights:

(a) (2)①において定められた行使価額に90%を乗じた価格（1円未満切り上げ）を下回る価格を対価とする当会社普通株式の発行等が行われた場合（払込金額が会社法第199条第3項，同第200条第2項に定める「特に有利な金額である場合」，株主割当てによる場合その他普通株式の株式価値とは異なると認められる価格で行われる場合を除く。）

(a) If the shares of common stock of the Company are issued at the per-share-price which is below 90% of the Exercise Price as determined in Sub-paragraph (2)(i) above (any fraction less than JPY 1 shall be rounded up to the nearest yen) except for the cases where such share price does not represent the value of the shares of common stock including those issued on specially favorable terms pursuant to Article 199, Paragraph 3 and Article 200, Paragraph 2 of the Companies Act of Japan or the shares were issued by way of shareholders allotment;

(b) 本新株予約権の目的である当会社普通株式が日本国内のいずれの登録証券取引所にも上場されていない場合，(2)①において定められた行使価額に90%を乗じた価格（1円未満切り上げ）を下回る価格を対価とする売買その他の取引が行われたとき（但し，資本政策目的等により当該取引時点における株式価値よりも著しく低いと認められる価格で取引が行われた場合を除く。）

(b) If the shares of common stock of the Company are not listed on any national securities exchange, in the case where the shares of the Company are privately traded at the per-share-price which is below 90% of the Exercise Price as determined in Sub-paragraph (2)(i) above (any fraction less than JPY 1 shall be rounded up to the nearest yen) except if such trade was conducted for a special purpose (e.g., capital policy purpose) at a price which is significantly lower than the then-current value of the shares;

(c) 本新株予約権の目的である当会社普通株式が日本国内のいずれかの登録証券取引所に上場された場合，当該証券取引所における当会社普通株式の普通取引の終値が，(2)①において定められた行使価額に90%を乗じた価格（1円未満切り上げ）を下回る価格となったとき

(c) If the shares of common stock are listed on any national securities exchange, in the case where the closing market price of the shares of common stock is below 90% of the Exercise Price as determined in Sub-paragraph (2) (i) above on any trading day (any fraction less than JPY 1 shall be rounded up to the nearest yen); or

(d) 本新株予約権の目的である当会社普通株式が日本国内のいずれの登録証券取引所にも上場されていない場合，当会社と利害関係のない第三者評価機関等により評価された株式評価額が(2)①において定められた行使価額に90%を乗じた価格（1円未満切り上げ）を下回ったとき（但し，株式評価額が一定の幅をもって示された場合，当会社の取締役会が当該評価機関と協議の上本項への該当を判断するものとする。）

(d) If the shares of common stock are not listed on any national securities exchange, in the case where any unrelated third party valuation specialist provides its valuation of the shares of the Company, which indicates that the per-share value of the common stock of the Company is less than 90% of the Exercise Price as determined in Sub-paragraph (2)(i) above (any fraction less than JPY 1 shall be rounded up to the nearest yen); provided that if such valuation shows the certain range of the share prices, the board of directors of the Company determines whether this item (d) has occurred upon discussion with such valuation specialist.

⑤ 当会社又は当会社関係会社と新株予約権者の雇用が新株予約権者の死亡により終了した場合，当該故人が保有する本新株予約権は，故人の遺産の法律上の代表者又は故人の遺言により遺産受取人に指定された者が行使期間満了に至るまでの間(1)割当日以降当会社取締役会が定める期間（新株予約権者が米国カリフォルニア在住の場合は，同人の雇用終了後6カ月間とする），(2)当会社取締役会が期間を定めない場合は，死亡日から12

カ月間，又は(3)(1)又は(2)のいずれか早く到来する期間，行使可能な本新株予約権又は当会社取締役会が決定する内容に従って行使することができる。

(v) If a holder's service with the Company or any of its affiliates terminates by reason of death, any Stock Acquisition Right held by such person may thereafter be exercised, to the extent then exercisable or on such accelerated basis as the board of directors may determine, at or after grant, by the legal representative of the estate or by the legatee of the holder under the will of the holder, for a period expiring (1) at such time as may be specified by the board of directors at or after the time of grant (which, in the event that the holder resides in the State of California, shall be no less than 6 months from the date of termination), (2) if not specified by the board of directors, then twelve (12) months from the date of death, or (3) if sooner than the applicable period specified under (1) or (2) above, then upon the expiration of the stated term of such Option.

⑥ 新株予約権者は，本新株予約権の全部又は一部を行使することができるが，各新株予約権の一部行使はできない。

(vi) The exercise of all or any of the Stock Acquisition Rights by the holders thereof is permitted, but partial exercise of each Stock Acquisition Right is not permitted.

⑦ 新株予約権者は，当会社との間で締結する新株予約権割当契約に違反した場合，本新株予約権を行使することができない。

(vii) The holders of the Stock Acquisition Rights will not be able to exercise the Stock Acquisition Rights, in case of a breach of the Stock Option Allotment (Grant) Agreement to be entered into by and between the Company and the holders of the Stock Acquisition Rights.

⑧ 本新株予約権の行使によって，当会社の発行済株式総数が当該時点における授権株式数を超過することとなるときは，当該本新株予約権の行使を行うことはできない。

(viii) If the issued and outstanding shares of the Company exceed the number of authorized shares of the Company at the time when the Stock Acquisition Rights are to be exercised, such Stock Acquisition Rights may not be exercised.

⑨ その他の条件は，取締役会の決議に基づき，当会社及び新株予約権者との間で締結する新株予約権割当契約に定めるところによる。

(ix) Other terms and conditions shall be as set forth in the Stock Option Allotment (Grant) Agreement to be entered into by and between the Company and the holders of the Stock Acquisition Rights, pursuant to a resolution adopted by the board of directors.

(10) その他の新株予約権の内容

(10) Other matters concerning Stock Acquisition Rights:

その他の新株予約権の募集事項については，別途開催される取締役会の決議において定める。

Other matters on the granting of Stock Acquisition Rights shall be prescribed by the resolution of a meeting of the board of directors to be held separately.

なお，非公開会社で取締役会設置会社であれば取締役会で決議する事項は，この募集事項全文及び割当日の設定を付加するだけであるため，取締役会議事録は割愛する。非公開会社で非取締役会設置会社では株主総会の決議によることになる。

〈例60 募集新株予約権総数引受契約〉

募集新株予約権総数引受契約
ALL STOCK ACQUISITION RIGHTS UNDERWRITING AGREEMENT

■（以下「引受人」という。）は，■株式会社（以下「発行会社」という。）が，■年３月30日付定時株主総会決議及び同日付普通株主による種類株主総会決議並びに■年３月30日付取締役会決議に基づき募集する新株予約権を，以下のとおり引き受ける。

■ (the "Subscriber") shall subscribe for the stock acquisition rights as set forth below, which will be issued by ■ KK (the "Company") based on the resolutions of the Ordinary General Meeting of Shareholders on March 30, ■, the Classified General Meeting of Common Shareholders on March 30, ■ and the Board of Directors resolution on March 30, ■.

発行会社は，募集新株予約権を下記の要領にて発行し，引受人は，当該募集新株予約権のうち下記(4)記載の個数を引き受ける。なお，別途，別紙１記載の者（引受人を除く。）が当該募集新株予約権のうち合計■個を引き受けることが予定されており，かかる者による引受けと，引受人による引受けにより，下記の募集新株予約権の総数が引き受けられる。

The Company shall issue the stock acquisition rights for subscription in accordance with the following particulars, and the Subscriber shall subscribe for the number of such stock acquisition rights for subscription as set forth in (4) below. Separately, the persons listed on Annex 1 attached hereto (except for the Subscriber) collectively subscribe for ■ stock acquisition rights of such stock acquisition rights for subscription. Accordingly, such stock acquisition rights to be subscribed for such persons and the Subscriber constitute the total number of the stock acquisition rights for subscription as set forth below.

(1)募集新株予約権の名称及び数: Name and Number of Stock Acquisition Rights:	■株式会社第２回ストックオプション　170,500個 ■ KK Series 2 Stock Acquisition Rights ; 170,500
(2)払込金額: Payment Amount:	引受人は，募集新株予約権１個あたり12円の払込みを要するものとする。 Subscriber will be required to pay JPY12 per stock acquisition right.
(3)割当日: Allotment Date:	[■年４月１日] [April 1, ■]

(4)割当 Allocation:	引受人に募集新株予約権■個を割り当てる。 ■ stock acquisition rights shall be allotted to the Subscriber.

その他募集新株予約権の募集事項については，別紙２「募集新株予約権の募集事項（発行要項)」に記載のとおりとする。
Other terms and conditions of the stock acquisition rights are set forth in "Details of Stock Options to be issued" which is attached as Annex 2 hereto.

本契約締結の証として，以下の日付で引受人及び発行会社のそれぞれが署名または記名押印する。
IN WITNESS WHEREOF, the Subscriber and the Company have executed this Agreement as of the date set forth below.

■年３月30日
March 30, ■

発行会社：
Company:
東京都■区■丁目■番■号

■ビル
■ Japan株式会社
代表取締役　■
■ Building,
■-■, ■ ■-chome, ■-ku, Tokyo
■ Japan, KK
■, Representative Director

引受人：
Subscriber:

［住所］
［Address］

［名前］
［Name］

別紙１
Annex 1

引受人一覧
List of Subscribers

5　減資手続

減資とは，法の手続に従い資本金の額を減少させることである（会社447条）。資本金の額は，貸借対照表の１項目で会社が配当等で株主に分配できる金額（配当可能額）を計算するための計数であり，株主から拠出された金額の総額ではない。資本金の額を減少させることは，配当可能額の増加につながり，そのことは債権者の関心事であり，また，株主にも重大な影響を与えるものである。減資については会社法で資本の減少等（会社447条～449条）を定めている。資本減少には，資本の流出を伴う減資と，資本の流失を伴わない減資とがある。

⑴　資本流失を伴う減資

資本の流失を伴う減資には，分配可能額を増加させる資本間の額の減少をいう。手続的には，株主総会特別決議，債権者異議申立手続，登記手続というフローになる。定時又は臨時株主総会において特別決議（会社309条２項９号）が必要で，その決議事項は，減少する資本金等の額，減少する資本金の額の全部又は一部を準備金とするときは，その旨及び準備金とする額，資本金の額の減少が効力を生じる日の３点である。

⑵　資本の流失を伴わない減資

資本の流失を伴わない減資とは，貸借対照表の純資産から総債務を差引いた純資産の額に変動を来さないもので，純資産内での科目振替である。言い換えれば欠損の補填である。そのため定時株主総会での普通決議になる（会社309条２項９号イ・ロ）。ただし，臨時株主総会では特別決議となる（会社309条２項９号）。

〈例61　臨時株主総会議事録〉

株式会社　臨時株主総会議事録
Minutes of Extraordinary General Shareholders' Meeting of
K.K.

議案　資本金の額の減少に関する件
議長は，資本金８千万円のうち金７千万円を減少して金１千万円としたい旨を述べ，その理由を詳細に説明した。議長が以下の事項につき承認を求めたところ，満場異議なくこれを承認可決した。

1．減少する資本金の額　金７千万円
2．資本金の額の減少の効力発生日　■■■■年12月28日

Item Reductions in Amount of Stated Capital
The Chairman stated that the amount of the stated capital should be reduced as following, and explained that reasons in detail and then caused those present to take a vote of pros and cons with respect to this matter. The proposal was unanimously approved as in the original.

1. The amount by which the stated capital is reduced; JPY 70,000,000
2. The day on which the reduction in the amount of stated capital takes effect; December 28, ■■■■

6　事業譲渡

会社ごと売買するのではなく会社の事業に関連する資産・負債のみを売買する方法で，店舗や工事用といった土地建物などの有形固定資産や売掛金，在庫等の流動資産，営業権（のれん），人材，ノウハウといった無形資産も譲渡対象になる。会社法は第７章・事業の譲渡等として467条から470条に規定している。

事業譲渡に該当する契約については，効力発生日前日までに，株主総会の決議によって承認を受けなければならない（会社467条）。

承認を受ける事業譲渡は下記の通りである。

①　事業の全部の譲渡

②　事業の重要な一部の譲渡（ただし，譲渡資産の帳簿価額が会社の総資産額の５分の１を超えるもの，総資産額については，法務省令で定める方法により算定される額，５分の１については，これを下回る割合を定款で定めた場合にあっては，その割合）

③　子会社の株式又は持分の全部又は一部の譲渡

ただし，子会社の株式又は持分の全部又は一部の帳簿価額が会社の総資産額の５分の１を超えるもので，且つ，会社が，効力発生日にお

いてその子会社の議決権総数の過半数の議決権を有しないとき（総資産額及び５分の１の定義については②に同じ）

④　他の会社の事業の全部の譲受け（ただし，資産の中に譲受会社の株式が含まれているときは，取締役は株主総会に当該株式に関する事項を説明しなければならない。）

⑤　事業の全部の賃貸，事業の全部の経営の委任，他人と事業上の損益の全部を共通にする契約その他これらに準ずる契約の締結，変更又は解約

⑥　会社の成立後２年以内におけるその成立前から存在する財産であってその事業のために継続して使用するものの取得（総資産額及び５分の１の定義については②に同じ）

7　組織再編

組織再編とは，会社の組織を改めて経営資源の有効活用や，事業の強化を図る行為で，会社合併，会社分割，株式交換，株式移転等が会社法上４種類を用意している。また，組織変更は，組織再編の一環ではあるが，法人格の変更はなく，株式会社より持株会社又は持株会社より株式会社へ組織変更をなすことにより，持株会社にすることにより会社組織の意思決定の迅速化を図り，又は株式会社にすることにより資金調達を容易にする意図の下に組織変更がなされていることが実務的には多い。

⑴　合　併

合併には，吸収合併と新設合併が用意されている。

ア　吸収合併

吸収合併とは，会社が他の会社とする合併であって，合併により消滅する会社の権利義務の全部を合併後存続する会社に承継させるものをいう（会社２条27号）。吸収合併は，全ての種類の会社との間ですることができ，存続会社が持分会社とすることもできる（会社748条）。ただし，特例有限会社を存続会社とする吸収合併はできない（会社法の施行に伴う関係法律の整備等に関する法律37条）。

(ア)　手　続

①　合併契約の締結（会社749条）

②　合併契約書に関する書面等の備置き・閲覧等（会社782条・794条）

③　合併契約の承認（会社783条・795条）

④　株券・新株予約権証券の提出に係る公告・通知（会社219条1項6号・293条1項3号）

⑤　株式買取請求の通知又は公告（会社785条・797条）

⑥　新株予約権買取請求の通知又は公告（787条）

⑦　債権者保護手続（会社789条・799条）

⑧　合併の効力発生（会社750条1項）

⑨　合併の登記（会社921条・750条）

(イ)　株主総会の決議を要しない場合

①　略式合併

消滅会社が存続会社の特別支配会社（議決権の10分の9以上保有されている。）である場合には，存続会社においては，株主総会の決議によって合併契約の承認を受けることを要しない（会社796条1項本文）。ただし，存続会社の合併対価が譲渡制限株式であり，非公開会社であるときは，株主総会の決議を省略できない（会社796条1項ただし書）。

②　簡易合併

簡易合併の条件としては，

i　消滅会社株主に対して交付する株式の数に1株あたり総資産額を乗じた額

ii　消滅会社株主に交付する社債，新株予約権又は新株予約権付社債その他の財産の帳簿価額の合計

iii　消滅会社株主に交付する株式等以外の財産の帳簿価額の合計額

以上の合計額が純資産として法務省例で定める方法で算定した額の5分の1（20パーセント）を超えない場合には，存続会社にお

いて株主総会の決議によって合併契約の承認を不要とする。

但し，下記の場合には，株主総会の承認を必要とする（会社796条２項）。

ⅰ　消滅会社の債務額が資産額を超える場合（存続会社に合併差損が生じる場合）

ⅱ　消滅会社株主に交付する金銭等（株式等を除く。）の帳簿価額が，承継負債から承継資産を控除後の額を超える場合（存続会社に合併差損が生じる場合）

ⅲ　消滅会社株主に交付する金銭等の全部又は一部が譲渡制限株式であり，存続会社が非公開会社であるとき

ⅳ　会社法施行規則197条で定める数の株式を有する反対株主のから通知を受けたとき

イ　新設合併

新設合併とは，二つ以上の会社がする合併であり，合併により消滅する会社の権利義務の全部を合併により新設する会社に承継させるものをいう（会社２条28号）。新設合併は当事会社の全部が解散し，新設会社が設立されるもので，全ての種類の会社の間においてでき，新設会社の種類についても消滅会社の種類を問わず，また，全ての種類の会社を新設会社とすることができる（会社748条）。

◎　**手続**

①　合併契約の締結（会社753条）

②　合併契約書に関する書面等の備置き・閲覧等（会社803条）

③　合併契約の承認（会社804条）

④　株券・新株予約権証券の提出に係る公告・通知（会社219条１項６号・293条１項３号）

⑤　株式買取請求手続（会社806条）

⑥　新株予約権買取請求手続（会社808条）

⑦　債権者保護手続（会社810条）

⑧　新設合併の登記（会社922条）

例62は，存続会社は非公開会社であり，株式譲渡制限を設けている会社で，消滅会社を完全子会社化のうえ吸収合併した一連の手続の書式である。

〈例62　株式譲渡承認請求書（存続会社が消滅会社の特定支配会社になるための株式譲渡承認手続）〉

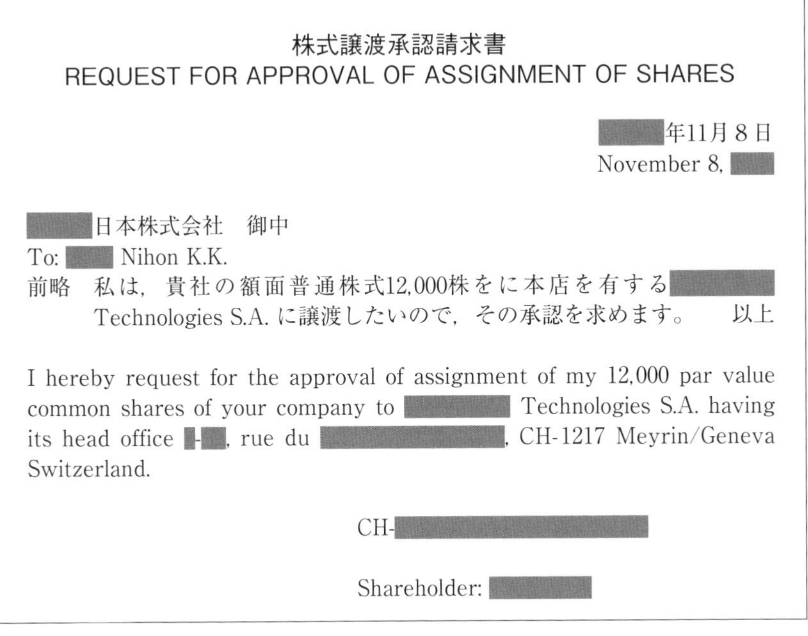

株式譲渡承認請求書
REQUEST FOR APPROVAL OF ASSIGNMENT OF SHARES

年11月８日
November 8,

日本株式会社　御中
To: Nihon K.K.
前略　私は，貴社の額面普通株式12,000株をに本店を有する Technologies S.A. に譲渡したいので，その承認を求めます。　以上

I hereby request for the approval of assignment of my 12,000 par value common shares of your company to Technologies S.A. having its head office -, rue du , CH-1217 Meyrin/Geneva Switzerland.

CH-

Shareholder:

〈例63　消滅会社の取締役会議事録（株式譲渡承認並びに合併承認のための株主総会招集の決議）〉

日本株式会社
取締役会議事録

Nihon K.K.
MINUTES OF MEETING OF BOARD OF DIRECTORS

年11月８日午前10時00分，横浜市区丁目番号所在の当会社本店において取締役会を開催した。

A meeting of the Board of Directors of the Company was held on November 8, ███ at 10:00 a.m. at the head office of the Company, located at █-█ ██████ █-chome, █████-ku, Yokohama.

取締役総数	5名
Total Number of Directors:	5
監査役総数	1
Total Number of Statutory Auditor:	1
出席取締役数	名
Directors Present:	
出席監査役数	名
Statutory Auditor Present:	

上記の出席があったので，取締役社長█████は，議長席につき開会を宣し，議事を進行した。
Whereupon, the above persons being present, the Director and President of the Company, ██████████, assumed the chair, declared the meeting in session and proceeded to the business at hand.

第１号議案：合併契約承認の件
First Proposal: Approval of Merger Agreement
議長は，株式会社██████・ジャパンと，████年11月15日開催予定の臨時株主総会の決定を得て，平成12年１月１日付で合併する旨を説明し，別紙合併契約書のとおり合併契約を締結したい旨提案したところ，出席取締役全員一致で承認可決された。
The Chairperson explained that the Company, upon approval of the shareholders at the Extraordinary General Meeting to be held in November 15,1999, will merge K.K. ██████ Japan on January 1, ███, and proposed to execute the Merger Agreement attached hereto. Upon motion duly made and seconded, the proposal was unanimously approved by the Directors present.

第２号議案　臨時株主総会召集に関する件
Second Proposal: Convocation of the Extraordinary General Meeting of the Shareholders

議長は，合併契約書承認の件を審議するために，当会社の臨時株主総会を█ ███年11月15日午前11時より当会社本店において開催したい旨諮ったところ，下記の要領で出席取締役の全員一致で承認可決された。
The Chairperson proposed that an Extraordinary General Meeting of Shareholders be held on November 15, ███ at 11:00 a.m. at the head office of the Company to consider the approval of the Merger Agreement.

Upon motion duly made and seconded, the convocation was approved unanimously without opposition in accordance with the following details.

臨時株主総会
The Extraordinary General Meeting of Shareholders:

日　　時　　　　　■■年11月15日午前11時00分
Date and Time: November 15,■■ at 11:00 a.m.
場　　所　　　　　■■日本株式会社
横浜市■■区■■丁目■番■号
Place:　　　　　　The head Office of the Company
■-■ ■■ 1-chome, ■■-Ku, Yokohama

会議の目的たる事項
Agenda:
第１号議案　　合併承認の件
First Proposal: Approval of Merger Agreement
なお，合併契約書は添付のとおり
Merger Agreement is attached to this minutes.

第３号議案　株式譲渡の承認について
Proposal: Approval of Assignment of Shares

議長は，株主■■ S.A.より次のとおり株式譲渡の承認請求が出されている旨を説明し，その賛否を諮ったところ全員異議なくこれを承認した。

The Chairman reported that a request had been received from shareholder ■■ S.A. for approval of assignment of shares as summarized below. Whereupon a motion was put and approved unanimously without opposition.

１）譲渡人　Assignor:
■■, Switzerland
■■ S.A.

２）譲受人　Assignee:
■■, rue du ■■
CH-1217 Meyrin/Geneva Switzerland
■■ Technologies S.A.

３）株数　　額面普通株式 12,000株
Number of Shares: 12,000 par value common shares

以上を持って議事を終了し，議長は午前10時30分閉会を宣した。
Whereupon, the proceedings having been concluded, the Chairperson closed the meeting at 10:30 a.m.

上記議事を明確にするためこの議事録を作成し，議長並びに出席取締役は署名または記名捺印する。
These Minutes are prepared as evidence of the above proceedings and bear the signatures or names and seals of the Chairperson and all Directors present.

███年11月８日
November 8, ███

███日本株式会社
███ Nihon K.K.

代表取締役 ███
Representative Director: ███ ____________

代表取締役 ███
Representative Director: ███ ____________

取締役 ███
Director: ███ ____________

取締役 ███
Director: ███ ____________

取締役 ███
Director: ███ ____________

監査役 ███
Statutory Auditor: ███ ____________

〈例64　譲渡承認通知書（取締役会後の株式譲受人に対する承認通知）〉

譲渡承認通知書
NOTICE OF APPROVAL OF ASSIGNMENT OF SHARES

To: ███ S.A.

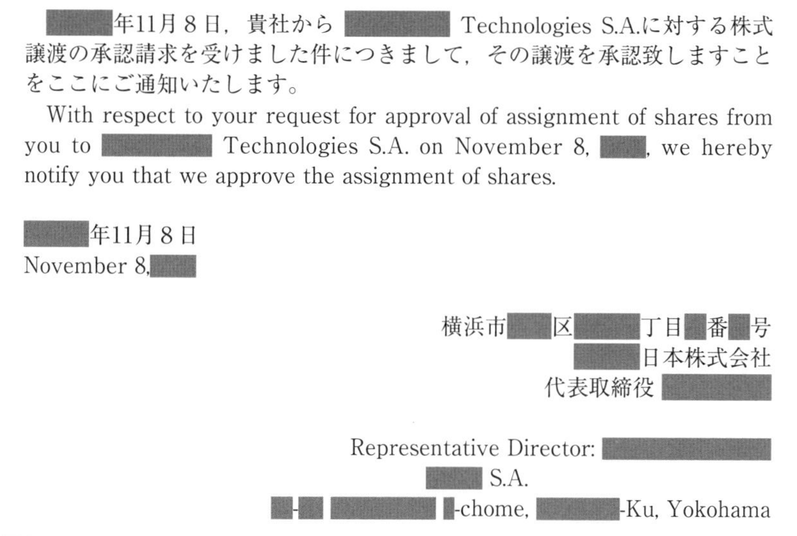

年11月８日，貴社から　Technologies S.A.に対する株式譲渡の承認請求を受けました件につきまして，その譲渡を承認致しますことをここにご通知いたします。

With respect to your request for approval of assignment of shares from you to Technologies S.A. on November 8, , we hereby notify you that we approve the assignment of shares.

年11月８日
November 8,

横浜市　区　丁目　番　号
日本株式会社
代表取締役

Representative Director:
S.A.
- -chome, -Ku, Yokohama

〈例65　存続会社の取締役会議事録（合併承認のための株主総会招集の決議）〉

株式会社　・ジャパン
取締役会議事録

K.K. Japan
MINUTES OF MEETING OF BOARD OF DIRECTORS

年11月８日午前10時00分，横浜市　区　丁目　番　号所在の当会社本店において取締役会を開催した。
A meeting of the Board of Directors of the Company was held on November 8, at 10:00 a.m. at the head office of the Company, located at - -chome, -ku, Yokohama.

取締役総数	４名
Total Number of Directors:	4
監査役総数	1
Total Number of Statutory Auditor:	1
出席取締役数	名
Directors Present:	
出席監査役数	名
Statutory Auditor Present:	

上記の出席があったので，取締役社長■■■は，議長席につき開会を宣し，議事を進行した。
Whereupon, the above persons being present, the Director and President of the Company, ■■■, assumed the chair, declared the meeting in session and proceeded to the business at hand.

第１号議案：合併契約承認の件
First Proposal: Approval of Merger Agreement

議長は，■■■日本株式会社と，■■■年11月15日開催予定の臨時株主総会の決定を得て，■■■年１月１日付で合併する旨を説明し，別紙合併契約書のとおり合併契約を締結したい旨提案したところ，出席取締役全員一致で承認可決された。
The Chairperson explained that the Company, upon approval of the shareholders at the Extraordinary General Meeting to be held in November 15, ■■■, will merge ■■■ Nihon K.K. on January 1, ■■■, and proposed to execute the Merger Agreement attached hereto. Upon motion duly made and seconded, the proposal was unanimously approved by the Directors present.

第２号議案　臨時株主総会召集に関する件
Second Proposal: Convocation of the Extraordinary General Meeting of the Shareholders

議長は，合併契約書承認の件を審議するために，当会社の臨時株主総会を■■■年11月15日午前11時より当会社本店において開催したい旨諮ったところ，下記の要領で出席取締役の全員一致で承認可決された。
The Chairperson proposed that an Extraordinary General Meeting of Shareholders be held on November 15, ■■■ at 11:00 a.m. at the head office of the Company to consider the approval of the Merger Agreement. Upon motion duly made and seconded, the convocation was approved unanimously without opposition in accordance with the following details.

臨時株主総会
The Extraordinary General Meeting of Shareholders:

日　　時	■■■年11月15日午前11時00分
Date and Time:	November 15,■■■ at 11:00 a.m.
場　　所	株式会社■■■・ジャパン
	横浜市■■■区■■■丁目■番■号
Place:	The head Office of the Company
	■-■ ■■■ ■-chome, ■■■-ku,

Yokohama

会議の目的たる事項
Agenda:
第１号議案　合併承認の件
First Proposal: Approval of Merger Agreement
なお，合併契約書は添付のとおり
Merger Agreement is attached to this minutes.

以上を持って議事を終了し，議長は午前10時30分閉会を宣した。
Whereupon, the proceedings having been concluded, the Chairperson closed the meeting at 10:30 a.m.

上記議事を明確にするためこの議事録を作成し，議長並びに出席取締役は署名または記名捺印する。
These Minutes are prepared as evidence of the above proceedings and bear the signatures or names and seals of the Chairperson and all Directors present.

■■■■年11月８日
November 8, ■■■■

株式会社■■■■・ジャパン

代表取締役 ■■■■
Representative Director: ■■■■ ________________

代表取締役 ■■■■
Representative Director: ■■■■ ________________

取締役 ■■■■
Director: ■■■■ ________________

取締役 ■■■■
Director: ■■■■ ________________

監査役 ■■■■
Statutory Auditor: ■■■■ ________________

〈例66　存続会社の臨時株主総会議事録（合併契約の承認の決議）〉

株式会社████・ジャパン
臨時株主総会議事録

K.K. ████ Japan
MINUTES OF EXTRAORDINARY GENERAL MEETING OF SHAREHOLDERS

███年11月15日午前11時，横浜市██区███丁目█番█号所在の株式会社████・ジャパン（以下「当会社」という）本店において臨時株主総会を開催した。
The Extraordinary General Meeting of Shareholders of K.K. ████ Japan (the "Company") was held on November 15,███ at 11:00 a.m. at the head office of the Company, located at █-█ █████ █-chome, ███-ku, Yokohama.

株主総数	1名
Total Number of Shareholders:	1
発行済株式総数	8,800株
Total Number of Shares Issued:	8,800 shares
出席株主数	1名
Number of Shareholders Represented in Person or by Proxy:	1
この議決権のある持株総数	8,800株
Total number of shares having voting right held by the above:	8,800 shares

上記の出席があったので，当会社の定款第条の定めに従い，取締役社長███が議長席につき開会を宣し，議事を進行した。
Whereupon, the above persons being present, the Director and President of the Company, █████, assumed the chair in accordance with Article of the Articles of Incorporation of the Company, declared the meeting in session and proceeded to the business at hand.

第1号議案：合併契約書承認の件
First Proposal: Approval of Merger Agreement

議長は，当会社と███日本株式会社の間でかねて交渉が進められてきた合併について，別紙契約書の記載のとおり両社代表者間において合併契約が成立した旨を報告し，合併の目的等を説明の後，合併契約書承認を求めたところ，満場異議なく承認可決した。
The Chairperson reported that regarding the merger which had been negotiated between the Company and ■■■ Nihon K.K. the Merger Agreement has been executed between the representatives of both companies. The Chairperson then sought for the approval of shareholders of the merger agreement after explaining the purpose of the merger. Upon motion duly made and seconded, the proposal was unanimously approved without opposition.

以上を持って議事を終了し，議長は午前11時40分閉会を宣した。
Whereupon, the proceedings having been concluded, the Chairperson closed the meeting at 11:40 a.m.

上記議事を明確にするためこの議事録を作成し，議長並びに出席取締役は署名または記名捺印する。
These Minutes are prepared as evidence of the above proceedings and bear the signatures or names and seals of the Chairperson and all Directors present.

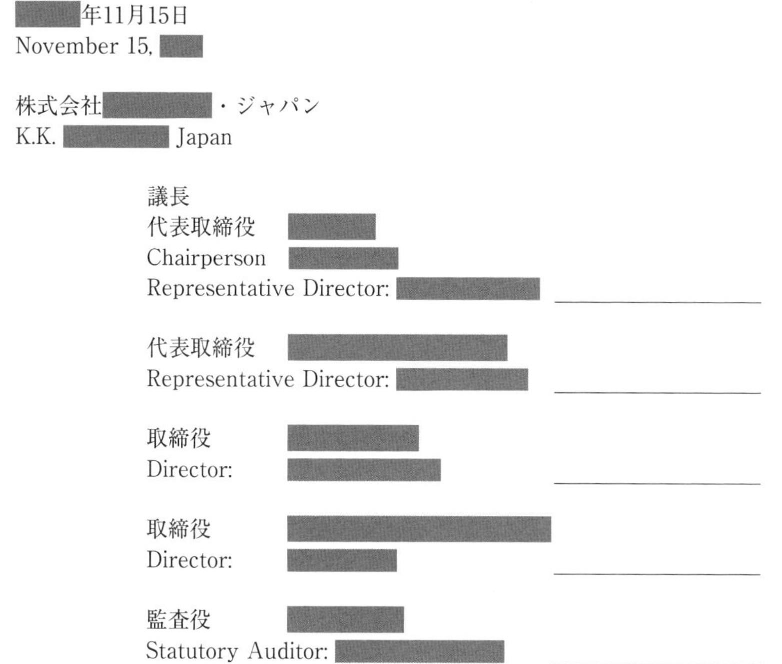

■■■年11月15日
November 15, ■■■

株式会社■■■・ジャパン
K.K. ■■■ Japan

議長
代表取締役 ■■■
Chairperson ■■■
Representative Director: ■■■ ________

代表取締役 ■■■
Representative Director: ■■■ ________

取締役 ■■■
Director: ■■■ ________

取締役 ■■■
Director: ■■■ ________

監査役 ■■■
Statutory Auditor: ■■■ ________

〈例67　消滅会社の臨時株主総会議事録（合併契約の承認の決議）〉

日本株式会社
臨時株主総会議事録

Nihon K.K.
MINUTES OF EXTRAORDINARY GENERAL MEETING OF SHAREHOLDERS

年11月15日午前11時，横浜市区丁目番号所在の日本株式会社（以下「当会社」という）本店において臨時株主総会を開催した。
The Extraordinary General Meeting of Shareholders of Nihon K.K. (the "Company") was held on November 15, at 11:00 a.m. at the head office of the Company, located at - -chome, -Ku, Yokohama.

株主総数	1名
Total Number of Shareholders:	1
発行済株式総数	12,000株
Total Number of Shares Issued:	12,000 shares
出席株主数	1名
Number of Shareholders Represented in Person or by Proxy:	1
この議決権のある持株総数	12,000株
Total number of shares having voting right held by the above:	12,000 shares

上記の出席があったので，当会社の定款第条の定めに従い，取締役社長雅昭が議長席につき開会を宣し，議事を進行した。
Whereupon, the above persons being present, the Director and President of the Company, , assumed the chair in accordance with Article of the Articles of Incorporation of the Company, declared the meeting in session and proceeded to the business at hand.

第1号議案：合併契約書承認の件
First Proposal: Approval of Merger Agreement

議長は，当会社と株式会社・ジャパンの間でかねて交渉が進められてきた合併について，別紙契約書の記載のとおり両社代表者間において合併契約が成立した旨を報告し，合併の目的等を説明の後，合併契約書承認を求めたところ，満場異議なく承認可決した。
The Chairperson reported that regarding the merger which had been negotiated between the Company and K.K. ████ Japan the Merger Agreement has been executed between the representatives of both companies. The Chairperson then sought for the approval of shareholders of the merger agreement after explaining the purpose of the merger. Upon motion duly made and seconded, the proposal was unanimously approved without opposition.

以上を持って議事を終了し，議長は午前11時40分閉会を宣した。
Whereupon, the proceedings having been concluded, the Chairperson closed the meeting at 11:40 a.m.

上記議事を明確にするためこの議事録を作成し，議長並びに出席取締役は署名または記名捺印する。
These Minutes are prepared as evidence of the above proceedings and bear the signatures or names and seals of the Chairperson and all Directors present.

████年11月15日
November 15, ████

████日本株式会社
████ Nihon K.K.

代表取締役 ████
Representative Director: ████ ______________

代表取締役 ████
Representative Director: ████ ______________

取締役 ████
Director: ████ ______________

取締役 ████
Director: ████ ______________

取締役 ████
Director: ████ ______________

監査役 ████
Statutory Auditor: ████ ______________

〈例68－1　合併契約書〉

合併契約書

（甲）　株式会社[redacted]・ジャパン

（乙）　[redacted]日本株式会社

合併契約書

株式会社[redacted]・ジャパン（以下「甲」という。）と、[redacted]日本株式会社（以下「乙」という。）は、合併に関し次のとおり契約を締結する。

（合併の方式）
第 1 条　甲および乙は合併して、甲は存続し、乙は解散する。

（合併による定款の変更）
第 2 条　甲は、合併により、その定款を次のとおり変更する。
1．定款第1条(商号)を、
「第1条(商号)
当会社は、株式会社[redacted]・ジャパンと称する。
英文では，[redacted] JAPAN LTD. と表示する。」
と改める。
2．定款第3条（本店の所在地）を
「第3条（本店の所在地）
当会社は、本店を横浜市[redacted]区に置く。」
と改める。
② 前各号については、合併期日より効力を生ずる。

（合併による新株式の割当と資本の額）
第 3 条 甲は、合併に際して普通額面株式（1株の額面金額 50,000円）1株を発行し、合併期日現在における乙の株主名簿に記載された株主に対して、その所有する乙の株式 （1株の額面金額 50,000円）7,660株につき、甲の株式（1株の額面金額 50,000円） 1株の割合をもって割当交付する。

（準備金に関する事項）
第 4 条　甲は、合併により、資本金を50,000円増加し、甲の資本金の額を440,050,000円とする。

② 甲は合併により生じる合併差益金のうち資本準備金からなる額を資本準備金、利益準備金からなる額を利益準備金とし、なお残額がある場合は任意積立金その他の留保利益とする。ただし、任意積立金その他の留保利益として積立てるべき項目は、甲および乙協議のうえ決定する。

(合併承認総会)

第5条 甲及び乙は、■■■■年11月15日にそれぞれ株主総会を招集し、本契約書の承認および合併に必要な事項に関する決議を求める。ただし、合併手続の進行に応じ必要あるときは、甲および乙協議のうえ、この期日を変更することができる。

(合併期日)

第6条 合併期日は、■■■■年1月1日とする。ただし、合併手続の進行に応じ必要あるときは、甲および乙協議のうえ、これを変更することができる。

(会社財産の引継ぎ)

第7条 乙は、■■■■年9月30日現在の貸借対照表その他同日現在の計算を基礎とし、その後合併期日までの間において、その資産または負債に変動を生じたものについては、別に計算書を添付してこれを明確にし、合併期日において、その資産、負債および権利義務一切を甲に引継ぎ、甲は、これを承継する。

(会社財産の善管注意義務)

第8条 甲および乙は、本契約締結後合併期日に至るまで、善良なる管理者の注意をもって、その資産および負債を管理し、かつ、それぞれの業務を執行するものとし、その資産および負債または権利義務に重大な影響を及ぼす行為を行うときは、あらかじめ甲および乙協議し、合意のうえこれを実行する。

（従業員の引継ぎ）

第 9 条　甲は、合併期日において、乙の従業員を甲の従業員として引き続き雇用し、従業員に関する取扱いについては、別に甲乙協議のうえこれを定める。

（合併前に就職した甲の監査役の任期）

第 10 条　甲の監査役であって、合併前に就職したものは、合併後最初の定時株主総会終結のときには退任しない。その任期は、甲の定款第17条の定めにしたがって取扱うものとする。

（合併に際して就任する取締役又は監査役）

第 11 条　合併に伴い新たに甲の取締役又は監査役となるべき者は、次のとおりとする。ただし就職すべき時期は合併の日とする。

取締役

監査役

（地位及び在職年数の合算）

第 12 条　乙の取締役又は監査役であって、合併に際して甲の取締役又は監査役に就職した者が、退職にあたって甲の株主総会の決議によって支払を受ける退職慰労金の額の算定にあたっては、乙における地位及び在職年数を、甲における地位及び在職年数に合算する。

（消滅会社の役員の退職慰労金）

第 13 条　乙の取締役又は監査役のうち、合併により甲の取締役又は監査役に就職しなかった者に対する退職慰労金は、第 5 条に定める乙の合併承認総会の承認を得て支給する。

（合併条件の変更および合併契約の解除）

第 14 条　本契約締結の日から合併期日までの間において、天災地変その他の事由により、甲および乙いずれかの財産もしくは経営状態に重大な変更を生じたときは、甲および乙協議のうえ、合併条件を変更し、または本契約を解除することができる。

（合併契約の効力）

第 15 条　本契約は第５条に定める甲及び乙の株主総会承認または法令に定める関係諸官庁の承認が得られないときは、その効力を失う。

（規定外事項）

第 16 条　本契約に定めるもののほか、合併の実現に関して必要な事項は、本契約の趣旨に従って、甲および乙協議のうえ、これを決定する。

本契約の成立を証するため、契約書２通を作成し、甲および乙記名押印のうえ、各１通を保有する。

年 11月10日

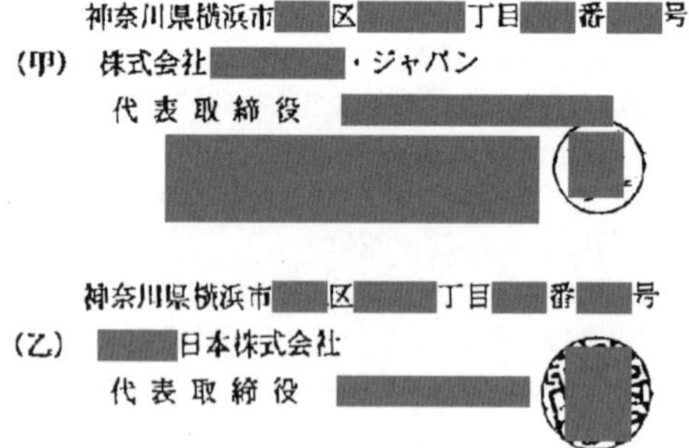

神奈川県横浜市　区　丁目　番　号

（甲）　株式会社　・ジャパン

代 表 取 締 役

神奈川県横浜市　区　丁目　番　号

（乙）　日本株式会社

代 表 取 締 役

〈例68－２　合併契約書（英文）〉

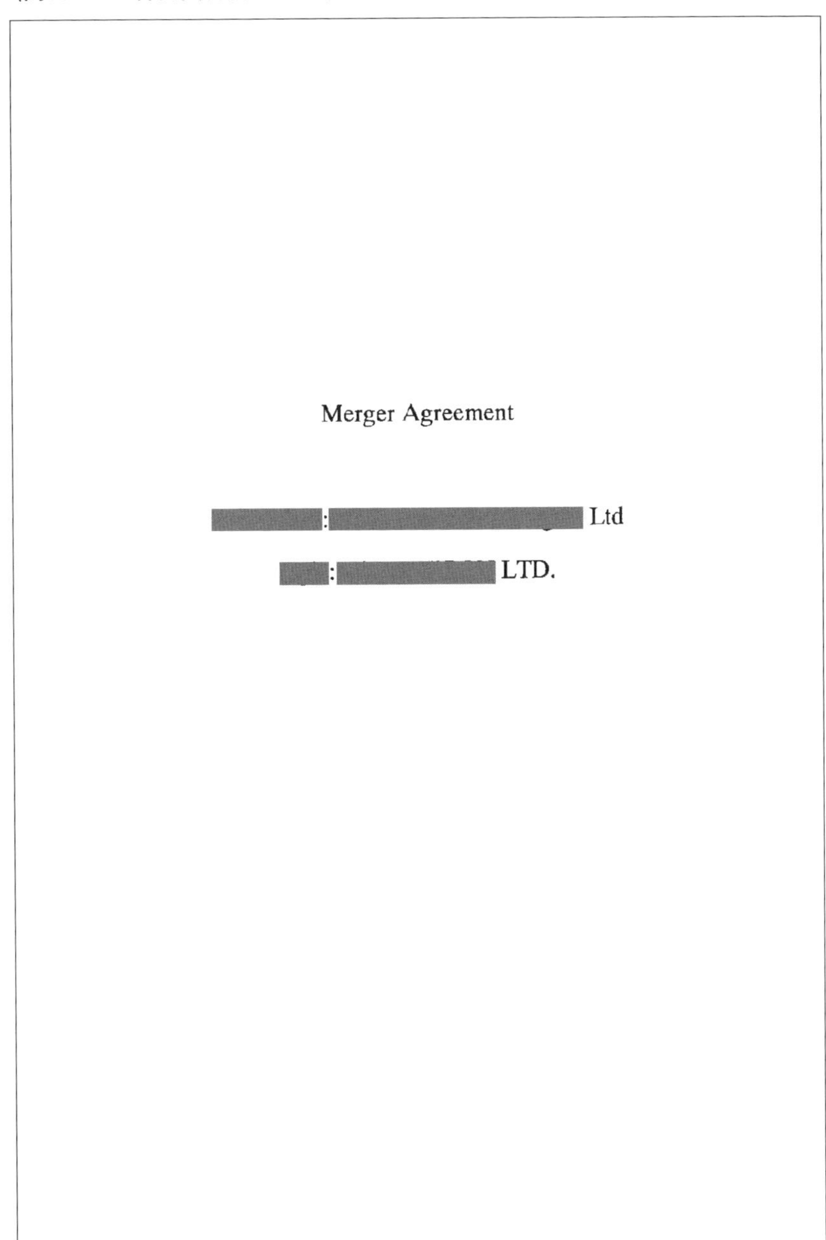

Merger Agreement

: Ltd

: LTD.

Merger Agreement

THIS AGREEMENT has made as set forth below by and between [redacted] Ltd., (hereinafter referred to as "[redacted]") and [redacted] LTD. (hereinafter referred to as "[redacted]"), in connection with their merger.

Article 1. Method of Merger.

[redacted] and [redacted] shall merge. [redacted] shall continue in existence and Agie shall cease to exist.

Article 2. Changes to Articles of Incorporation Through Merger.

1. [redacted] shall through the merger change its Articles of Incorporation in the manner prescribed below:

i. Article 1 (Company Name) of the Articles of Incorporation shall be amended to read as follows:

Article 1. Company Name.

The name of the company shall be [redacted] Japan Ltd, and the name in Roman letters shall be [redacted] Japan Ltd.

ii. Article 3 (Location of Head Office) of the Articles of Incorporation shall be amended to read as follows:

Article 3. Location of Head Office.

The head office of the Company shall be in [redacted], Yokohama.

2. Each of the preceding items shall take effect from the date of the merger.

Article 3. Allocation of New Shares and Amount of Capital as a Result of the Merger.

[redacted] shall issue one common par value share (with a par value of ¥50,000 per share) at the time of the merger, and shall allocate one share of [redacted] (with a par value of ¥50,000 per share) per 7,660 shares of [redacted] (with a par value of 50,000 per share) to shareholders listed in [redacted]'s registry of shareholders.

Article 4. Particulars Concerning Reserve.

- 2 -

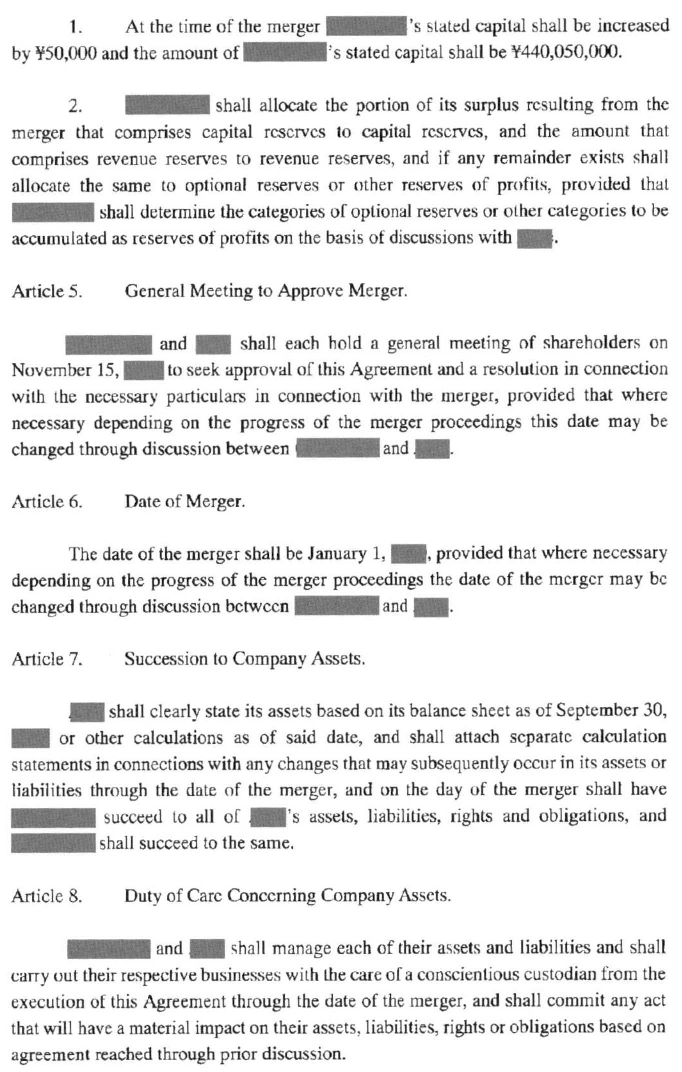

1. At the time of the merger 's stated capital shall be increased by ¥50,000 and the amount of 's stated capital shall be ¥440,050,000.

2. shall allocate the portion of its surplus resulting from the merger that comprises capital reserves to capital reserves, and the amount that comprises revenue reserves to revenue reserves, and if any remainder exists shall allocate the same to optional reserves or other reserves of profits, provided that shall determine the categories of optional reserves or other categories to be accumulated as reserves of profits on the basis of discussions with .

Article 5. General Meeting to Approve Merger.

and shall each hold a general meeting of shareholders on November 15, to seek approval of this Agreement and a resolution in connection with the necessary particulars in connection with the merger, provided that where necessary depending on the progress of the merger proceedings this date may be changed through discussion between and .

Article 6. Date of Merger.

The date of the merger shall be January 1, , provided that where necessary depending on the progress of the merger proceedings the date of the merger may be changed through discussion between and .

Article 7. Succession to Company Assets.

shall clearly state its assets based on its balance sheet as of September 30, or other calculations as of said date, and shall attach separate calculation statements in connections with any changes that may subsequently occur in its assets or liabilities through the date of the merger, and on the day of the merger shall have succeed to all of 's assets, liabilities, rights and obligations, and shall succeed to the same.

Article 8. Duty of Care Concerning Company Assets.

and shall manage each of their assets and liabilities and shall carry out their respective businesses with the care of a conscientious custodian from the execution of this Agreement through the date of the merger, and shall commit any act that will have a material impact on their assets, liabilities, rights or obligations based on agreement reached through prior discussion.

- 3 -

第2章　株式会社

Article 9. Succeeding to Employees.

[redacted] shall continue to employ [redacted]'s employees from the date of the merger, and the treatment of employees shall be determined through separate discussions between [redacted] and [redacted].

Article 10. Period of Office of Statutory Auditors of [redacted] Who Have Been Installed Prior to Merger.

Statutory auditors of [redacted] who are installed prior to the merger shall not retire from their office at the time of the conclusion of the first ordinary general meeting of shareholders after the merger, and their terms of office shall be treated as set forth in Article 17 of [redacted]'s Articles of Incorporation.

Article 11. Directors and Officers Installed at the Time of the Merger.

Directors and statutory auditors of [redacted] who are newly installed at the time of the merger shall be as follows, and the date on which they are to be installed shall be the date of the merger:

Director: [redacted]
Statutory Auditor: [redacted]

Article 12. Status and Totalization of Years of Service.

For the purposes of calculation of the retirement bonus payable through resolution of the general meeting of shareholders of [redacted], of a person who is a director or statutory auditor of [redacted] and who at the time of the merger is installed as a director or statutory auditor of [redacted], the status and number of years of service at [redacted] shall be added to the status and number of years of service at [redacted].

Article 13. Retirement Bonus of Officers of the Company to Be Extinguished.

The retirement bonus of a director or statutory auditor of [redacted] who is not installed as a director or statutory auditor of [redacted] as a result of the merger shall be paid on approval being obtained by the general meeting of shareholders of [redacted] to approve the merger as set forth in Article 5.

Article 14. Amending Conditions of Merger or Canceling Merger Agreement.

The conditions of the merger may be amended or this Agreement may be canceled through discussion between [redacted] and [redacted] if a significant change

- 4 -

occurs in the assets or operating position of [redacted] or [redacted] as a result of a force majeure or other reason between the date of execution of this Agreement and the date of the merger.

Article 15. Effect of Merger Agreement.

This Agreement shall be void and of no effect if approval cannot be obtained from the general meeting of shareholders of [redacted] or [redacted] as set forth in Article 5 hereof, or from a relevant supervising governmental body.

Article 16. Discussion.

In addition to the particulars set forth in this Agreement, [redacted] and [redacted] shall separately discuss and determine any particulars necessary to implement this merger in the spirit of this Agreement.

IN WITNESS WHEREOF, this document has been executed in duplicate, with the names and seals of [redacted] and [redacted] affixed below, and with each party retaining one original in each of their possessions.

November 10, [redacted]

For [redacted]:

[redacted]
Representative Director
[redacted] Ltd.
[redacted]-[redacted] [redacted] [redacted]-chome
[redacted]-ku
Yokohama-shi, Kanagawa

For [redacted]:

[redacted]
Representative Director
[redacted] LTD.
[redacted]-[redacted] [redacted] 1-chome
[redacted]-ku,
Yokohama-shi, Kanagawa

(2) 組織変更

例69は株式会社より合同会社への組織変更に関する書式である。

〈例69 組織変更の必要書類一覧〉

Japan株式会社
組織変更

Japan, KK
Re: Entity Conversion

	Documents	Signatory/Seal
1	取締役会決議事項に関する取締役の提案及びその同意のお願い Director's Proposal concerning Matters to be Resolved at Meeting of Board of Directors and Request for Consent	
2	取締役及び監査役の同意書 Written Consents by Directors and Statutory Auditor	, , , z, and (sign/personal seal)
3	取締役会議事録 Minutes of the Board of Directors	Japan (company seal)
4	株主総会決議事項に関する取締役の提案及びその同意のお願い Director's Proposal concerning Matters to be Resolved at General Meeting of Shareholders and Request for Consent	
5	取締役の提案に対する株主の同意書 Written Consent by the Shareholder to Director's Proposal	Inc. (sign)
6	臨時株主総会議事録 Minutes of the Extraordinary General Meeting of Shareholders	Japan (company seal)
7	組織変更計画書 Entity Conversion Plan	
8	定款 Articles of Incorporation	Inc. (sign)* all pages

〈例70　取締役会決定事項に関する取締役の提案及びその同意のお願い〉

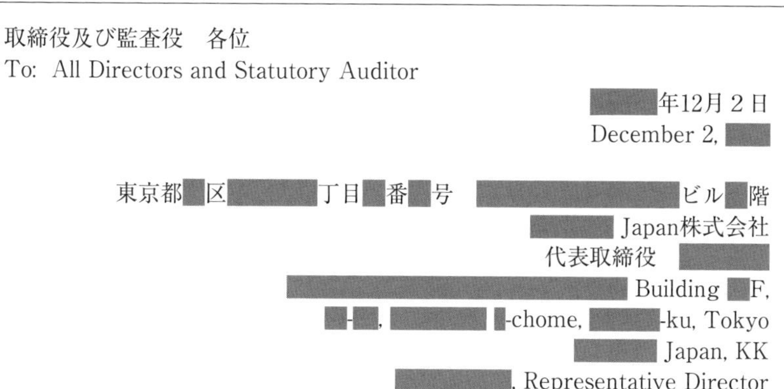

取締役及び監査役　各位
To: All Directors and Statutory Auditor

■年12月2日
December 2, ■

東京都■区■丁目■番■号　■ビル■階
■Japan株式会社
代表取締役　■
■Building ■F,
■-■, ■■-chome, ■-ku, Tokyo
■Japan, KK
■, Representative Director

取締役会決議事項に関する取締役の提案及びその同意のお願い
Director's Proposal concerning
Matters to be Resolved at Meeting of Board of Directors and
Request for Consent

この度，会社法第370条及び当会社定款第30条の規定に基づき，取締役会の目的である事項について別紙記載のとおりご提案致します。

つきましては，かかる取締役の提案の内容につき異議なくご同意いただける場合には，同封の同意書にご署名又はご捺印の上，ご返送下さいますようお願い申し上げます

In accordance with the provisions of Article 370 of the Companies Act and Article 30 of the Articles of Incorporation of the Company, I hereby propose the matters to be resolved at the meeting of the Board of Directors as described in the Annex attached hereto.

If you consent without any objection to the particulars of such proposal by the Director, please sign or affix your seal to the Letter of Consent enclosed herewith and return it to us.

以上
End

〈例71　取締役及び監査役の同意書（監査役については省略）〉

Japan株式会社 御中
To: Japan, KK

取締役会決議事項の取締役の提案の内容に対する同意書
Consent to Director's Proposal concerning Matters to be Resolved at Meeting of Board of Directors

Japan株式会社（以下「当会社」という。）の取締役である私は，会社法第370条及び当会社定款第30条の規定に基づき，取締役会の決議事項に関する別紙記載の取締役の提案の内容につき，これに異議を述べず同意します。

I, Director of Japan, KK (hereinafter the "Company"), hereby consent to, and do not raise any objection to, the proposal by the Director concerning the matters to be resolved at the meeting of the Board of Directors as described in the Annex attached hereto, in accordance with the provisions of Article 370 of the Companies Act and Article 30 of the Articles of Incorporation of the Company.

以上
End

年12月２日
December 2,

取締役 
Director

〈例72　取締役会議事録（同意書があっても議事録作成は必要）〉

Japan株式会社
取締役会議事録
MINUTES OF MEETING OF BOARD OF DIRECTORS OF JAPAN, KK

Japan株式会社（以下「当会社」という。）は，年12月２日付をもって，取締役会決議事項につき取締役の提案を行い，同日付をもって当該事項につき議決に加わることができる取締役の全員より，かかる提案に同意する旨の同意書の提出を受けたので，会社法第370条及び当会社定款

第30条の規定に基づき，次のとおり取締役会の決議があったものとみなされた。なお，監査役からの異議はなかった。
In accordance with the provisions of Article 370 of the Companies Act and Article 30 of the Articles of Incorporation of ████ Japan, KK (hereinafter the "Company"), a Director of the Company proposed the matters to be resolved at the meeting of the Board of Directors and obtained the written consents from all Directors entitled to vote as of December 2, ███. Accordingly, the resolution of the Board of Directors was deemed to have been adopted as follows. The Statutory Auditor raised no objection to the proposal.

Ⅰ．取締役会の決議があったものとみなされた事項の内容
Matters passed by resolution of the meeting of the Board of Directors

別紙記載のとおり
As described in the Annex attached hereto

Ⅱ．Ⅰ．の事項の提案をした取締役の氏名
Name of the Director who proposed the matters described in I above

代表取締役　████
████, Representative Director

Ⅲ．取締役会の決議があったものとみなされた日
Date of resolution of the meeting of the Board of Directors

███年12月２日
December 2, ███

Ⅳ．議事録の作成に係る職務を行った取締役の氏名
Name of the Director preparing these minutes

代表取締役　████
████, Representative Director

上記を証するため，本議事録を作成する。
IN WITNESS WHEREOF, these minutes have been prepared.

████ Japan株式会社

第2章　株式会社

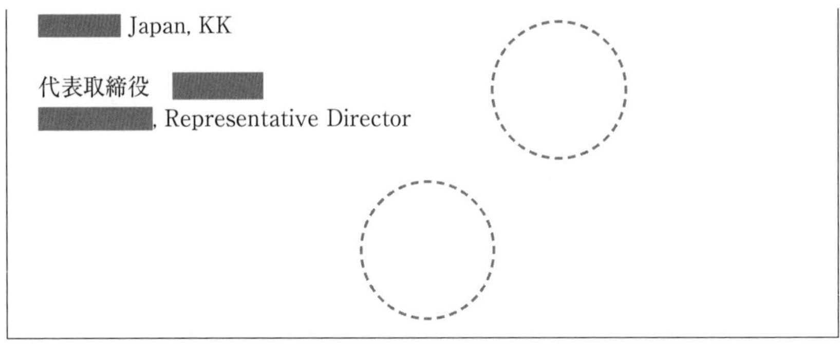
■■■ Japan, KK

代表取締役 ■■■
■■■, Representative Director

〈例73　株主総会議事事項に関する取締役の提案及びその同意のお願い（株主に対する）〉

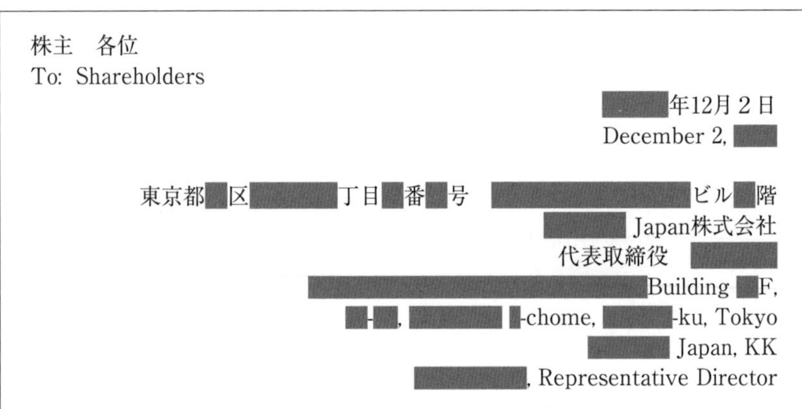
株主　各位
To: Shareholders

■■■年12月2日
December 2, ■■■

東京都■区■■■丁目■番■号　■■■ビル■階
■■■Japan株式会社
代表取締役　■■■
■■■Building ■F,
■-■, ■■■ ■-chome, ■■■-ku, Tokyo
■■■ Japan, KK
■■■, Representative Director

株主総会決議事項に関する取締役の提案及びその同意のお願い
Director's Proposal concerning
Matters to be Resolved at General Meeting of Shareholders and
Request for Consent

この度，会社法第319条の規定に基づき，株主総会の目的である事項について別紙記載のとおりご提案致します。

つきましては，かかる取締役の提案の内容につき異議なくご同意いただける場合には，同封の同意書にご署名又はご捺印の上，ご返送下さいますようお願い申し上げます

In accordance with the provisions of Article 319 of the Companies Act, I hereby propose the matters to be resolved at the meeting of the General Meeting of Shareholders as described in the Annex attached hereto.

If you consent without any objection to the particulars of such proposal by the Director, please sign or affix your seal to the Letter of Consent enclosed herewith and return it to us.

以上
End

〈例74　取締役の提案に対する株主の同意書（全株主の同意が必要）〉

██████ Japan株式会社　御中
To: ██████ Japan, KK

株主総会決議事項の取締役の提案の内容に対する同意書
Consent to the Proposals by the Director on the Matters to be resolved by the General Meeting of Shareholders

私は，会社法第319条に基づき，別紙の取締役の提案の内容につき，これに異議を述べず同意します。

Pursuant to the provisions of Article 319 of the Companies Act, the undersigned hereby consent, without any objection, to the proposals submitted by the director stated in the Annex attached hereto.

█████年12月２日
December 2, ███

普通株式（6,500,000株）
A種優先株式（3,496,503株）
Common Stock（6,500,000 shares）
Series A Preferred Stock（3,496,503 shares）

株主　██████, Inc.
Shareholder:　██████, Inc.

██████, Inc.

____
██████████
Chief Executive Officer

【別紙】
Annex

決議事項
Matters to be resolved

1．組織変更計画承認の件
1．Approval of the entity conversion plan
当会社を合同会社に組織変更するため，別紙のとおり組織変更計画を承認する。
In order to convert the Company to a limited liability company, the Company shall approve the entity conversion plan as attached.

以上
End

〈例75　臨時株主総会議事録（同意書があっても議事録作成は必要）〉

[redacted] Japan株式会社
臨時株主総会議事録
MINUTES OF THE EXTRAORDINARY GENERAL MEETING OF SHAREHOLDERS OF [redacted] JAPAN, KK

私は，[redacted] Japan株式会社（以下「当会社」という。）が，会社法第319条の定めに基づき，下記のとおり株主総会を開催することなく当会社株主に対する提案を行い，当会社株主が取締役の提案を可決したことをここに証明いたします。

I hereby certify that the matters below were proposed to the shareholder of [redacted] Japan, KK (the "Company"), and that such resolutions were adopted by the shareholders as proposed by the director, without holding a general meeting of the shareholders in accordance with the provisions of Article 319 of the Companies Act.

記
Note

決議事項
Matters to be resolved

Ⅰ．株主総会の決議があったものとみなされた事項の内容
Matters deemed to have been resolved at a general meeting of shareholders

別紙のとおり
As described in the Annex attached hereto

Ⅱ．Ⅰ．の事項の提案をした者の氏名または名称
Name of the person who proposed the matters described in Note I above

代表取締役

, Representative Director

Ⅲ. 株主総会の決議があったものとみなされた日
Date of the deemed resolutions of the general meeting of shareholders

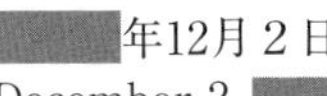
年12月２日
December 2,

Ⅳ. 議事録の作成に係る職務を行った取締役の氏名
Name of the director preparing the minutes

代表取締役

, Representative Director

以上
End

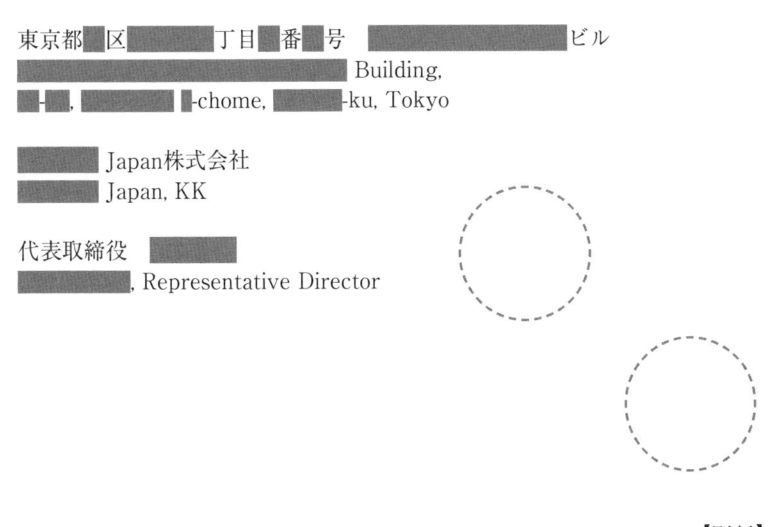
東京都 区 丁目 番 号 ビル
Building,
- , -chome, -ku, Tokyo

Japan株式会社
Japan, KK

代表取締役
, Representative Director

【別紙】
Annex

決議事項
Matters to be resolved

1. 組織変更計画承認の件
1. Approval of the entity conversion plan
当会社を合同会社に組織変更するため，別紙のとおり組織変更計画を承認する。

In order to convert the Company to a limited liability company, the Company shall approve the entity conversion plan as attached.

以上

End

〈例76　組織変更計画書〉

組織変更計画書

Entity Conversion Plan

1．組織変更後持分会社の会社種別　合同会社

1．Type of membership companies after entity conversion: Limited Liability Company

2．目的

(1)　ソーシャルメディア管理その他の分野に関連するソフトウェア，技術の開発，販売

(2)　情報技術サービスの提供

(3)　データ収集・利用に関するコンサルティングサービスの提供

(4)　前各号に付帯関連する一切の事業

2．Purpose:

(1)　To develop and sale of software and technologies related to social media management and other areas

(2)　To provide information technology services

(3)　To provide consulting services on data collection and use

(4)　Any and all businesses incidental or related to the foregoing

3．商号　■■■■ Japan合同会社

3．Trade name: ■■■■ Japan, GK

4．本店 東京都■区

4．Location of head office: ■■■■-ku, Tokyo

5．組織変更後社員の氏名又は名称及び住所，無限責任社員又は有限責任社員の別，出資の価額

アメリカ合衆国ニューヨーク州■■■■，■■■■ストリート■，■F

有限責任社員　■■■■・インク 金10億9858円

5．Name, address, liability and amount of capital subscription of the member after entity conversion:

■ West ■th Street, ■th Floor, ■■■■, NY 10001 USA
Member with limited liability ■■■■, Inc. 1,000,009,858 yen

6．新株予約権者に対して交付する当該新株予約権に代わる金銭の額及び割当方法
■■■■ Japan株式会社第２回ストックオプション
その有する新株予約権１個につき 金105円の割合をもって金銭を割当交付する。

6．Amount and allocation method of money in place of share options to be issued to holders of share options:
2nd stock option of ■■■■ Japan, KK
The money will be allotted and delivered at the rate of 105 yen for each share option.

7．組織変更後の定款で定める事項 別紙定款案のとおり

7．Matters prescribed by articles of incorporation after entity conversion: As per the attached draft articles of incorporation

8．効力発生日　■■■■年２月１日

8．Effective day:　February 1, ■■■■

〈例77　定款（組織変更後の合同会社の定款）〉

■■■■ Japan合同会社
■■■■ Japan, GK
定　款
Articles of Incorporation

第１章　総則
Chapter I General Provisions

第１条（商号）
当会社は，■■■■ Japan合同会社と称し，英文では■■■■ Japan, GKと表示する。

Article 1 (Trade Name)
The Company is called "■■■■ Japan Godo-Kaisha" and in English "■■■■ Japan, GK."

第２条（目的）
当会社は，次の事業を行うことを目的とする。
1．ソーシャルメディア管理その他の分野に関連するソフトウェア，技術の開発，販売
2．情報技術サービスの提供
3．データ収集・利用に関するコンサルティングサービスの提供

4．前各号に付帯関連する一切の事業
Article 2（Purposes）
Purposes of the Company are to engage in the following businesses:
1．To develop and sale of software and technologies related to social media management and other areas
2．To provide information technology services
3．To provide consulting services on data collection and use
4．Any and all businesses incidental or related to the foregoing

第３条（本店の所在地）
当会社は，本店を東京都■区に置く。
Article 3（Location of Head Office）
The Company has its head office in ■-ku, Tokyo.

第４条（公告の方法）
当会社の公告は，官報に掲載する方法により行う。
Article 4（Method of Public Notices）
Public notices of the Company are carried in Official Gazette（Kampo）.

第２章　社員及び出資
Chapter Ⅱ Members and Capital Contributions

第５条（社員の氏名又は名称，住所，出資及び責任）
当会社の社員の氏名又は名称，住所及び出資の価額は，次の通りである。
アメリカ合衆国ニューヨーク州■，ウエスト■ストリート■，■F
■・インク 金10億9,858円
2．当会社の社員は，すべて有限責任社員とする。
Article 5（Name, Address and Capital Subscription and Liability of Member）
Name, address and amount of capital subscription of the member are as follows:
■ West ■th Street, ■th Floor, ■, NY 10001 USA
■, Inc. 1,000,009,858 yen
2．Members of the Company shall be all the member with limited liability

第３章　業務執行権及び代表権
Chapter Ⅲ Right to Execute Business and Authority of Representation

第６条（業務執行社員）
当会社の業務執行社員は，■・インクとする。
Article 6（Executive Member）
The executive member［Gyomu Shikko Shain］of the Company shall be ■, Inc.

第７条（代表社員）
当会社の代表社員は，■・インクとする。
Article 7（Representative Member）
The representative member［Daihyo Shain］of the Company shall be ■, Inc.

第４章　職務執行者
Chapter Ⅳ Managing Officer

第８条（職務執行者の任命）
法人が業務執行員である場合には，当会社の業務執行社員は，当会社の日々の業務の執行につき全ての責任を負い権限を有する職務執行者を任命する。

Article 8 (Appointment of Managing Officer)

In cases where corporation act as executive member, the executive member of the Company shall appoint the managing officer (s) which shall have full responsibility and authority for management of day-to-day operations of the Company.

第９条（職務執行者の任期）

職務執行者の任期は，その後任者が選任された時点，又はそれよりも早く辞任し若しくは解任された時点までとする。

Article 9 (Term of Office)

The managing officer shall hold office until the successor are chosen and qualify or until the earlier resignation or removal.

第10条（報酬）

職務執行者の報酬は，当会社の業務執行社員の決議により決定されるものとする。

Article 10 (Compensation)

The compensation of the managing officer of the Company shall be fixed by the resolution of the executive member (s) of the Company.

第５章　社員の加入及び退社

Chapter V Incoming and Withdrawal Members

第11条（社員の加入）

新たに社員を加入させる場合は，総社員の同意によって定款を変更しなければならない。

Article 11 (Incoming Members)

Incoming members shall be subject to change in the articles of incorporation of the Company pursuant to unanimous consent of all members.

第12条（任意退社）

社員は，事業年度の終了の時において退社をすることができる。この場合においては，社員は，２ヶ月前までに会社に退社の予告をしなければならない。

２．前項の規定にかかわらず，社員は，やむを得ない事由があるときは，いつでも退社することができる。

Article 12 (Voluntary Withdrawal)

Each member may withdraw from the Company at the end of each business year by giving 2 months prior notice to the Company.

2. Notwithstanding the preceding clause, each member may withdraw from the Company any time due to unavoidable reasons.

第13条（法定退社）

各社員は，会社法第607条の規定により，退社する。

Article 13 (Statutory Withdrawal)

Each member shall withdraw from the Company pursuant to the provision of article 607 of Company Law of Japan.

第６章　計算

Chapter VI Accounts

第14条（事業年度）

当会社の事業年度は，毎年２月１日から翌年１月31日までの年１期とする。

Article 14 (Business Year)

The business year of the Company shall commence on February 1 and end on January 31 next year.

第15条（会計帳簿及び計算書類）
当会社は，適用される法務省令で定めるところにより，適時に，正確な会計帳簿及び計算書類（貸借対照表その他法務省令で定める書類をいう。）を作成しなければならない。
Article 15 (Accounting books and financial statement)
The Company must prepare accurate accounting books and financial statements (balance sheet and other statements as prescribed by the applicable Ordinance of the Ministry of Justice) in a timely manner as prescribed by the applicable Ordinance of the Ministry of Justice.

第16条（会計帳簿の維持）
当会社は，その会計帳簿，計算書類及びその事業に関する重要な資料を会計帳簿の閉鎖の時から10年間維持しなければならない。
Article 16 (Retention of books and records)
The Company must retain its accounting books, financial statements and important materials regarding its business for ten years from the time of the closing of the accounting books.
以上，　Japan合同会社設立のため，本定款を作成し，社員はこれに署名する。
For the incorporation of 　Japan, GK, the articles of incorporation are prepared and the Member affixes the signature thereto.

年２月１日
February 1,

有限責任社員　・インク
Member with limited liability: , Inc.
最高経営責任者

Chief Executive Officer

Chief Executive Officer

8　解散手続・清算結了

(1)　会社解散

会社解散とは，会社の法人格を消滅させる原因事実で，会社清算の準備段階である。ただし，法人格は，会社合併を除き清算の目的の範囲内において清算結了するまで間存続することになる（会社476条）。

解散事由は下記の通りである（会社471条）。

① 定款で定めた存続期間の満了
② 定款で定めた解散の事由の発生
③ 株主総会の決議
④ 合併（合併により当該会社が消滅する場合に限る。）

⑤　破産手続開始の決定

⑥　公益確保を理由とする裁判所の解散命令又は解散訴訟判決による解散

⑦　最後の登記の日から12年経過している休眠会社のみなし解散（会社472条）。法務大臣による公告及び登記所からの通知があったにもかかわらず，公告の日から２か月以内に役員変更登記又は事業を廃止していない旨の届出をしない場合には登記官の職権によるみなし解散登記がされることになる（商業登記法72条）。

(2)　会社清算

会社清算とは，合併又は破産手続開始決定を除き，会社の資産及び負債を清算のため処分しなければならず，そのためには一人又は二人以上の清算人を選任することになる（会社477条１項）。定款の定めにより清算人会，監査役又は監査役会を置くことができる（会社477条２項）。会計参与，会計監査人，監査等委員会又は指名委員会は設置できない（会社477条７項）。公開会社又は大会社は監査役設置義務がある（会社477条４項）。

〈例78　取締役会議事録（株主総会の決議による解散，清算人選任のための招集決議）〉

取締役会議事録
MINUTES OF MEETING OF BOARD OF DIRECTORS

■■■年８月15日午前９時，当会社本店会議室において，取締役会を開催した。
A meeting of the board of directors was held on August 15, ■■■, at 9:00 am at the meeting room of the head office of the Company.

取締役総数	３名	Total number of Directors:	3
出席取締役数	２名	Number of Directors present:	2

上記のとおり出席があり本取締役会は適法に成立したので，代表取締役■■■は選ばれて議長となり開会する旨を宣し，直ちに議事に入った。
Whereupon the above directors being present, this meeting of the

board of directors was lawfully constituted, and Representative Director [redacted] was selected as a chairman, assumed the chair, declared the meeting in session and proceeded immediately with the business at hand.

議　案　臨時株主総会の招集に関する件
Proposal: Concerning Convening of the Extraordinary General Shareholders' Meeting

議長は，臨時株主総会を次の要領で開催したい旨を議場に諮ったところ，出席取締役慎重審議の結果，全員異議なく承認可決した。

The Chairperson proposed that the Extraordinary General Shareholders' Meeting should be held as described below. Upon motion duly made and seconded, the convocation was approved unanimously without opposition.

記
Particulars

(1)　日　時　[redacted]年８月15日　午前10時
Date and Time: August 15, [redacted] at 10：00 am
(2)　場　所　東京都[redacted]区[redacted]丁目[redacted]番[redacted]号[redacted]
当会社本店会議室
Place: [redacted] [redacted]-[redacted], Uehara 2-chome, Shibuya-ku, Tokyo,
Meeting Room of the headquarter office of the Company
(3)　会議の目的　Purpose:
第１号議案　当会社解散の件
Proposal 1: Concerning Dissolution of the Company
第２号議案　清算人選任の件
Proposal 2: Concerning Appointment of the Liquidator
[redacted]氏を候補者とする。
The candidate for the Liquidator is Mr. [redacted].

議長は，以上をもって本日の議事を終了した旨を述べ，午前９時15分閉会した。

Whereupon, all business before the Board as of this date having been concluded, the Chairperson declared the meeting closed at 9:15 am.

上記の決議を明確にするため，本議事録を作り，議長及び出席取締役全員がこれに記名押印する。

These minutes have been prepared as evidence of the above resolution, with the names and seals of the Chairperson and the Directors present affixed hereto.

年８月15日
August 15,

株式会社
K.K.

議長兼出席取締役
Chairperson & Director Present: ( )
出席取締役
Director Present: ( )

〈例79　株主の議決権行使の委任状〉

委　任　状
Proxy

私は，東京都　区　丁目　番　-　号に居住する　を代理人と定め，下記権限を委任する。

I hereby appoint　residing at #　-　,　-chome,　-ku, Tokyo, as my proxy and delegate all powers to perform the following:

年　月　日開催の　株式会社の臨時株主総会及びその継続会又は延会に出席し，下記議案につき私の指示（○印で表示）に従い，次のとおり議決権を行使すること。なお，賛否を明記しないとき及び修正案が提出されたときは，いずれも白紙委任いたします。

To attend the Extraordinary General Meeting of Shareholders of　K.K. to be held on　,　and any continuation thereof or adjourned meeting and execute the voting rights regarding the proposals below according to my instruction（which is circled）. Where there is no instruction regarding the vote or where there is an amended proposal, I delegate a blank vote.

第１号議案：当会社解散の件 Proposal 1: Concerning Dissolution of the Company	（賛・否） （Approved / Disapproved）
第２号議案：清算人の選任の件 Proposal 2: Concerning Appointment of the Liquidator	（賛・否） （Approved / Disapproved）

以上のとおり相違なく委任した。　I hereby delegated the above.

年　月　日

,

住所（Address）

資格（Title）

氏名（Name）

〈例80　臨時株主総会議事録（会社解散及び清算人選任決議）〉

臨時株主総会議事録
MINUTES OF EXTRAORDINARY GENERAL MEETING OF SHAREHOLDERS

年８月15日午前10時，当会社本店会議室において，臨時株主総会を開催した。

At 10:00a.m. on August 15, , an extraordinary general meeting of shareholders of the Company was held at the meeting room of the head office of the Company.

議決権のある当会社株主総数　17名
Total number of shareholders having voting rights of the Company: 17
議決権のある発行済株式総数　162万3320株
Total number of issued shares having voting rights: 1,623,320 shares
出席株主数（委任状による者を含む）　17名
Number of shareholders present（including attendance by proxy） 17
この議決権のある持株総数　162万3320株
Total number of shares having voting rights held by the above: 1,623,320shares

以上のとおり株主の出席があったので，定款第13条の規定により代表取締役社長は議長席につき，臨時総会は適法に成立したので，開会する旨を宣し，直ちに議事に入った。

With the attendance of shareholders shown above, in accordance with the provisions of Article 13 of the Articles of Incorporation of the Company, , President and Representative Director, assumed the chair, and, since the meeting was duly called and held, declared the meeting in session, and immediately proceeded the business at hand.

第１号議案　当会社解散の件
Proposal 1: Concerning Dissolution of the Company

議長は，その理由を詳細に説明した上で，当会社を解散したい旨を議場に諮ったところ，総会は全員異議なくこれを承認した。
The Chairperson proposed that the Company should be dissolved with a detailed explanation. Subsequently, the Chairperson requested the discussion thereof and all the shareholders present at the meeting approved the same.

第２号議案　清算人の選任の件
Proposal 2: Concerning Appointment of the Liquidator

議長は，解散に伴い清算人に下記の者を選任したい旨を総会に諮ったところ，総会は全員一致でこれを承認した。
The Chairperson nominated the following person as a candidate of the liquidator. All the shareholders presented at the meeting approved the same.

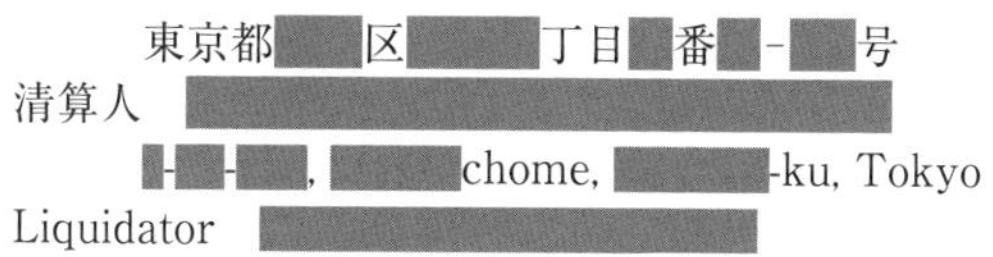
東京都　区　丁目　番 - 号
清算人
- - , chome, -ku, Tokyo
Liquidator

なお，被選任者は，総会においてその就任を承諾した。
The above person accepted his election to such office.

議長は，以上をもって本日の議事を終了した旨を述べ，午前10時30分閉会した。以上の決議を明確にするため，この議事録を作り，議長および出席取締役がこれに記名押印する。
Whereupon, the proceedings having been concluded, the chairperson declared the meeting was closed at 10:30 a.m. In order to certify the above resolutions, these minutes have been prepared and the chairperson and all the directors present have affixed their names and seals hereto.

年８月15日
August 15,

株式会社　臨時株主総会
Extraordinary general meeting of shareholders of　KK

議長兼出席取締役

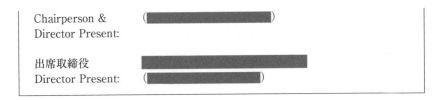

Chairperson & Director Present:	(　　　　)
出席取締役 Director Present:	 (　　　　)

〈例81　清算人就任承諾書〉

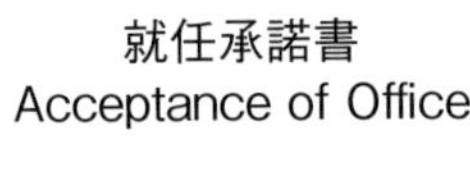

就任承諾書

Acceptance of Office

私は，　　年8月15日開催の貴社臨時株主総会において，貴社の清算人に選任されましたが，その就任を承諾いたします。

I have been elected as a Liquidator of your Company at the Extraordinary General Meeting of Shareholders held on, August 15, 　　 and I hereby accept such office.

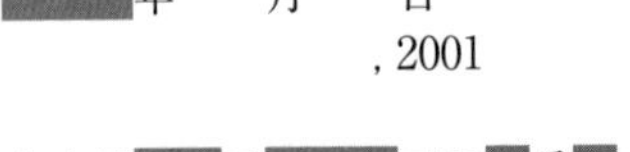

　　年　　月　　日

, 2001

東京都　　区　　丁目　番　-　号

-　-　,　-　chome, 　　-ku, Tokyo

清算人

Liquidator:

〈例82　清算人決定書（臨時株主総会招集のための決定）〉

清算人決定書

Minutes of Liquidator's Decision

　　年　月　日午前　時，当会社本店会議室において，清算人　　　は次のとおり定めた。

On　,　　, at the meeting room of the head office of the Company Liquidator　　　resolved as follows:

記

Particulars

臨時株主総会の招集に関する件

Concerning Convening of the Extraordinary General Shareholders' Meeting

(1)　日　時　　　　年　月　日　午前　時
Date and Time:　,　　at　:　am

(2)　場　所　東京都　区　丁目　番　号
当会社本店会議室
Place:　　,　-　,　-chome,　-ku, Tokyo,
Meeting Room of the headquarter office of the Company

(3)　会議の目的　Purpose:
議　案　財産目録及び貸借対照表承認の件
Proposal: Concerning Approval of Inventory and Balance sheet

上記の決定事項を明確にするために，この決定書を作り，清算人が次に記名押印する。
In witness of the above determined items, this determination has been executed with the name and seal of the Liquidator affixed hereto.

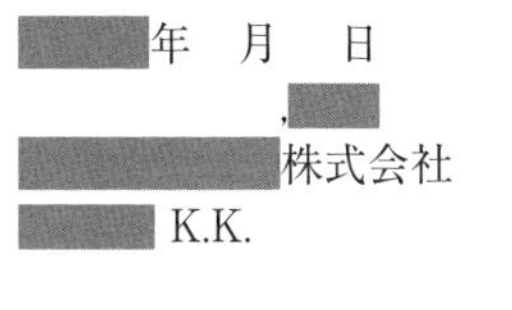

　年　月　日
,
株式会社
K.K.

議長兼清算人
Chairperson & Liquidator: (　)

〈例83　清算事務報告書（株主総会決議後清算結了登記添付書面）〉

清算事務報告書
Statement of Liquidation Affairs

清算人は，株主総会において，清算事務について説明し，別添の財産目録，貸借対照表及び残余財産処分計算書とともに総会の承認を得た。
The liquidator explained the liquidation affairs before the general meeting of shareholders and obtained approval from the general meeting together with the attached Inventory and the Balance Sheet for approval as well as the Statement of Calculation of Disposition of Remaining Assets.

以上のとおり清算結了した。
Whereupon liquidation was completed as stated above.

■■年　月　日
, ■■

東京都■■区■■丁目■番■号　■■■■
■■■■株式会社
清算人　■■■■■■
■■■■, ■-■, ■■■-chome, ■■■-ku, Tokyo
■■■ K.K.
Liquidator ■■■■■■

〈例84　残余財産処分計算書（清算事務報告書添付書面）〉

残余財産処分計算書
Statement of Calculation of Liquidation of Assets:

1．残余財産　　　　円
Remaining Assets　　¥＿＿＿＿＿＿

2．発行済株式数　　162万3,320株
内　普通株式　100万株
優先株式　62万3320株
Number of Shares Issued　　1,623,320 shares
Of which 1,000,000 are common shares, and 623,320 are preferred shares

3．1株当り分配額　　普通株式　　円
優先株式　　円

Distribution Per Share　　Common Shares　¥＿＿＿＿＿＿
Preferred Shares　¥＿＿＿＿＿＿

残余財産処分については，上記のとおりであります。
The distribution of remaining assets is as set forth above.

■■年　月　日
, ■■

東京都　区　丁目　番　号
株式会社
清算人
, -, -chome, -ku, Tokyo
K.K.
Liquidator:

〈例85　決算報告書（残余財産がない場合の書面）〉

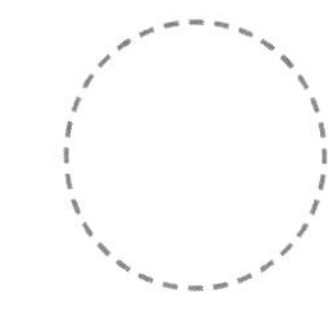

決算報告書
Settlement of accounts

Company Seal

1．債務の弁済，清算に係る費用の支払いによる費用の額：　金　0　円
1．Amount of cost by paying for the Performance of Obligations and the Cost on Liquidation: Nil yen

1．債権の取立て，資産の処分によって得た収入の額：　金　0　円
1．Amount of revenue received by the Collection of Debts and the Disposal of Assets: Nil yen

1．残余財産の額：　金　0　円
1．Amount of Residual assets: Nil yen

（支払税額）：　金　0　円
（Paid amount of tax）: Nil yen

当該税額を控除した後の財産額：　金　0　円
Amount of assets after subtracted such amount of tax: Nil yen

1．発行済株式数：　普通株式　200株
1．Total number of the Issued Shares: Ordinary shares: 200 shares

1．1株当り分配額：　金　0　円
1．Distributed amount per share: Nil yen

上記のとおり清算結了したことを報告する。
I hereby report the Conclusion of Liquidation as mentioned above.

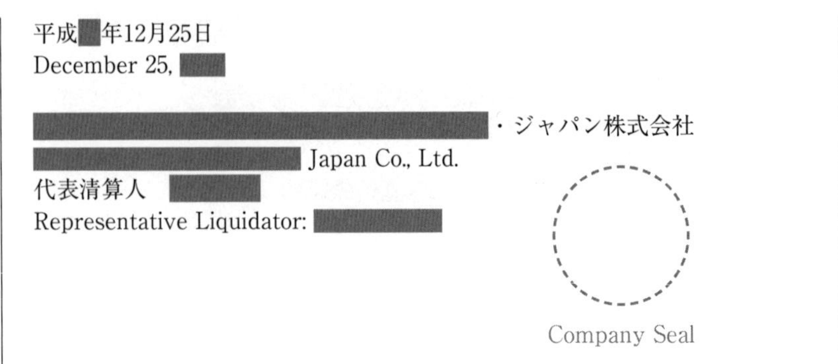
平成■年12月25日
December 25, ■

■・ジャパン株式会社
■ Japan Co., Ltd.
代表清算人　■
Representative Liquidator: ■

第3章 合同会社

1 設 立

合同会社は，株式会社，合資会社，合名会社とともに日本における会社形態の一つであり，アメリカの州法で認められているLLC（Limited Liability Company）をモデルにして会社法において採用された会社形態である。

合同会社の全ての社員は，株式会社の株主と同様に，会社の債務については有限責任である。合名会社の社員又は合資会社の無限責任社員は，会社の債務について無限責任であるところに相違がある。また，株主が出資し意思決定は取締役のように出資と経営が分離している株式会社とは異なり，合同会社は出資と経営が一体となっており，意思決定手続が簡素であるため，新設を認められなくなった有限会社に代わって小規模企業設立のために多く利用されている。

合同会社を設立するに当たり，社員，商号，事業目的，本店所在地，公告方法，決算期，資本金等の基本的事項を決定しなければならない。社員は１名以上で，数名の社員で設立するときは，業務執行社員（代表権を有する者）を定めなければならない。社員の中から業務執行社員を定めないときは全員が業務執行社員となる。資本金について，最低資本金制度はないため１円からスタートできるが，実際的にはなくある程度の資本金は必要になる。ただし，株式会社のように出資比率にしたがって利益配当する必要はなく定款に別段の定めをすることができる。定款作成は必要であるが，公証人の認証は不要である。

設立登記のための添付書面として，①定款，②代表社員及び資本金決定書，③代表社員の就任承諾書（社員１名のときは不要），④代表者の印鑑証明書・資本金の払込証明書，⑤法人が社員である場合の資格証明書（登記事項証明書），⑥法人が社員である場合の職務執行者の選任に関する書面，⑦法人が社員である場合の職務執行者の就任承諾書，⑧代表社員の印鑑届出書となっている。

例86は，社員は法人１名で設立された合同会社の事案である。

〈例86 定款（合同会社）〉

ARTICLES OF INCORPORATION

合同会社
GK

定 款
Articles of Incorporation

第１章 総 則
Chapter I General Provisions

（商号）
第１条 当会社は，■■■■合同会社と称し，英文では■■■■GKと表示する。
Article 1 (Trade name) The Company is called "■■■■ Godo-kaisha" and in English "■■■■ GK."

（目的）
第２条 当会社は，次の事業を行うことを目的とする。
1．発電事業及びその管理・運営，電力の売買，発電設備の建設並びに太陽光発電設備の運営等及び保守管理業務
2．上記の事業を営む会社，その他の法人及び外国会社の株式または持分を保有することによる当該会社の事業活動の支配並びに管理
3．前各号に附帯し又は関連する一切の事業

Article 2 (Purposes) Purposes of the Company are to engage in the following businesses:
1. Power generating business and related management and administration, purchasing and selling of electricity, and administration and maintenance of solar power generating facilities.
2. To control and manage the activities of companies or organizations conducting above-mentioned businesses by owning their shares or ownership.
3. Any and all businesses incidental to the foregoing

（本店の所在地）
第３条 当会社は，本店を東京都■■■に置く。
Article 3 (Location of Head Office)
The Company has its head office in ■■■■ Tokyo.

（公告の方法）
第４条　当会社の公告は，官報に掲載してする。
Article 4 (Method of Public Notices) Public notices of the Company are carried in Official Gazette (Kampo).
第２章　社員及び出資
Chapter Ⅱ Members and Capital Contributions

（社員の氏名，住所，出資及び責任）
第５条　当会社の社員の氏名，住所及び出資の価額は次の通りである。
　　県　　市　　丁目10番24号
　　株式会社　金１万円
２　当会社の社員は，すべて有限責任社員とする。
Article 5 (Name, Address and Capital Subscription and Liability of Member) Name, address, capital subscription and liability of the Member are as follows:
10-24, , -shi,
K.K., 10 thousand yen
2. Members of the Company shall be all the members with Limited Liability

第３章　業務執行権及び代表権
Chapter Ⅲ Right to Execute Business and Authority of Representation

（業務執行社員）
第６条　当会社の業務執行社員は，　株式会社とする。
Article 6 (Managing Partner) The Managing Partner of the Company and execute the operation shall be　K.K..

（代表社員）
第７条　当会社の代表社員は，　株式会社とする。
Article 7 (Representative Member) The representative member of the company shall be　K.K..

第４章　社員の加入及び退社
Chapter Ⅳ Incoming and Withdrawal Members

（社員の加入）
第８条　新たに社員を加入させる場合は，総社員の同意によって定款を変更しなければならない。
Article 8 (Incoming Members) Incoming Members shall be subject to change in the articles of incorporation of the company pursuant to unanimous consent of all Members.

（任意退社）
第９条　各社員は，事業年度の終了の時において退社をすることができる。この場合においては，各社員は，２か月前までに会社に退社の予告をしなければならない。
２　前項の規定にかかわらず，各社員は，やむを得ない事由があるときは，いつでも退社することができる。
Article 9 (Voluntary Withdrawal) Each member may withdraw from the Company at the end of each business year by giving 2 months notice to the Company.
2. Notwithstanding the preceding clause, each member may withdraw from the Company any time due to unavoidable reasons.

（法定退社）
第10条　各社員は，会社法第607条の規定により，退社する。

第3章　合同会社

Article 10 (Statutory Withdrawal) Each member shall withdraw from the Company pursuant to the provision of article 607 of Company Law of Japan.

第５章　計算
Chapter V Accounts

(事業年度)
第12条　当会社の事業年度は，毎年１月１日から同年12月31日までの年１期とする。
Article 12 (Business Year) The business year of the Company shall commence on January 1 of every year and end on December 31 of the same year.

(決算に係る事項)
第12条の２　事業年度末日の翌日から３ヶ月以内に決算を確定する。
Article 12-2 (Settlement of Account) Account of the Company shall be settled within 3 months from the immediately following day of the end of the business year.

附　則
Supplemental Provisions

(最初の事業年度)
第13条　当会社の最初の事業年度は，当会社設立の日から■■年12月31日までとする。
Article 13 (The First Business Year) The first business year of the Company shall commence on the day of incorporation of the Company and end on December 31, ■■.

(設立時の資本金)
第14条　当会社の設立時資本金は金１万円とする。
Article 14 (Capital upon Incorporation of Company) The capital upon Incorporation of the Company is 10 thousand yen.

(設立当初の本店所在地)
第15条　当会社の設立当初の本店は，東京都■■23番４号■■ビル７階に置く。
Article 15. (Address of the Head office) The address of the head office at incorporation is ■■. 23-4 ■■, Tokyo.

(定款に定めのない事項)
第16条　本定款に定めのない事項については，会社法その他の法令の定めるところによる。
Article 16. (Any matter not Stipulated herein) Any matter not stipulated herein shall be settled by company law or other applicable laws and regulations.

以上，■■合同会社を設立するため，社員■■株式会社の定款作成代理人である司法書士■■は，電磁的記録である本定款を作成し，これに電子署名をする。

For the incorporation of ■■ GK, the articles of incorporation are prepared in the form of electromagnetic record and ■■, Shiho-shoshi, affixes his digital signature thereto as the agent of the Member, ■■ K.K..

■■年３月17日
March 17, ■■

有限責任社員　■■株式会社
Member with Limited Liability: ■■ K.K.

上記社員の定款作成代理人	司法書士 ■■■
Agent mentioned above	Shiho-shoshi ■■■

〈例87　就任承諾書（代表社員の就任）〉

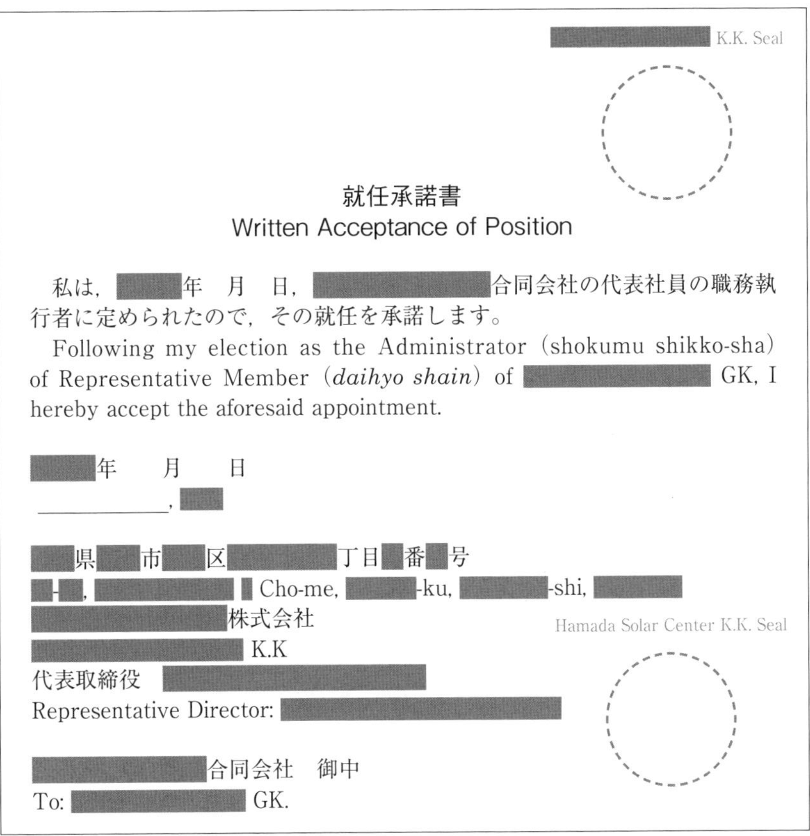

■■■ K.K. Seal

就任承諾書
Written Acceptance of Position

私は，■■年　月　日，■■■合同会社の代表社員の職務執行者に定められたので，その就任を承諾します。

Following my election as the Administrator (shokumu shikko-sha) of Representative Member (*daihyo shain*) of ■■■ GK, I hereby accept the aforesaid appointment.

■■年　月　日
＿＿＿＿＿, ■■

■県■市■区■■丁目■番■号
■-■, ■■■ ■ Cho-me, ■■-ku, ■■-shi, ■■
■■■株式会社
■■■ K.K
代表取締役 ■■■
Representative Director: ■■■

Hamada Solar Center K.K. Seal

■■■合同会社　御中
To: ■■■ GK.

〈例88 職務執行者選任決定書（代表社員が法人の場合）〉

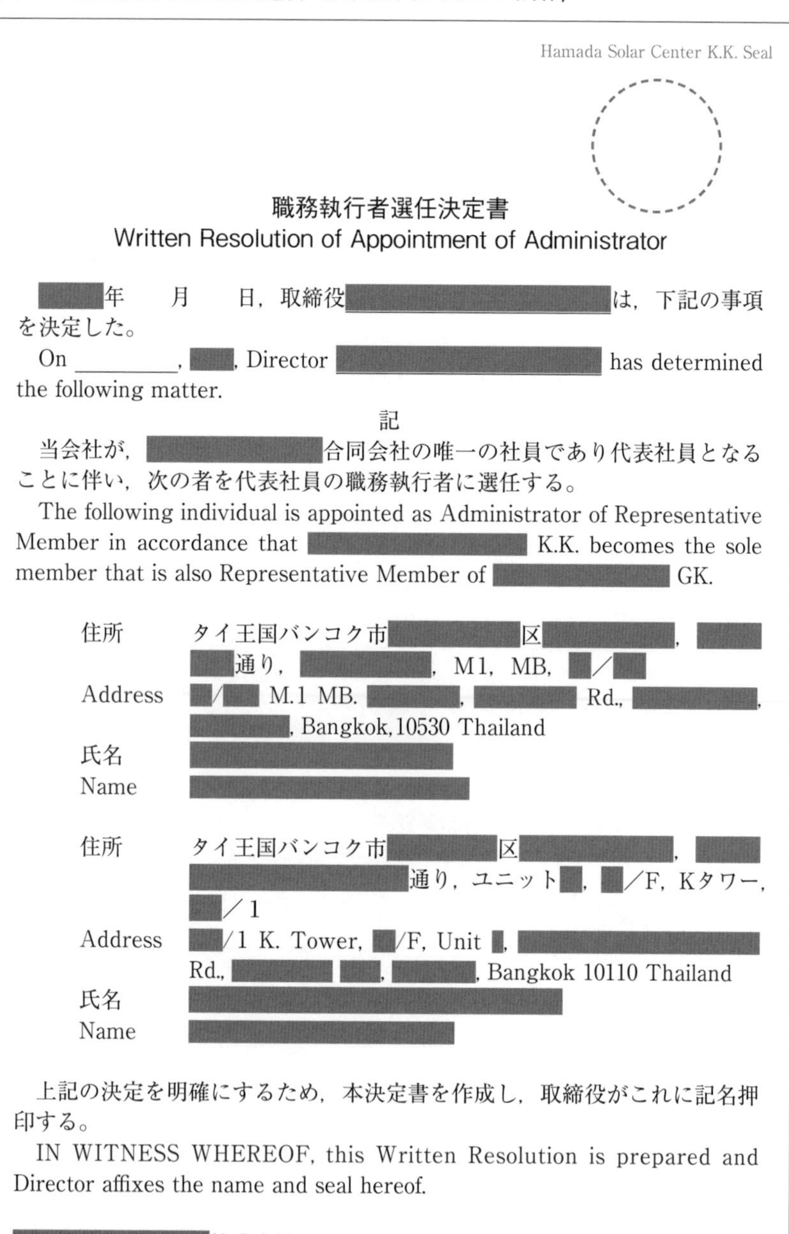

Hamada Solar Center K.K. Seal

職務執行者選任決定書
Written Resolution of Appointment of Administrator

年　月　日，取締役　　は，下記の事項を決定した。

On ______, , Director　　has determined the following matter.

記

当会社が，　合同会社の唯一の社員であり代表社員となることに伴い，次の者を代表社員の職務執行者に選任する。

The following individual is appointed as Administrator of Representative Member in accordance that　K.K. becomes the sole member that is also Representative Member of　GK.

住所　タイ王国バンコク市　区　，　通り，　，M1，MB，／

Address　／　M.1 MB.　，　Rd.，　，　，Bangkok, 10530 Thailand

氏名

Name

住所　タイ王国バンコク市　区　，　通り，ユニット　，　／F，Kタワー，　／1

Address　／1 K. Tower,　／F, Unit　，　Rd.，　　，　，Bangkok 10110 Thailand

氏名

Name

上記の決定を明確にするため，本決定書を作成し，取締役がこれに記名押印する。

IN WITNESS WHEREOF, this Written Resolution is prepared and Director affixes the name and seal hereof.

株式会社

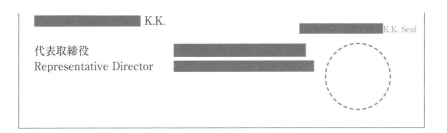
K.K.

K.K. Seal

代表取締役
Representative Director

〈例89 就任承諾書（代表社員たる法人より選任された職務執行者）〉

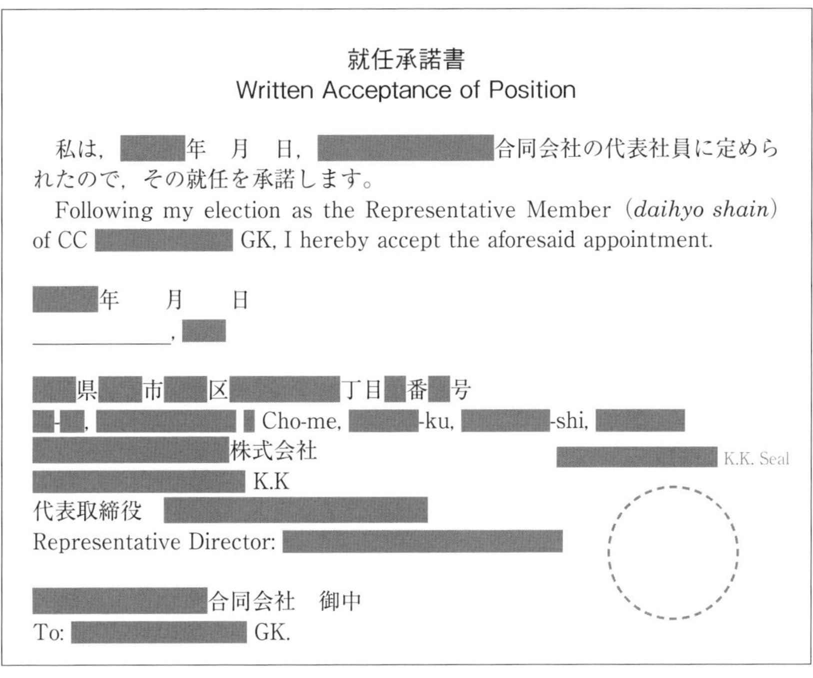
就任承諾書
Written Acceptance of Position

私は，　年　月　日，　合同会社の代表社員に定められたので，その就任を承諾します。
Following my election as the Representative Member (*daihyo shain*) of CC　GK, I hereby accept the aforesaid appointment.

年　月　日
＿＿＿＿＿＿＿，

県　市　区　丁目　番　号
-　,　Cho-me,　-ku,　-shi,
株式会社　K.K. Seal
K.K
代表取締役
Representative Director:

合同会社　御中
To:　GK.

〈例90　証明書（資本金の払込みを証する書類）〉

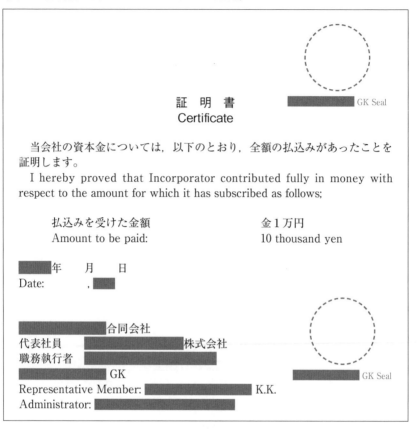

GK Seal

証　明　書
Certificate

当会社の資本金については，以下のとおり，全額の払込みがあったことを証明します。

I hereby proved that Incorporator contributed fully in money with respect to the amount for which it has subscribed as follows;

払込みを受けた金額	金１万円
Amount to be paid:	10 thousand yen

年　月　日
Date: ,

合同会社
代表社員　株式会社
職務執行者
GK
Representative Member: K.K.
Administrator:

GK Seal

〈例91　委任状（代表社員による定款作成のための委任状）〉

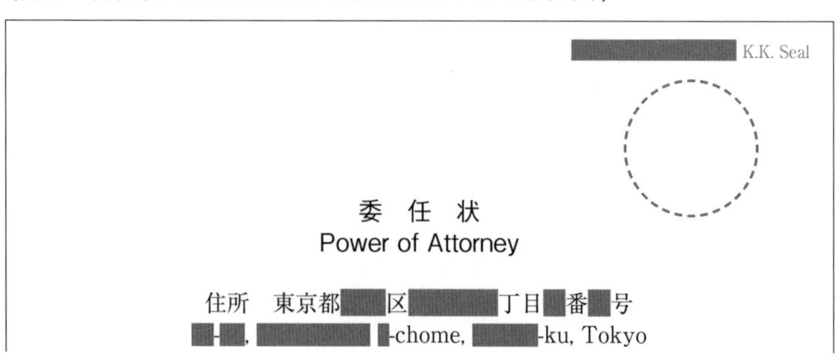

K.K. Seal

委　任　状
Power of Attorney

住所　東京都区丁目番号
-, -chome, -ku, Tokyo

氏名 司法書士 ■■■■

Shiho-shoshi ■■■■

私は，上記の者を代理人と定め，次の権限を委任する。

I hereby appoint the person mentioned above as my attorney-in-fact and authorize him to perform the following:

1．■■■■合同会社の設立に際し，添付のとおり電磁的記録であるその原始定款を作成する手続に関する一切の件

To take any and all procedures necessary to make its original Articles of Incorporation that is electromagnetic record for Incorporation of ■■■■ GK as attached.

2．復代理人の選任を許諾する

To grant authority to appoint Sub-agent

■■年　月　日

, , ■■

■■県■■市■■区■■■■丁目■■番■■号

■-■, ■■■■ ■ Cho-me, ■■■-ku, ■■■-shi, ■■■

有限責任社員 ■■■■株式会社 ■■■■ K.K. Seal

Member with Limited Liability: ■■■■ K.K.

代表取締役 ■■■■

Representative Director: ■■■■

〈例92 委任状（職務執行者による登記申請のための委任状）〉

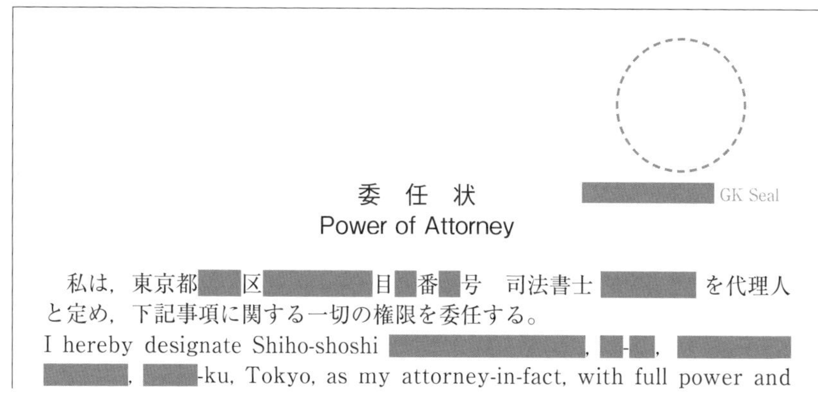

■■■■ GK Seal

委 任 状

Power of Attorney

私は，東京都■■区■■■■目■■番■■号 司法書士 ■■■■ を代理人と定め，下記事項に関する一切の権限を委任する。

I hereby designate Shiho-shoshi ■■■■, ■-■, ■■■■ ■■■■, ■■■-ku, Tokyo, as my attorney-in-fact, with full power and

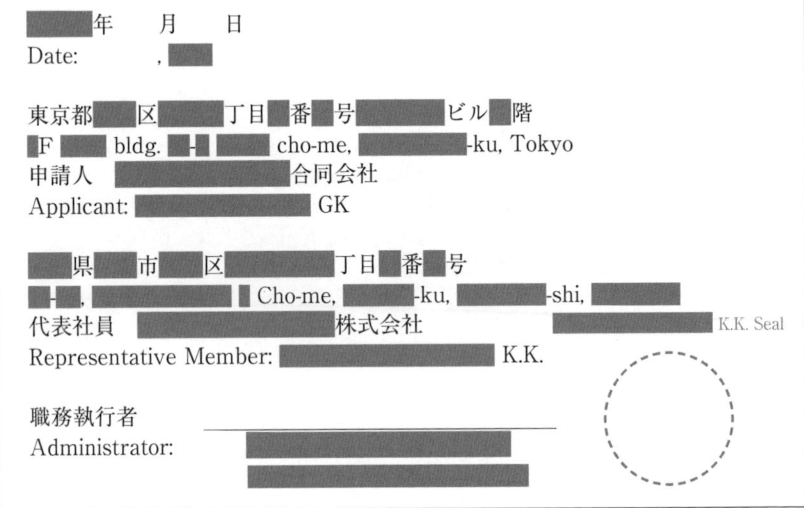
authority to perform the following:

1．当会社の設立登記の申請に関する一切の件
1．To handle all matters relating to the application for company recording of the incorporation of the Company.

2．原本還付の請求並びに受領に関する件
2．To request and receive the original documents related to the above application.

3．上記登記に係る登録免許税の還付金の受領に関する件
3．To receive the registration and license tax refund related to the above application.

年　月　日
Date: ,

東京都　区　丁目　番　号　ビル　階
F　bldg. -　cho-me, -ku, Tokyo
申請人　合同会社
Applicant: GK

県　市　区　丁目　番　号
-, Cho-me, -ku, -shi,
代表社員　株式会社　K.K. Seal
Representative Member: K.K.

職務執行者
Administrator:

2　増資手続

合同会社での増資方法については，新たに社員を加入させて出資する方法と，既存の社員が改めて出資する方法がある。

(1)　新規社員加入増資

例93は，社員増加による増資手続である。

〈例93　業務執行社員決定書（増資手続の決定・社員一人のため）〉

業務執行社員決定書
Written decision of Managing Members

1．業務執行社員の全員一致をもって，次の事項を決定した。
Sole Managing Member of the company unanimously decided the following matter:

資本金の額の増加の件
Capital increase of the Company

増加すべき資本金の額	金35,874,030円
Increased amount	JPY 35,874,030

上記の決定を明確にするため，この決定書を作成し，各業務執行社員はこれに記名押印する。

In order to clarify the above decisions, these written decision have been prepared and the seal beside printed name was affixed by Managing Members who were present at the meeting.

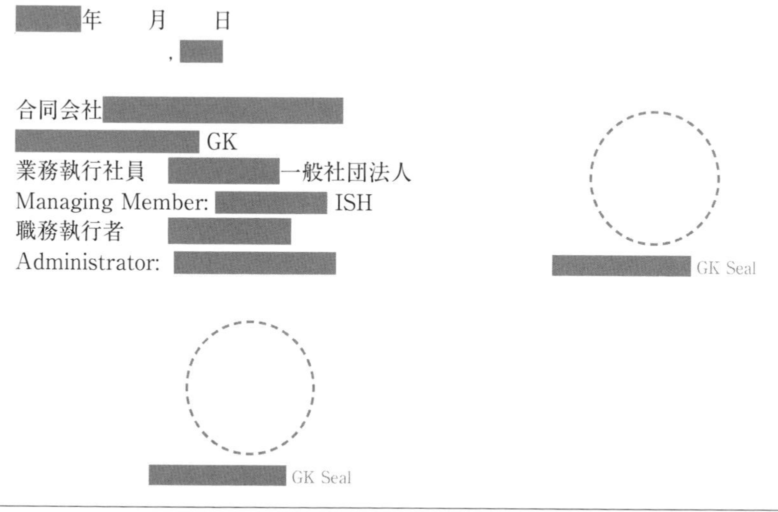
年　月　日
,

合同会社
GK
業務執行社員　一般社団法人
Managing Member: ISH
職務執行者
Administrator:

〈例94　総社員の同意書（新規社員加入についての総社員の同意）〉

総社員の同意書
Written Consent of All Members of GK

合同会社（以下，「当会社」という。）の社員は，下記の事項について同意致します。

The member of the GK (the "Company") hereby consent to the following matters.

記

当会社の新規有限責任社員として，株式会社が出資，加入するため，当会社の定款を下記のとおり変更する。

The Articles of Incorporation of the Company is amended as follows in order for K.K. to invest in and join as a new member with limited liability of the Company.

下線部変更箇所
Changes are indicated by underline

変更前 Before Amendment	変更後 After Amendment
第２章　社員及び出資 CHAPTER 2 MEMBERS AND EQUITY （社員の氏名，住所，出資の目的と価額） 第５条　社員の氏名又は名称，住所，出資の目的及びその価額は，以下のとおりとする。 住所　東京都区 丁目番号 ビル号室 名称　一般社団法人 出資の目的　金銭 出資の価額　金10,000円 (Name of the member, address, purpose of investment and capital) Article 5 The name of each member, address, and invested	第２章　社員及び出資 CHAPTER 2 MEMBERS AND EQUITY （社員の氏名，住所，出資の目的と価額） 第５条　社員の氏名又は名称，住所，出資の目的及びその価額は，以下のとおりとする。 住所　東京都区 丁目番号 ビル号室 名称　一般社団法人 出資の目的　金銭 出資の価額　金10,000円 <u>住所　東京都区</u> <u>丁目番号</u> ビル階 <u>名称</u>

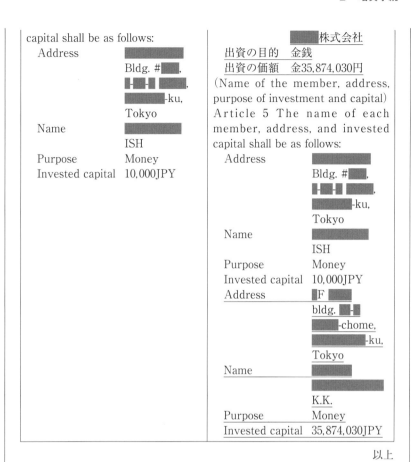

capital shall be as follows: Address　Bldg. #, -- , -ku, Tokyo Name　ISH Purpose　Money Invested capital　10,000JPY	株式会社 出資の目的　金銭 出資の価額　金35,874,030円 (Name of the member, address, purpose of investment and capital) Article 5 The name of each member, address, and invested capital shall be as follows: Address　Bldg. #, -- , -ku, Tokyo Name　ISH Purpose　Money Invested capital　10,000JPY Address　F bldg. -, -chome, -ku, Tokyo Name　K.K. Purpose　Money Invested capital　35,874,030JPY

以上
End

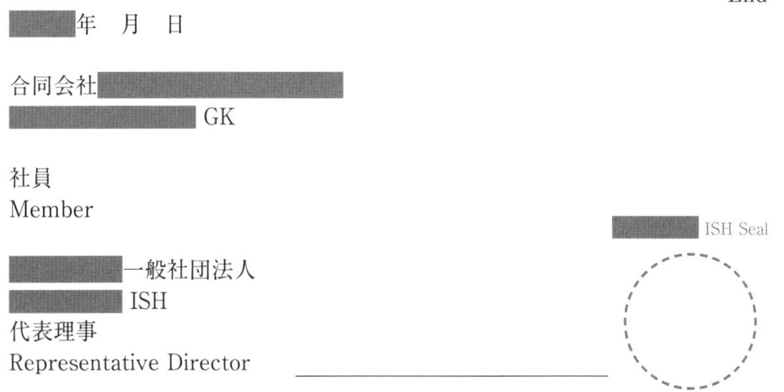

年　月　日

合同会社
GK

社員
Member

ISH Seal

一般社団法人
ISH
代表理事
Representative Director

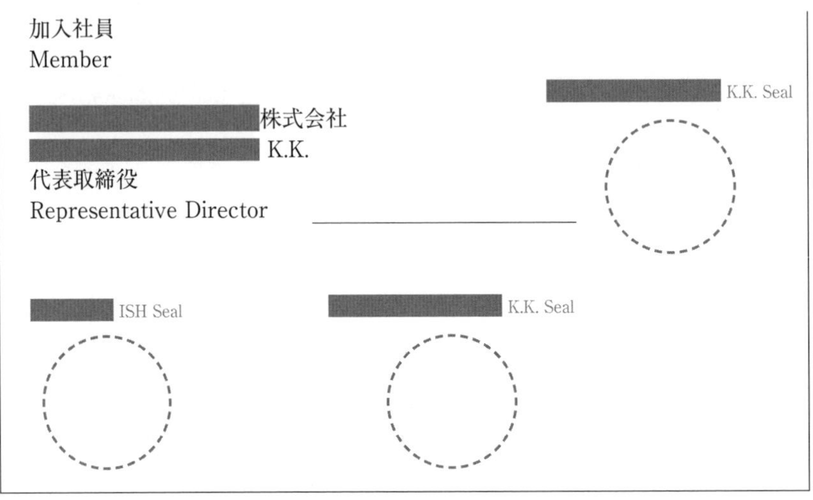
加入社員
Member

株式会社
K.K.
代表取締役
Representative Director

K.K. Seal

ISH Seal

K.K. Seal

〈例95　証明書（抄，資本金の払込みを証する書類）〉

証　明　書
Certificate

当会社の資本金については，以下のとおり，全額の払込みがあったことを証明します。

It is hereby certified that capital of the Company has been fully paid as follows. I hereby prove that Incorporator contributed fully in money with respect to the amount for which it has subscribed as follows;

払込みを受けた金額	金35,874,030円
Amount to be paid:	JPY 35,874,030

〈例96　領収書（抄，新規社員に対しての払込金の領収を証する書類）〉

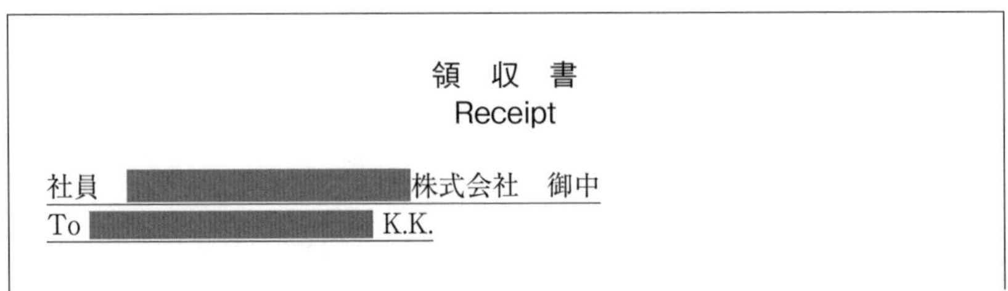
領　収　書
Receipt

社員　株式会社　御中
To　K.K.

金35,874,030円也
ただし，合同会社[redacted]の増資に係る払込金として領収しました。
JPY 35,874,030
We have received as capital Increased amount of [redacted] GK.

〈例97　委任状（抄，増資登記申請のため）〉

委　任　状
Power of Attorney

私は，上記の者を代理人と定め，次の権限を委任する。
I hereby delegate the above individual as my attorney-in-fact with full power and authority to perform the following.

1．当会社の資本金の額の変更登記に関する一切の件
All matters relating to the application for company recording of the capital increase of the Company.

2．原本還付の請求及び受領に関する件
Request of the original documents and receipt thereof.

3．上記登記に係る登録免許税の還付金の受領に関する件
Receive repayment money of registration tax related to the above applications.

⑵　既存社員の増資

例98は既存社員の追加出資による増資手続である。

〈例98　業務執行社員決定書（抄，増資手続の決定・社員一人のため）〉

業務執行社員決定書
Written decision of Managing Members

1．業務執行社員の全員一致をもって，次の事項を決定した。
Sole Managing Member of the company unanimously decided the following matter:

第3章　合同会社

資本金の額の増加の件
Capital increase of the Company

増加すべき資本金の額	金990,000円
Increased amount	JPY 990,000

上記の決定を明確にするため，この決定書を作成し，各業務執行社員はこれに記名押印する。

In order to clarify the above decisions, these written decision have been prepared and the seal beside printed name was affixed by Managing Members who were present at the meeting.

〈例99　総社員の同意書（抄，既存社員の出資増加のため定款変更の同意書）〉

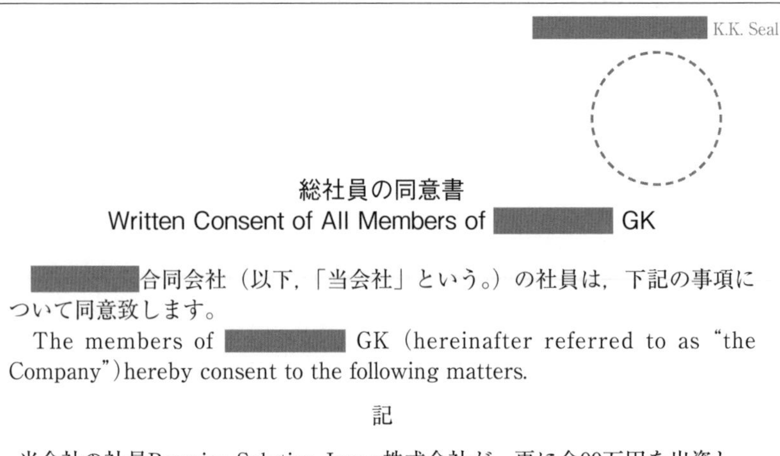

K.K. Seal

総社員の同意書
Written Consent of All Members of GK

合同会社（以下，「当会社」という。）の社員は，下記の事項について同意致します。

The members of GK (hereinafter referred to as "the Company") hereby consent to the following matters.

記

当会社の社員Premier Solution Japan株式会社が，更に金99万円を出資し，その出資額を金100万円とすることに伴い，当会社の定款を下記のとおり変更する。

The Articles of Incorporation of the Company is amended as follows in accordance with K.K., the member of the Company, shall invest additionally 990,000 yen and make its amount investment of 1,000,000 yen.

下線部変更箇所
Amendments are indicated by underline.

変更前 Before Amendment	変更後 After Amendment
第2章　社員及び出資	第2章　社員及び出資

Chapter Ⅱ Members and Capital Contributions	Chapter Ⅱ Members and Capital Contributions
（社員の氏名，住所，出資及び責任） 第５条　当会社の社員の氏名，住所及び出資の価額は次の通りである。 東京都■■区■■丁目■番■号 ■■■ビル７階 ■■■■■■■■株式会社 金１万円 ２　当会社の社員は，すべて有限責任社員とする。	（社員の氏名，住所，出資及び責任） 第５条　当会社の社員の氏名，住所及び出資の価額は次の通りである。 東京都■■区■■丁目■番■号 ■■■ビル７階 ■■■■■■■■株式会社 金100万円 ２　当会社の社員は，すべて有限責任社員とする。
Article 5 (Name, Address and Capital Subscription and Liability of Members) Name, address, capital subscription and liability of the Members are as follows: ■F ■■■ building ■-■ ■-chome, ■■■-ku, Tokyo Japan ■■■■■■■■ KK., 10 thousand yen 2. Members of the Company shall be all the members with Limited Liability	Article 5 (Name, Address and Capital Subscriptions and Liability of Members) Name, address, capital subscriptions and liability of the Members are as follows: ■F ■■■ building ■-■ ■-chome, ■■■-ku, Tokyo Japan ■■■■■■■■ KK., 1,000,000 yen 2. Members of the Company shall be all the members with Limited Liability

〈例100　領収書（抄，資本金の払込みを証する書類）〉

領　収　書

Receipt

社員 ■■■■■■■■株式会社　御中

To ■■■■■■■■ K.K.

金990,000円也

ただし，■■■■合同会社の増資に係る払込金として領収しました。

JPY 990,000

We have received as capital Increased amount of ■■■■ GK.

3　合同会社のM&A

社員の持分権を第三者に譲渡し，譲渡人は持分権の譲渡により退社し，譲受人が新規社員として入社することになる。但し，社員全員の同意を必要とする（会社585条１項）。

〈例101　持分譲渡契約書（第三者へ持分を譲渡する契約）〉

持分譲渡契約書
Agreement for Assignment of Equity Interest

■■■合同会社（以下，「当会社」という。）の業務執行社員である合同会社■■■（以下，「甲」という。）と■■■株式会社（以下，「乙」という。）は，甲が，当会社に対して有する持分金１万円分を金＿＿＿＿円で乙に譲渡することにより当会社を退社することについて合意した。

Managing member of ■■■ GK (the "Company"), ■■■ GK (the "Assignor"), and ■■■ K.K. (the "Assignee") hereby agree that the Assignor resigns the Company as the Assignor assigns its equity interest worth 10,000 yen in the Company for ＿＿＿＿ yen to the Assignee.

この契約の証として，本書２通を作成し，甲乙各署名押印のうえ，各１通を保持する。

IN WITNESS WHEREOF, the parties hereto have prepared and executed this Agreement in duplicate by affixing their name and seal and each party shall keep one copy hereof.

■■年　月　日
, ■■

譲渡人（甲）/Assigner

東京都品川区■■■23番４号■■■７階
7F ■■■. 23-4 ■■■, Shinagawa-ku, Tokyo
合同会社■■■
■■■ GK
代表社員　■■■一般社団法人
Representative Member: ■■■ ISH　　■■■ GK Seal
職務執行者　■■■
Administrator: ■■■

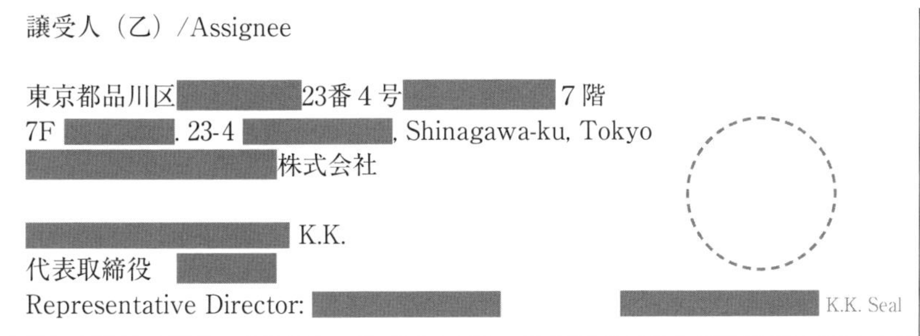
譲受人（乙）/Assignee

東京都品川区■■■■23番４号■■■■７階
7F ■■■■. 23-4 ■■■■, Shinagawa-ku, Tokyo
■■■■株式会社

■■■■ K.K.
代表取締役　■■■■
Representative Director: ■■■■　　■■■■ K.K. Seal

〈例102　総社員の同意書（持分譲受人の加入につき定款変更の同意）〉

総社員の同意書
Written Consent of All Members of ■■■■ GK

■■■■合同会社（以下，「当会社」という。）の総社員は，下記の事項について同意致します。

All of the members of ■■■■ GK (the "Company")hereby undersigned consent to the following matters.

記

当会社の業務執行社員である合同会社■■■■は，その有する当会社の持分全部を，■■年　月　日，■■■■株式会社に譲渡して退社するため，当会社の定款を下記のとおり変更する。

The Articles of Incorporation of the Company is amended as follows due to the resignation of ■■■■ GK Managing Member, after assignment of all equity interest in the Company to ■■■■ Japan K.K. on　　, ■■.

下線部変更箇所
Changes are indicated by underline

変更前 Before Amendment	変更後 After Amendment
第２章　社員及び出資 Chapter Ⅱ Members and Capital Contributions （社員及び出資） 第５条　当会社の社員の氏名又は名称及び住所，社員の出資の目的及びその価額は，次のとおりである。	第２章　社員及び出資 Chapter Ⅱ Members and Capital Contributions （社員及び出資） 第５条　当会社の社員の氏名又は名称及び住所，社員の出資の目的及びその価額は，次のとおりである。

第3章　合同会社

1　金1万円 東京都品川区　23番4号　7階 合同会社	1　金1万円 東京都品川区　23番4号　7階 株式会社
(Members and Capital Contributions) Article 5 The name, address and the purpose and value of the contribution of a member of the company are as follows. 1. Value of Contribution: 10,000 yen Address: 7F　. 23-4　, Shinagawa-ku, Tokyo Name:　GK	(Members and Capital Contributions) Article 5 The name, address and the purpose and value of the contribution of a member of the company are as follows. 1. Value of Contribution: 10,000 yen Address: 7F　. 23-4　, Shinagawa-ku, Tokyo Name:　K.K.
第3章　業務執行権及び代表権 Chapter Ⅲ Right to Execute Business and Authority of Representation	第3章　業務執行権及び代表権 Chapter Ⅲ Right to Execute Business and Authority of Representation
(業務執行社員) 第7条　当会社の業務執行社員は，社員合同会社　とし，当会社の業務を執行するものとする。 (Managing Member) Article 7 The managing member of the company shall be the member,　GK and shall execute business of the Company.	(業務執行社員) 第7条　当会社の業務執行社員は，社員　株式会社とし，当会社の業務を執行するものとする。 (Managing Member) Article 7 The managing member of the company shall be the member,　K.K. and shall execute business of the Company.
(代表社員) 第8条　当会社の代表社員は，合同会社　とする。 (Representative Member) Article 8 The representative member of the company shall be　GK	(代表社員) 第8条　当会社の代表社員は，　株式会社とする。 (Representative Member) Article 8 The representative member of the company shall be　K.K.

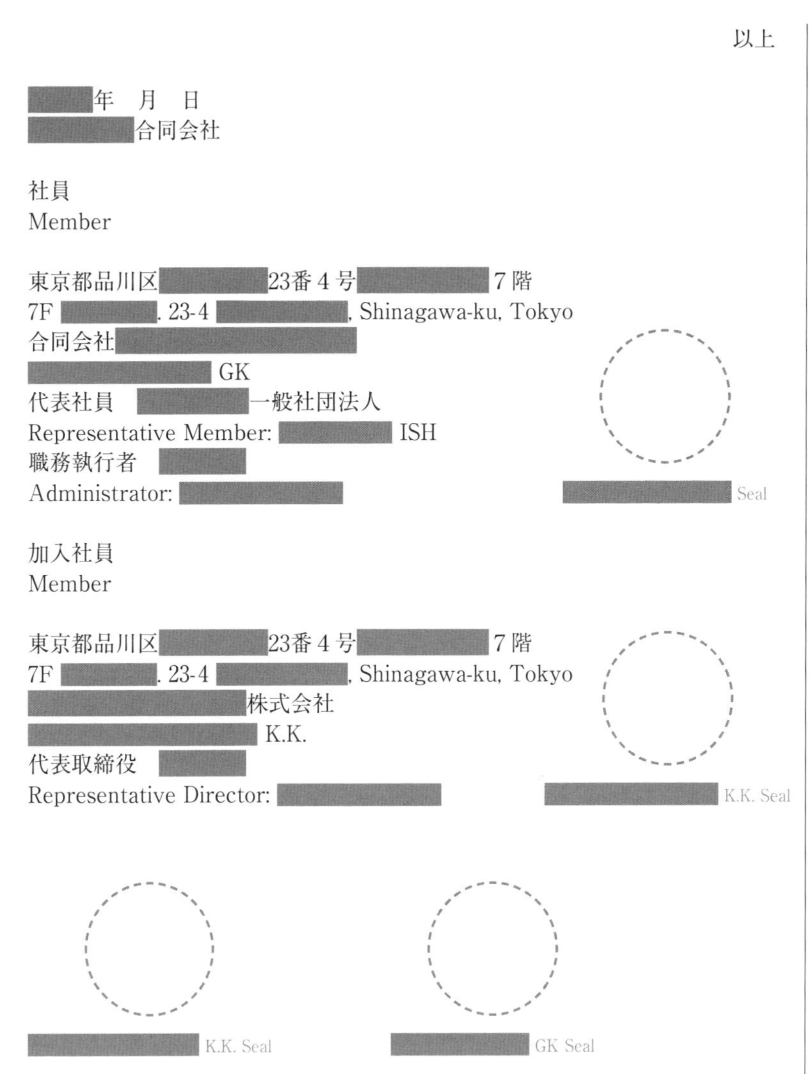

以上

年　月　日
合同会社

社員
Member

東京都品川区23番4号7階
7F . 23-4 , Shinagawa-ku, Tokyo
合同会社
GK
代表社員　一般社団法人
Representative Member: ISH
職務執行者
Administrator:
Seal

加入社員
Member

東京都品川区23番4号7階
7F . 23-4 , Shinagawa-ku, Tokyo
株式会社
K.K.
代表取締役
Representative Director:
K.K. Seal

K.K. Seal
GK Seal

〈例103　就任承諾書（抄，譲受人が代表社員に就任した承諾書）〉

就任承諾書
Written Acceptance of Position

私は，　　年　月　日，　　　　合同会社の代表社員の職務執行者に定められたので，その就任を承諾します。
Following my election as the Administrator (shokumu shikko-sha) of Representative Member (*daihyo shain*) of 　　　　 GK, I hereby accept the aforesaid appointment.

〈例104　職務執行者に関する決定書（抄，代表社員が法人の場合）〉

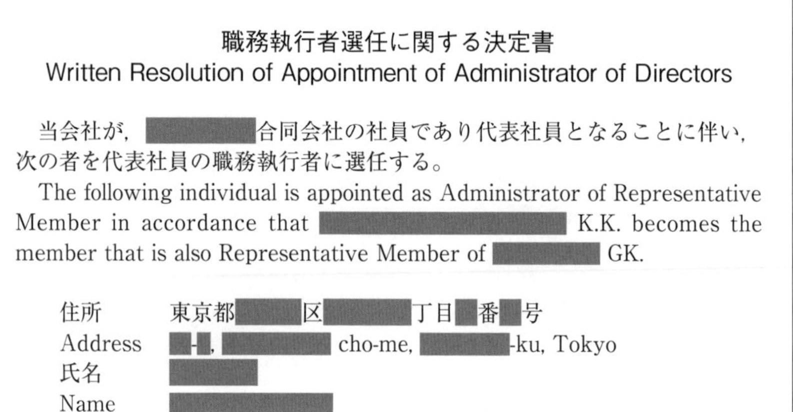

職務執行者選任に関する決定書
Written Resolution of Appointment of Administrator of Directors

当会社が，　　　　合同会社の社員であり代表社員となることに伴い，次の者を代表社員の職務執行者に選任する。
The following individual is appointed as Administrator of Representative Member in accordance that 　　　　 K.K. becomes the member that is also Representative Member of 　　　　 GK.

住所　東京都　　区　　　丁目　番　号
Address 　-　, 　　　 cho-me, 　　　 -ku, Tokyo
氏名
Name

〈例105　就任承諾書（抄，職務執行者の就任の承諾）〉

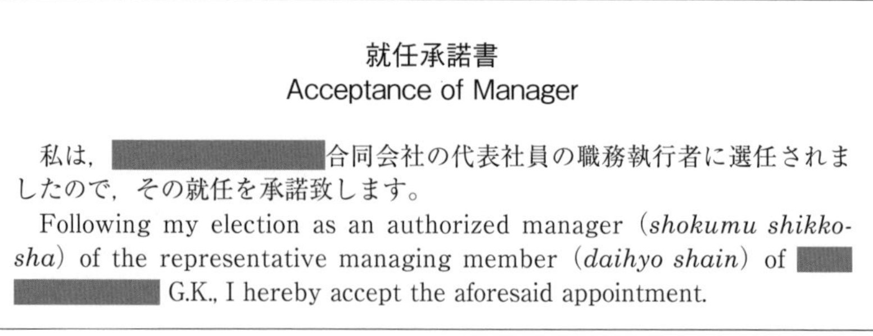

就任承諾書
Acceptance of Manager

私は，　　　　合同会社の代表社員の職務執行者に選任されましたので，その就任を承諾致します。
Following my election as an authorized manager (*shokumu shikko-sha*) of the representative managing member (*daihyo shain*) of 　　　　 G.K., I hereby accept the aforesaid appointment.

4　外国会社の業務執行者及び職務執行者の交代

例106は，LLC外国会社が日本の合同会社の代表者に就任した場合で，その代表社員たるLLC外国会社の財務役（Treasurer）が会社を代表して，職務執行者を選任した旨並びにその変更登記申請に関する権限を有する旨の宣誓供述書である。

〈例106－1　宣誓供述書（外国会社が代表社員である旨，職務執行者を選任した旨並びに職務執行者に対する保証に関して）〉

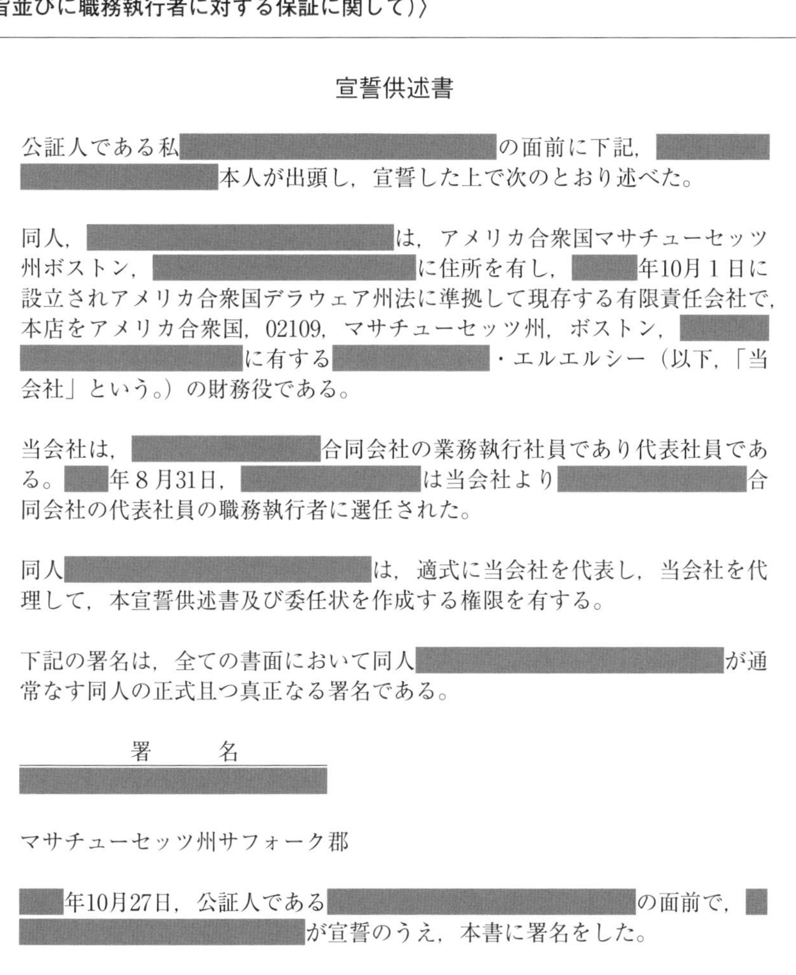

宣誓供述書

公証人である私　　の面前に下記，　　本人が出頭し，宣誓した上で次のとおり述べた。

同人，　　は，アメリカ合衆国マサチューセッツ州ボストン，　　に住所を有し，　　年10月１日に設立されアメリカ合衆国デラウェア州法に準拠して現存する有限責任会社で，本店をアメリカ合衆国，02109，マサチューセッツ州，ボストン，　　に有する　　・エルエルシー（以下，「当会社」という。）の財務役である。

当会社は，　　合同会社の業務執行社員であり代表社員である。　　年８月31日，　　は当会社より　　合同会社の代表社員の職務執行者に選任された。

同人　　は，適式に当会社を代表し，当会社を代理して，本宣誓供述書及び委任状を作成する権限を有する。

下記の署名は，全ての書面において同人　　が通常なす同人の正式且つ真正なる署名である。

署　　名

マサチューセッツ州サフォーク郡

　　年10月27日，公証人である　　の面前で，　　が宣誓のうえ，本書に署名をした。

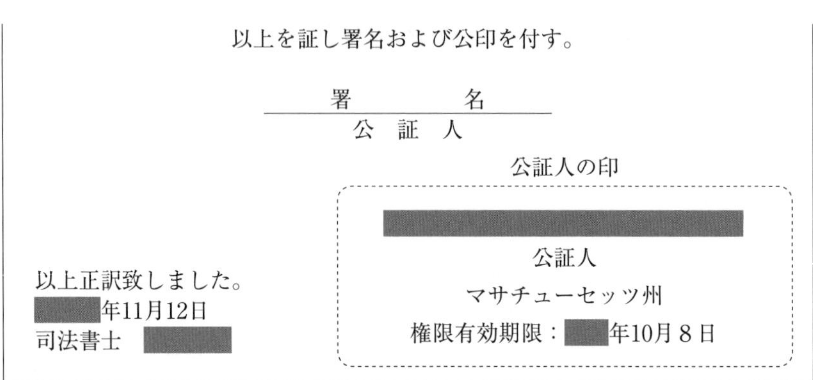

以上を証し署名および公印を付す。

署　　名

公　証　人

公証人の印

公証人

マサチューセッツ州

権限有効期限：年10月８日

以上正訳致しました。

年11月12日

司法書士

〈例106－２　Affidavit（外国会社が代表社員である旨，職務執行者を選任した旨並びに職務執行者に対する保証に関する宣誓供述書）〉

AFFIDAVIT

Before me, ______________, a/the Notary Public, duly commissioned and qualified, personally appeared , who being duly sworn, deposed and said:

THAT he, , presently residing at , Boston, Massachusetts , U.S.A., is the Treasurer of LLC (hereinafter the "Company"), which is a limited liability company formed on October 1, and existing under the laws of the State of Delaware, the United States of America, and has its registered office located at Boston, MA , U.S.A.

THAT the Company is the duly authorized managing member (*gyoumu shikko shain*) and representative managing member (*daihyo shain*) of GK, a Japan godo kaisha, and has been appointed by the Company as the duly authorized manager (*shokumu shikko-sha*) for the representative managing member of GK as of August 31, .

THAT he is duly authorized to represent the Company, with respect to the registration of the change of the representative managing member of GK and has been authorized and vested with the power to execute this Affidavit on behalf of the Company.

THAT the following signature is his true and genuine signature which he customarily uses for execution of any and all documents which require his signature.

____

COMMONWEALTH OF MASSACHUSETTS

COUNTY OF SUFFOLK

On ____________, [redacted] before me, ________________ personally appeared [redacted] personally known to me to be the person whose name is subscribed to the within instrument and acknowledged to me that he/she executed the same in his/her authorized capacities and that by his/her signature on the instrument the person or the entity upon behalf of which the person acted, executed the instrument.

Witness my hand and official seal

____

[Signature of Notary]

[Seal]

[redacted] v2

〈例107　就任承諾書（職務執行者の就任を承諾）〉

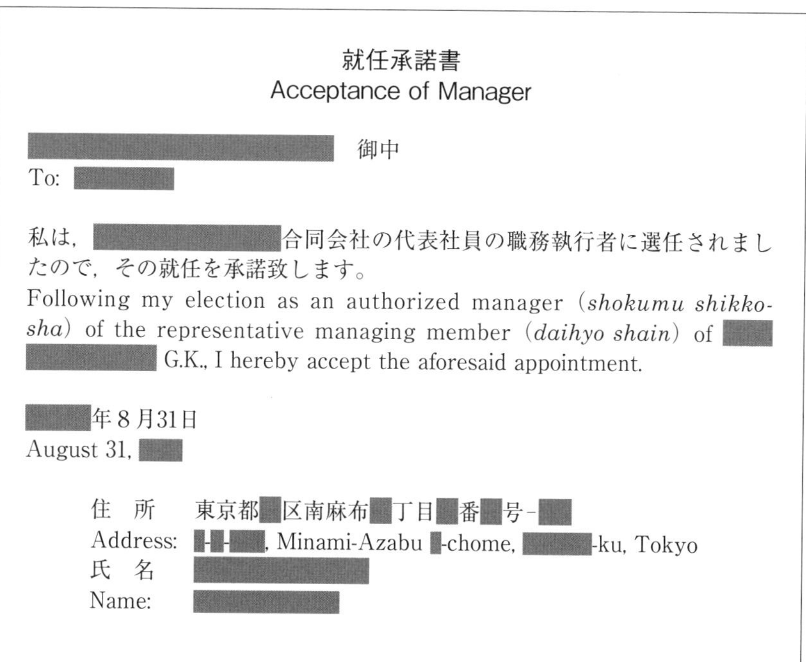

就任承諾書
Acceptance of Manager

[redacted] 御中
To: [redacted]

私は，[redacted]合同会社の代表社員の職務執行者に選任されましたので，その就任を承諾致します。
Following my election as an authorized manager (*shokumu shikko-sha*) of the representative managing member (*daihyo shain*) of [redacted] G.K., I hereby accept the aforesaid appointment.

[redacted]年８月31日
August 31, [redacted]

住　所　東京都[redacted]区南麻布[redacted]丁目[redacted]番[redacted]号－[redacted]
Address: [redacted], Minami-Azabu [redacted]-chome, [redacted]-ku, Tokyo
氏　名　[redacted]
Name: [redacted]

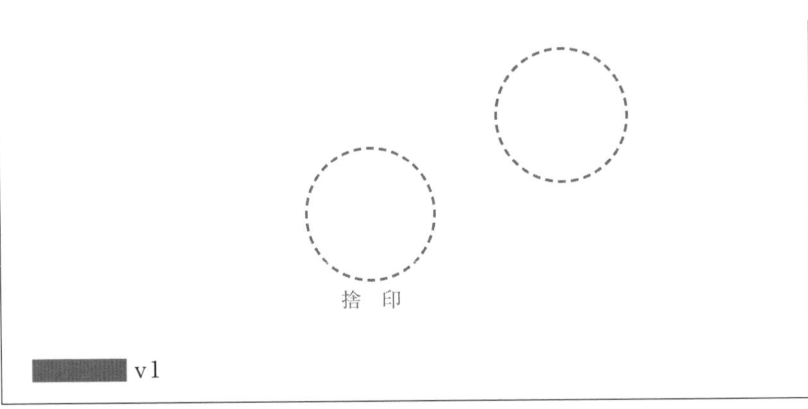

〈例108　署名証明書（職務執行者が外国籍のため印鑑証明書に代替）〉

CERTIFICATE OF SIGNATURE

I, ■■■■■, presently residing at ■ Devonshire Street, Boston, Massachusetts ■■■, U.S.A., certify that the signature that appears below is, for all intents and purposes, my true and correct signature.

____
■■■■■

COMMONWEALTH OF MASSACHUSETTS

COUNTY OF SUFFOLK

On ______________, ■■ before me, __________________ personally appeared ■■■■■ personally known to me to be the person whose name is subscribed to the within instrument and acknowledged to me that he/she executed the same in her authorized capacities and that by his/her signature on the instrument the person or the entity upon behalf of which the person acted, executed the instrument.

Witness my hand and official seal

____

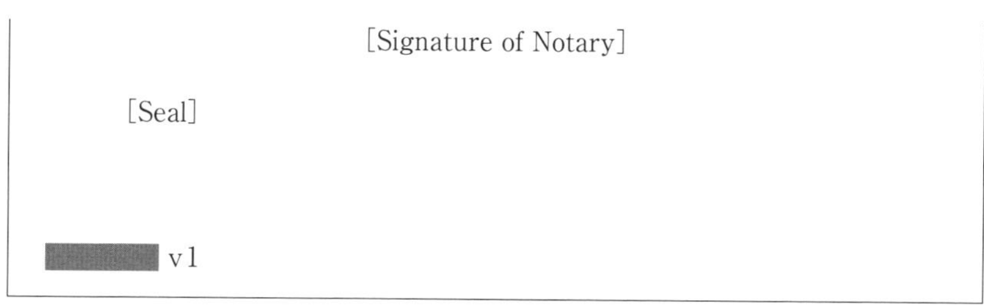
[Signature of Notary]

[Seal]

████ v1

〈例109　保証書（代表社員の職務執行者の代表印を保証）〉

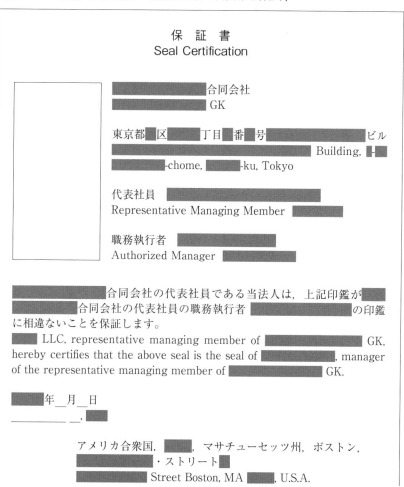

保　証　書
Seal Certification

████合同会社
████ GK

東京都█区██丁目█番█号████ビル
████ Building, █-█
████-chome, ████-ku, Tokyo

代表社員 ████
Representative Managing Member ████

職務執行者 ████
Authorized Manager ████

████合同会社の代表社員である当法人は，上記印鑑が████合同会社の代表社員の職務執行者 ████の印鑑に相違ないことを保証します。
████ LLC, representative managing member of ████ GK, hereby certifies that the above seal is the seal of ████, manager of the representative managing member of ████ GK.

████年__月__日
_________ __, ████

アメリカ合衆国，████，マサチューセッツ州，ボストン，
████・ストリート█
████ Street Boston, MA ████, U.S.A.

[redacted]・エルエルシー
FMR LLC

____
Name: [redacted]
Title: Treasurer

____
[redacted]

東京法務局 [redacted]出張所　御中
To: Tokyo Legal Affairs Bureau, [redacted] branch

[redacted] v1

〈例110　委任状（抄，職務執行者変更登記用）〉

委　任　状
(Power of Attorney)

私は，上記の者を代理人と定め当会社のために下記の行為をなす権限を授与します。
The undersigned does hereby appoint and authorize the above person to act its lawful attorney and to conduct the following acts on behalf of the undersigned:

1．当会社の職務執行者の変更登記に関する一切の件
To carry out all necessary registration procedures in connection with change of manager of [redacted] GK;
2．原本還付請求ならびに受領の件
To request the return of original documents and to receive them;
3．上記登記申請の取下げ手続をなす件
To proceed to dismiss this application; and
4．上記事項遂行のため，復代理人を選任する件
To appoint a substitute attorney or substitute attorneys for the performance of the foregoing acts.

〈例111　辞任届（抄，代表社員の辞任）〉

辞　任　届
Notice of Resignation

私は，█████年　月　日をもって，██████████合同会社の代表社員の職務執行者を辞任したいので，お届けいたします。
I do hereby give notice of my resignation as an administrator（shokumu-shikkosha）of representative member（daihyo-shain）of ██████████ GK as of 　　　　, ███.

〈例112　辞任届（抄，職務執行者の辞任）〉

辞　任　届
RESIGNATION

私は，██████████████合同会社の代表社員の職務執行者を███年8月31日をもって辞任いたしたくここに届け出ます。
I hereby tender my resignation as authorized manager（*shokumu shikko-sha*）of representative managing member（*daihyo shain*）of ████ ██████████ GK effective as of August 31, ███.

5　解散・清算

合同会社は，①定款で定めた存続期間の満了，②定款で定めた解散の事由の発生，③総社員の同意，④社員が欠けたとき，⑤合併により会社が消滅するとき，⑥破産手続の開始の決定，⑦公益確保を理由とする裁判所の解散命令又は解散訴訟判決による解散，以上七つの事由により解散することになる（会社641条）。解散したときは，清算の目的の範囲内において清算が結了するまでなお存続することになる（会社645条）。そこで，その期間中の清算手続の権限を持つものとして清算人の選任が必要になる（646条）。

例113は，社員を一人にして解散・清算手続が容易になるよう，社員が持分を一人の社員に譲渡して，最後の一人の社員が清算人に就任し，清算結了手続をする場合の書式である。

〈例113　持分譲渡契約（抄，社員一人にするため社員間で持分譲渡契約）〉

持分譲渡契約書
Agreement for Assignment of Equity Interest

■■■■■■■■合同会社（以下，「当会社」という。）の業務執行社員である■■■■（以下，「甲」という。）と当会社の社員である■■■■■■■■■■■■■■（以下，「乙」という。）は，甲が，当会社に対して有する持分金１万円分を金■■円で乙に譲渡することにより当会社を退社することについて合意した。

Managing Member of ■■■■■■ GK (the "Company"), ■■■■ (the "Assignor"), and Member of the Company, ■■■■■■■■■■ LIMITED, (the "Assignee")hereby agree that the Assignor resigns the Company as the Assignor assigns its equity interest worth 10,000 yen in the Company for ＿＿＿＿＿yen to the Assignee.

〈例114　総社員同意書（社員の持分譲渡による社員，持分の変動による定款変更のための社員の同意）〉

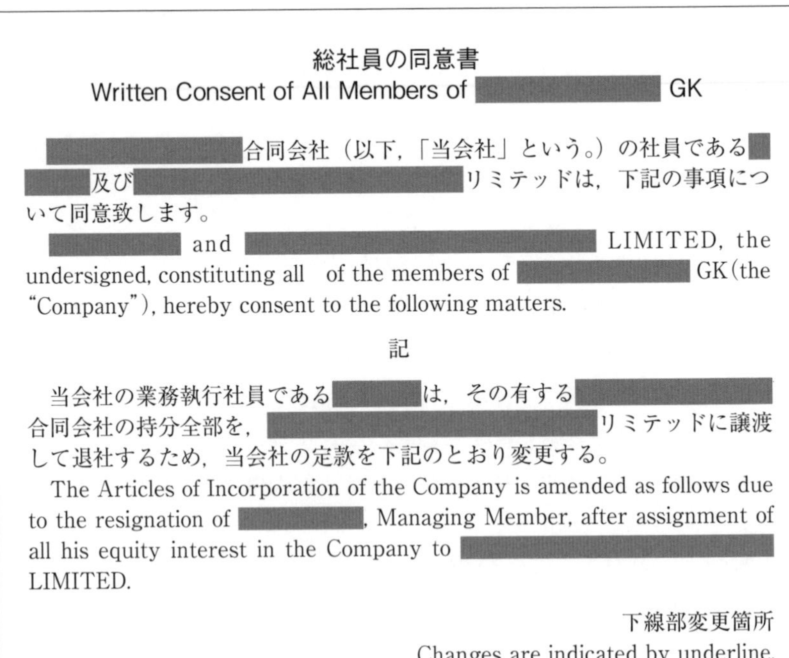

総社員の同意書
Written Consent of All Members of ■■■■■■ GK

■■■■■■■■合同会社（以下，「当会社」という。）の社員である■■■■及び■■■■■■■■■■■■■■リミテッドは，下記の事項について同意致します。

■■■■ and ■■■■■■■■■■ LIMITED, the undersigned, constituting all of the members of ■■■■■■ GK(the "Company"), hereby consent to the following matters.

記

当会社の業務執行社員である■■■■は，その有する■■■■■■■■合同会社の持分全部を，■■■■■■■■■■■■■■リミテッドに譲渡して退社するため，当会社の定款を下記のとおり変更する。

The Articles of Incorporation of the Company is amended as follows due to the resignation of ■■■■, Managing Member, after assignment of all his equity interest in the Company to ■■■■■■■■■■ LIMITED.

下線部変更箇所
Changes are indicated by underline.

変更前 Before Amendment	変更後 After Amendment
第２章　社員及び出資 Chapter Ⅱ Members and Capital Contributions 第５条（社員及び出資） Article 5 Members and Capital Contributions 社員は全員有限責任社員とし，社員の名称及び住所並びに出資の目的及びその価額は，次のとおりである。 All members shall be limited liability members. The name, address and the purpose and value of the contribution of each member are as follows. 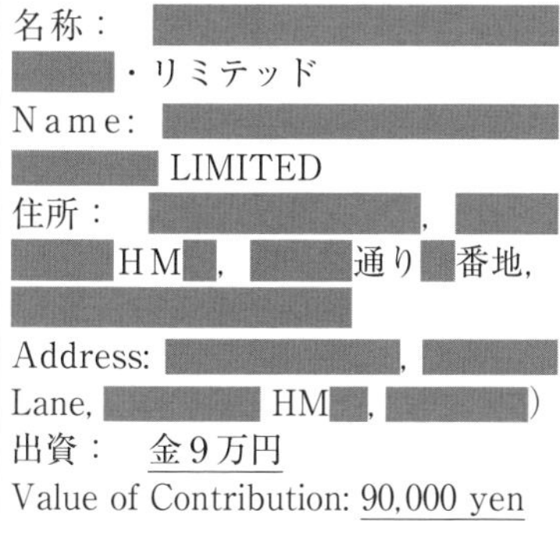 名称： ・リミテッド Name: LIMITED 住所：　, HM　,　通り　番地, Address:　, Lane,　HM　,　) 出資：　金９万円 Value of Contribution: 90,000 yen 氏名： Name: 住所：　東京都　区　丁目 番　号 Address:　-　, -chome,　-ku, Tokyo 出資：　金１万円 Value of Contribution: 10,000 yen	第２章　社員及び出資 Chapter Ⅱ Members and Capital Contributions 第５条（社員及び出資） Article 5 Members and Capital Contributions 社員は全員有限責任社員とし，社員の名称及び住所並びに出資の目的及びその価額は，次のとおりである。 All members shall be limited liability members. The name, address and the purpose and value of the contribution of each member are as follows. 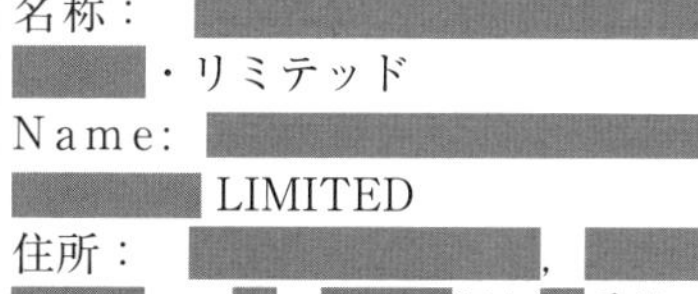 名称： ・リミテッド Name: LIMITED 住所：　, HM　,　通り　番地, Address:　, Lane, Pembroke HM19, Bermuda) 出資：　金10万円 Value of Contribution: 100,000 yen （以下，削除） (The rest is deleted.)

第3章　合同会社

第３章　業務執行 Chapter Ⅲ Business Operations	第３章　業務執行 Chapter Ⅲ Business Operations
第６条（業務執行） Article 6 Business Operations	第６条（業務執行） Article 6 Business Operations
２．当会社の業務執行社員は，■■■とする。 （以下，記載省略） 2. The Managing Member of the Company shall be ■■■. (The rest is omitted.)	２．当会社の業務執行社員は，■■■リミテッドとする。 （以下，記載省略） 2. The Managing Member of the Company shall be ■■■ LIMITED. (The rest is omitted.)
第５章　計算 Chapter　V Calculation	第５章　計算 Chapter　V Calculation
第11条（利益の配当） Article 11　Distribution of Profit	（削除） (Deleted)
利益の配当は，■■■・■■■・リミテッドと■■■に対して，99,999.9999：0.0001の配当割合で行う。 Profit shall be distributed on a basis; 99,999.999% to ■■■ LIMITED and 0.0001% to ■■■.	

以上
END

〈例115　職務執行者選任決定書（代表社員による職務執行者を選任）〉

職務執行者選任決定書
Written Resolution of Appointment of Administrator

年　月　日，取締役 は，下記の事項を決定した。
On ________, , Director Allan Pelvang has determined the following matter.

記

当会社が， 合同会社の唯一の社員であり代表社員となることに伴い，次の者を代表社員の職務執行者に選任する。
The following individual is appointed as Administrator of Representative Member in accordance that Limited becomes the sole member that is also Representative Member of GK.

東京都 区 丁目 番 - 号
Unit #, -, -chome, -ku, Tokyo

上記の決定を明確にするため，本決定書を作成し，取締役がこれに記名押印する。
IN WITNESS WHEREOF, this Written Resolution is prepared and Director affixes the name and seal hereof.

〈例116　就任承諾書（抄，職務執行者の就任の承諾）〉

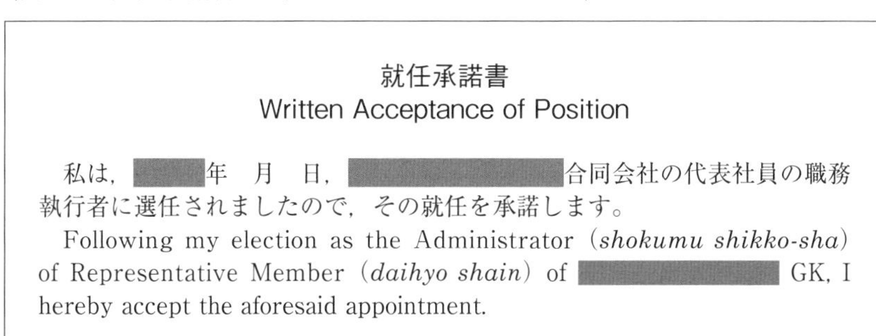
就任承諾書
Written Acceptance of Position

私は， 年　月　日， 合同会社の代表社員の職務執行者に選任されましたので，その就任を承諾します。
Following my election as the Administrator (*shokumu shikko-sha*) of Representative Member (*daihyo shain*) of GK, I hereby accept the aforesaid appointment.

〈例117　保証書（代表社員の職務執行者の代表社員であることの保証）〉

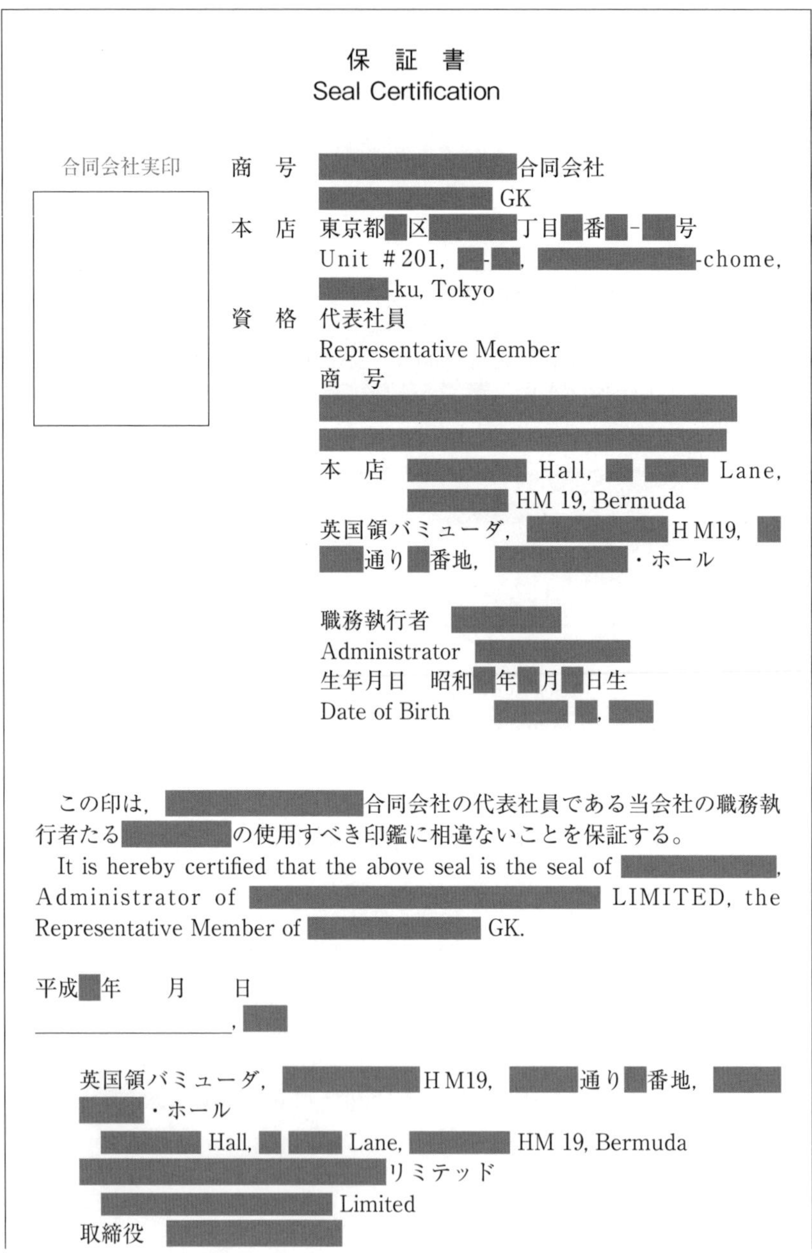

保　証　書
Seal Certification

合同会社実印

商　号　合同会社
GK

本　店　東京都 区 丁目 番 - 号
Unit #201, -, -chome,
-ku, Tokyo

資　格　代表社員
Representative Member
商　号

本　店　Hall, Lane,
HM 19, Bermuda
英国領バミューダ, HM19,
通り 番地, ・ホール

職務執行者
Administrator
生年月日　昭和 年 月 日生
Date of Birth ,

この印は, 合同会社の代表社員である当会社の職務執行者たる の使用すべき印鑑に相違ないことを保証する。
It is hereby certified that the above seal is the seal of , Administrator of LIMITED, the Representative Member of GK.

平成 年　　月　　日
＿＿＿＿＿＿＿＿＿＿,

英国領バミューダ, HM19, 通り 番地, ・ホール
Hall, Lane, HM 19, Bermuda
リミテッド
Limited
取締役

Director ████████　　　　________________________
Signature　署名

〈例118　委任状（抄，業務執行社員，代表社員（職務執行者）変更登記用）〉

委　任　状
Power of Attorney

私は，上記の者を代理人と定め，次の権限を委任する。
I hereby delegate the above individual as my attorney-in-fact with full power and authority to perform the following

1．当会社の業務執行社員，代表社員（代表社員の職務執行者の登記を含む）の変更登記に関する一切の件
All matters regarding registrations for change in Managing Member and Representative Member（including the registration for Administrator of Representative Member）of our company.

2．原本還付の請求及び受領に関する件
Request of the original documents and receipt thereof.

〈例119　同意書（代表社員による解散，清算人選任についての同意）〉

同　意　書
Written Consent of All Members of ████████ GK

当会社の解散に関し，社員全員の一致をもって次の事項を決議する。
In respect to the dissolution of this company, the following matters are resolved with unanimous consent of all members of ████████ GK (hereinafter the "Company").

1．当会社は，████年　月　日総社員の同意により解散するものとする。
On __________, ███, the Company shall be dissolved with consent of all members of the Company.

1．当会社の解散に伴い，清算人として次の者を選任する。
Upon the dissolution of the Company, the following individual is appointed as Liquidator.
東京都██区██████丁目██番██-██号

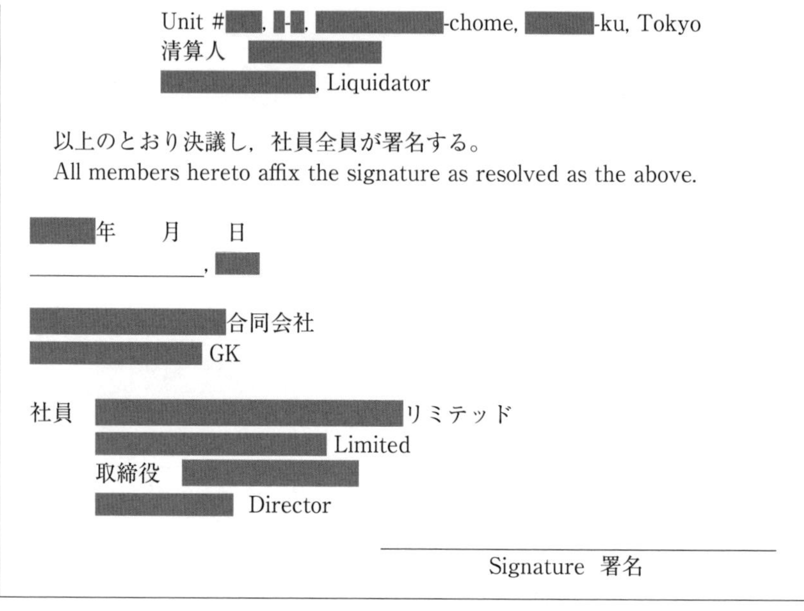

Unit #[redacted], [redacted], [redacted]-chome, [redacted]-ku, Tokyo
清算人　[redacted]
[redacted], Liquidator

以上のとおり決議し，社員全員が署名する。
All members hereto affix the signature as resolved as the above.

[redacted]年　　月　　日
________________, [redacted]

[redacted]合同会社
[redacted] GK

社員　[redacted]リミテッド
[redacted] Limited
取締役　[redacted]
[redacted] Director

Signature　署名

〈例120　同意書（職務執行者の清算人選任についての同意）〉

会社代表印

同　意　書
Written Consent of All Managing Members of [redacted] GK

当会社の清算人の選任に関し，業務執行社員全員の一致をもって次の事項を決議する。
In respect to the appointment of liquidator of [redacted] GK (hereinafter the "Company"), the following matters are resolved with unanimous consent of all managing members of the Company.

当会社の解散に伴い，清算人として次の者を選任する。
Upon the dissolution of the Company, the following individual is appointed as Liquidator.

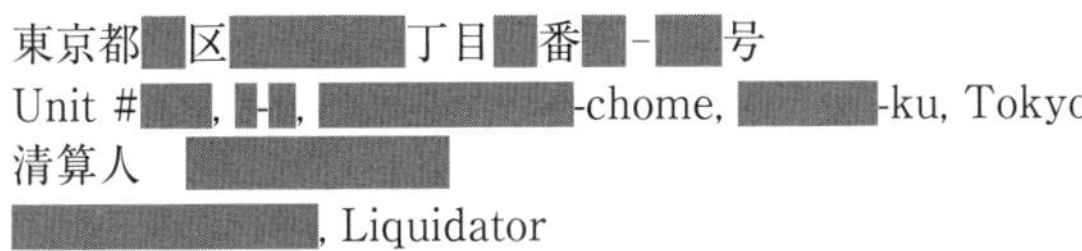

東京都 区 丁目 番 - 号
Unit #, -, -chome, -ku, Tokyo
清算人
, Liquidator

以上のとおり決議し，業務執行社員全員が署名する。

All managing members hereto affix the signature as resolved as the above.

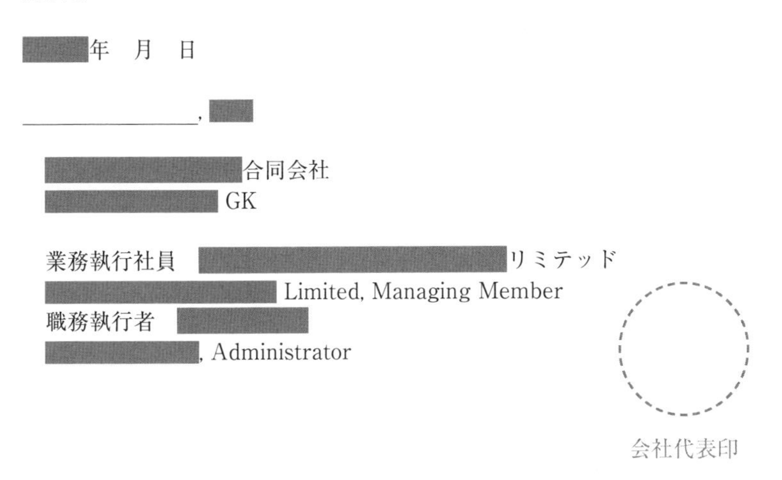

年　月　日

______________,

合同会社
GK

業務執行社員 リミテッド
Limited, Managing Member
職務執行者
, Administrator

会社代表印

〈例121　就任承諾書（清算人としての就任の承諾）〉

就任承諾書
Written Acceptance of Position

私は，年　月　日貴社の清算人に選任されましたので，その就任を承諾致します。

Following my election as the Liquidator (*seisan nin*) of GK, I hereby accept the aforesaid appointment.

年　月　日

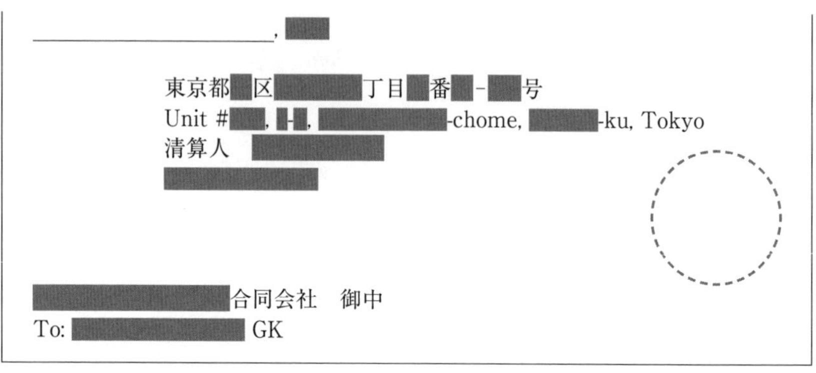
＿＿＿＿＿＿＿＿＿＿＿＿＿＿＿＿, ■■

東京都■区■■■丁目■番■-■号
Unit #■, ■-■, ■■■-chome, ■■■-ku, Tokyo
清算人　■■■
■■■

■■■合同会社　御中
To: ■■■ GK

〈例122－１　催告書（官報公告用）〉

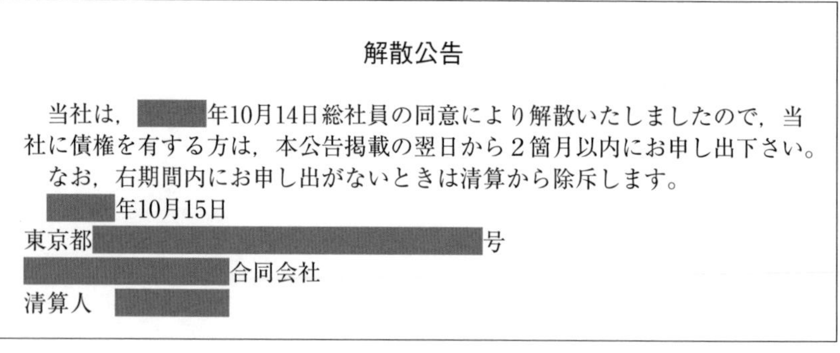
解散公告

当社は，■■年10月14日総社員の同意により解散いたしましたので，当社に債権を有する方は，本公告掲載の翌日から２箇月以内にお申し出下さい。
なお，右期間内にお申し出がないときは清算から除斥します。
■■年10月15日
東京都■■■号
■■■合同会社
清算人　■■■

（注）実際は縦組みで作成

〈例122－２　催告書（クライアント報告用，英文）〉

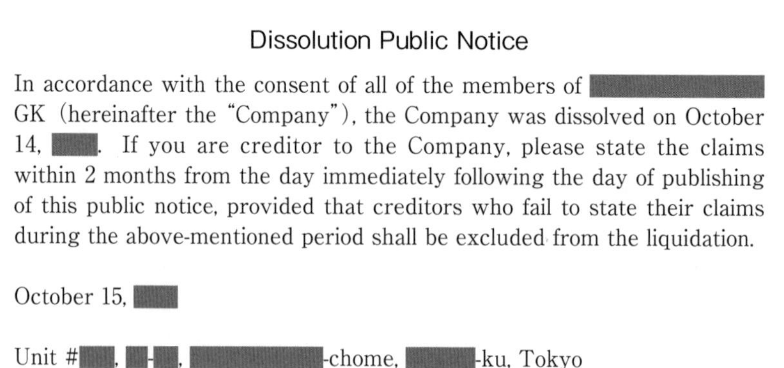
Dissolution Public Notice

In accordance with the consent of all of the members of ■■■ GK (hereinafter the "Company"), the Company was dissolved on October 14, ■■. If you are creditor to the Company, please state the claims within 2 months from the day immediately following the day of publishing of this public notice, provided that creditors who fail to state their claims during the above-mentioned period shall be excluded from the liquidation.

October 15, ■■

Unit #■, ■-■, ■■■-chome, ■■■-ku, Tokyo

GK
, Liquidator

〈例123　決算報告書（清算結了に際しての決算報告）〉

会社代表印
Seal

決　算　報　告　書
Settlement of Accounts

計　算　書 Financial Statement	
貸　方 Credit	借　方 Debit
合　計　　円 Total　　Yen	合　計　　円 Total　　Yen

財　産　目　録 Inventory of Property	
資　産　の　部 Asset	負　債　の　部 Liability
合　計　　円 Total　　Yen	合　計　　円 Total　　Yen

1．借入金：　金　　円（　年　月　日返済）
Debt:　　yen（Paid back on　　）

1．買掛金：　金　　円（　年　月　日返済）
Account Payable:　　yen（Paid back on　　）

1．売掛金：　金　　円（　年　月　日返済）
Account Receivable:　　yen（Collected on　　）

1．残余財産の額：　金　　円

第3章　合同会社

Amount of Residual Asset: ________________ yen

1. ████年　月　日，上記残余財産を，各社員の出資額に応じて分配した。
On　　　, ███, the above-mentioned residual asset is allocated on a pro rata basis in accordance with the amount of contribution by respective members.

上記のとおり清算結了したことを報告する。
It is hereby reported that the liquidation is completed as above.

████年　月　日
________________, ███

東京都█区█████丁目█番█-██号
Unit #██, █-█, ████████-chome, ████-ku, Tokyo
██████████合同会社
████████ GK
清算人 ████████
████████, Liquidator

会社代表印
Seal

〈例124　清算結了承認書（社員による清算結了の承認）〉

清算結了承認書
Authorization of Completion of Liquidation

当会社の清算は，下記決算書のとおり結了したことを承認する。
It is hereby authorized that the liquidation of ██████████ GK is completed as described below.

計　算　書 Financial Statement	
貸　方 Credit	借　方 Debit

合　計　　　　　　円 Total　　　　　　Yen	合　計　　　　　　円 Total　　　　　　Yen

財　産　目　録 Inventory of Property	
資　産　の　部 Asset	負　債　の　部 Liability
合　計　　　　　　円 Total　　　　　　Yen	合　計　　　　　　円 Total　　　　　　Yen

1．借入金：　金　　　　　円（平成　年　月　日返済）
Debt:　　　　　yen（Paid back on　　　　）

1．買掛金：　金　　　　　円（平成　年　月　日返済）
Account Payable:　　　　　yen（Paid back on　　　　）

1．売掛金：　金　　　　　円（████年　月　日返済）
Account Receivable:　　　　　yen（Collected on　　　　）

1．残余財産の額：　金　　　　　円
Amount of Residual Asset:　　　　　yen

1．████年　月　日，上記残余財産を，各社員の出資額に応じて分配した。
On　　　, ███, the above-mentioned residual asset is allocated on a pro rata basis in accordance with the amount of contribution by respective members.

████年　月　日
＿＿＿＿＿＿＿＿, ███

████████合同会社

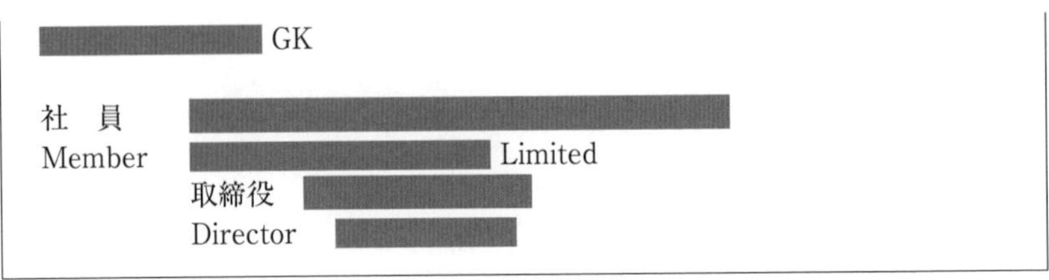

GK

社　員
Member　　　　Limited
取締役
Director

〈例125　委任状（抄，清算結了登記用）〉

委　任　状
Power of Attorney

私は，上記の者を代理人と定め，次の権限を委任する。

I hereby delegate the above individual as my attorney-in-fact with full power and authority to perform the following.

1．当会社の清算結了の登記申請に関する一切の件
All matters regarding registration for completion of liquidation of GK.

1．原本還付の請求及び受領に関する件
Request of the original documents and receipt thereof.

第４章　一般社団法人，一般財団法人

一般社団法人又は一般財団法人とは，「一般社団法人及び一般財団法人に関する法律」に基づき設立される非営利法人であり，二人以上の者（社員）により設立されるのが株式会社又は合同会社との相違点である。また，社員には個人であれ，法人であれ社員として参加ができ，法人の重要事項を議決する最高意思決定機関の社員総会に出席し，その議決権を行使することができる。

一般社団法人又は一般財団法人は，必ずしも公益的な事業を行う必要はなく，営利法人と同様に基本的にはどのような事業でも事由に行うことができる。非営利性を担保（剰余利益については，それを社員に配当できない。）しておけば，収益を上げることを目的とすることも法人内部の共益を目的とすることもできる，

1　一般社団法人の設立

一般社団法人を設立するには，社員になろうとする者が，共同して定款を作成し，その全員がこれに署名し，又は記名押印しなければならない（一般法人10条１項)。

定款には，①目的，②名称，③主たる事務所の所在地，④設立時社員の氏名又は名称及び住所，⑤社員の資格の得喪に関する規定，⑥公告方法，⑦事業年度を記載しなければならない（一般法人10条２項)。

2　一般財団法人の設立

一般財団法人を設立するには，設立者（設立者が二人以上あるときは，その全員）が定款を作成し，これに署名し，又は記名押印しなければならない（一般法人152条１項)。また，設立者は，遺言で，定款記載事項を定めて一般財団法人を設立する意思を表示することができる。この場合においては，遺言執行者は，当該遺言の効力が生じた後，遅滞なく，当該遺言で

定めた事項を記載した定款を作成し，これに署名し，又は記名押印しなければならない（一般法人152条２項）。

定款には，①目的，②名称，③主たる事務所の所在地，④設立者の氏名又は名称及び住所，⑤設立に際して設立者（設立者が二人以上あるときは，各設立者）が拠出をする財産及びその価額，⑥設立時評議員，設立時理事及び設立時監事の選任に関する事項，⑦設立しようとする一般財団法人が会計監査人設置一般財団法人であるときは，設立時会計監査人の選任に関する事項，⑧評議員の選任及び解任の方法，但し，理事又は理事会が評議員を選任又は解任する旨の定款の意定めはすることができない，⑨公告方法，⑩事業年度，を記載しなければならない（一般法人153条１項）。

また，設立者が拠出する財産の価額の合計額は，300万円を下回ってはならない（一般法人153条２項）。

更に，設立者に剰余金又は残余財産の分配を受ける権利を与える旨の定款の定めを設けることはできない。

〈例126　定款（一般社団法人の非営利目的の定款）〉

定　　款

ARTICLES OF INCORPORATION

一般社団法人
General Incorporated Association

定　款
ARTICLES OF INCORPORATION

第１章　総則
CHAPTER 1 GENERAL PROVISIONS

（名称）

第１条　当法人は，一般社団法人[redacted]と称し，英文では[redacted]と表示する。
Article 1 (Name) The Association is called "Ippan shadan houjin [redacted]" and in English "[redacted]".

（事務所）
第２条　当法人は，主たる事務所を東京都港区に置く。
Article 2 (Location of Principal Office) The Association shall have its principal office in [redacted]-ku, Tokyo.

（目的）
第３条　当法人は，科学探査[redacted]船[redacted]号による各種調査・研究を通じて，地球の温暖化に警鐘を鳴らすとともに，地球環境問題に対する理解の促進，教育，改善及び解決に向けた取組みを推進，実施することを目的とする。
Article 3 (Purposes) Purposes of the Association are to implement and promote an approach toward solving educating about, improving and promoting better understanding of the global environmental problems with sounding the alarm about global warming through the research and study by the [redacted] for the science expedition.

（事業）
第４条　当法人は，前条の目的を達成するため，次の事業を行う。
(1)　[redacted]号の研究成果及び調査結果の紹介及び啓蒙活動
(2)　[redacted]号寄港地における乗組員による船内見学の実施，これまでの調査結果，研究成果及び今後の活動計画に対する説明及び教育プログラム
(3)　学校及び研究者を対象とした海洋調査及び環境保護問題に関する共同研究，調査の実施及び援助
(4)　前各号に掲げるもののほか，当法人の目的を達成するために必要な事業全般
(5)　前各号に附帯又は関連する一切の事業
Article 4 (Projects) The Association shall operate the following projects for the purpose of achieving the objective set forth in the preceding Article.
(i)　Awareness campaign and Introduction of findings and research results of the [redacted]
(ii)　Ship tour by the crew, Explanation or Educational program for previous findings and research results and about the future activity plan at a port of call of the [redacted]
(iii)　Implement and Assistance of the collaborative research and investigation of the ocean research and matter of environmental protection targeted at the student and researcher.
(iv)　In addition to what is listed in each of the preceding items, those entire projects necessary for the attainment of purposes of the association.
(v)　Any and all projects incidental to each of the foregoing.

（公告の方法）
第５条　当法人の公告は，当法人の主たる事務所の公衆の見やすい場所に掲示する方法により行う。
Article 5 (Method of public notice) Public notice of the Association shall be the method of posting the object in question at a place accessible to the public at the principal office of the Association.

第２章　社員
CHAPTER 2 MEMBERS

（法人の構成員）

第６条　当法人は，当法人の事業に賛同する個人又は団体であって，次条の規定により当法人の社員となった者をもって構成する。
Article 6 (Members of an association) The Association shall consist of the person who has become a member of the Association pursuant to the provision of the following Article in addition to the condition that an individual or entity that agrees with the project of the Association.

（社員の資格取得）
第７条　当法人の社員になるには，当法人の目的に賛同する入社希望者が当法人所定の書式による入社届を提出の上，入社時点における他の社員全員の書面による同意を得なければならない。
Article 7 (Acquisition of membership status) In order to become a member of the Association, an applicant for membership who or which agrees with the purpose of the Association shall submit a written enrollment notice in the prescribed format of the Association and obtain written consent of all the other members at the time of the application of the membership.

（退社）
第８条　社員は，別に定める退社届を提出することにより，任意に退社することができる。
Article 8 (Withdrawal of Members) A member may freely withdraw by submitting the letter of registration separately provided.

（除名）
第９条　社員が次のいずれかに該当する場合には，社員総会の決議によって，当該社員を除名することができる。
(1)　本定款その他の規則に違反したとき。
(2)　当法人の名誉を傷つけ，又は目的に反する行為をしたとき。
(3)　その他除名すべき正当な事由があるとき。
Article 9 (Expulsion) The Association may dismiss such member by resolution at a General Assembly where a member falls under any of the following;
(i)　where a member has violated these articles of incorporation or other rules
(ii)　where a member injures the reputation or acts against the purposes of the Association
(iii)　where there are justifiable grounds to be expelled

（社員の資格喪失）
第10条　前二条の場合のほか，社員は，次のいずれかに該当する場合には，その資格を喪失する。
(1)　成年被後見人又は被保佐人になったとき。
(2)　死亡し，若しくは失踪宣告を受け，又は解散したとき。
(3)　総社員の同意があったとき。
Article 10 (Loss of member qualifications) If a member comes to fall under any of the following conditions in addition to what is provided for in the preceding two Articles, the member shall lose his/her qualification.
(i)　when a member becomes an adult ward or person under curatorship
(ii)　when a member has died, has become the subject of an adjudication of disappearance or is dissolved
(iii)　when all members agree

第３章　社員総会
CHAPTER 3 THE GENERAL ASSEMBLY

（構成）

第11条　社員総会は，全ての社員をもって構成する。
Article 11 (Constitution of General Assembly) The General Assembly shall consist of all members.

（開催）
第12条　定時社員総会は，毎事業年度末日の翌日から３か月以内に開催し，臨時社員総会は，必要がある場合に開催する。
Article 12 (Holding the general assembly) The annual meeting of the general assembly shall be held within three(3)months from the day following the last date of each business year, and the extraordinary meeting of the general assembly shall be held whenever necessary.

（招集）
第13条　社員総会は，理事の過半数の決定に基づき代表理事が招集する。代表理事に事故又は支障があるときは，あらかじめ定めた順序により，他の理事がこれに当たる。
２　社員総会を招集するには，社員総会の日の３日前までに，社員に対してその通知を発しなければならない。ただし，社員の全員の同意があるときは，招集の手続を経ることなく開催することができる。
Article 13 (Convocation) Meetings of the general assembly may be called by its representative director by a majority rule among the directors. If the Representative Director is involved in an accident or is in trouble, one of the other Directors shall act in his place in accordance with the order prescribed by the Directors in advance and shall convene the Meeting.
2 When calling a meeting of the general assembly, the director shall issue notice of said meeting to the members at least three days before the date of the meeting of the general assembly; provided, however, that where the consent of all members is obtained, a meeting of the general assembly may be held without convocation procedures.

（議長）
第14条　社員総会の議長は，代表理事がこれに当たる。代表理事に事故又は支障があるときは，当該社員総会において議長を選出する。
Article 14 (Chairperson) The Representative Director shall assume chairperson at the general assembly; provided, however, that where the Representative Director is involved in an accident or is in trouble, such general assembly shall elect a chairperson.

（議決権）
第15条　社員は，各１個の議決権を有する。
Article 15 (Votes) Each member shall have one vote.

（決議）
第16条　社員総会の決議は，法令又はこの定款に別段の定めがある場合を除き，総社員の議決権の過半数を有する社員が出席し，出席した当該社員の議決権の過半数をもって行う。
２　前項の規定にかかわらず，次に掲げる社員総会の決議は，総社員の半数以上であって，総社員の議決権の３分の２以上に当たる多数をもって行わなければならない。
(1)　社員の除名
(2)　定款の変更
(3)　解散
(4)　その他法令で定められた事項
Article 16 (Resolutions) Except as otherwise prescribed in the laws and regulations or the articles of incorporation, a resolution at a meeting of the general assembly shall be effected by a majority vote of the members in attendance who have voting rights, provided that the members with a majority of the voting rights are present.

2. Notwithstanding the provisions of the preceding paragraph, resolutions at the following meetings of the general assembly shall be effected by at least a two-thirds majority of the votes of all members and with a quorum of at least one-half of the total number of members:
(i) Expulsion of a member
(ii) Changing the Articles of Incorporation
(iii) Dissolution
(iv) Matters prescribed by laws and regulations

（社員総会の決議の省略）
第17条　理事又は社員が社員総会の目的である事項について提案をした場合において，当該提案につき社員の全員が書面又は電磁的記録により同意の意思表示をしたときは，当該提案を可決する旨の社員総会の決議があったものとみなす。
Article 17 (Omission of a Resolution at a General Assembly) In cases where a director or a member makes a proposal regarding a matter for the purpose of a meeting of the general assembly and where all members manifest their intention to agree with said proposal either in writing or by electromagnetic records, a resolution of the general assembly that affirms the proposal shall be deemed to have passed.

（社員総会への報告の省略）
第18条　理事が社員の全員に対して社員総会に報告すべき事項を通知した場合において，当該事項を社員総会に報告することを要しないことにつき社員の全員が書面又は電磁的記録により同意の意思表示をしたときは，当該事項の社員総会への報告があったものとみなす。
Article 18 (Omission of a Report to the General Assembly) In cases where a director provides notice to all members regarding matters to be reported to the general assembly and all members have manifested their intentions, either in writing or by electromagnetic records, to agree that such matters need not be reported to the general assembly, such matters shall be deemed to have been reported to the general assembly.

（議決権の代理行使）
第19条　社員は，代理人によってその議決権を行使することができる。この場合においては，当該社員又は代理人は，代理権を証明する書面を当法人に提出しなければならない。
2　前項の代理権の授与は，社員総会ごとにしなければならない。
Article 19 (Exercising Voting Rights by Proxy) Members may exercise their voting rights by proxy. In such cases, the subject member or proxy shall submit a document certifying the authority of representation to the association.
2. The granting of the authority of representation shall be made for each meeting of the general assembly.

（議事録）
第20条　社員総会の議事については，法務省令で定めるところにより，議事録を作成しなければならない。
2　社員総会の日から10年間，前項の議事録をその主たる事務所に備え置かなければならない。
Article 20 (Minutes) With respect to the agenda of a meeting of the general assembly, minutes of the meeting shall be prepared as prescribed by the applicable Ordinance of the Ministry of Justice.
2. The general incorporated association shall keep the minutes set forth in the preceding paragraph at its principal office for ten years from the date of the meeting of the general assembly.

第４章　役員
CHAPTER 4 OFFICERS

（役員）
第21条　当法人に，理事３名以上を置く。
２　理事のうち１名を代表理事とする。
Article 21 (Officers) The Association shall have three or more Directors.
2. The Association shall designate a representative director from among the directors.

（役員の選任）
第22条　理事は，社員総会の決議によって選任する。
２　理事の互選によって，理事の中から代表理事を定める。
３　理事のうち，当該理事及びその配偶者又は三親等内の親族である理事の合計数は，理事の総数の３分の１を超えてはならない。
Article 22 (Appointments of Officers) Directors shall be appointed by a resolution of the general assembly.
2. A representative director shall be designated from among the directors by choosing a director from among their members.
3. With respect to each director, the total number of said director and his or her spouse or relatives within the third degree of kinship who are directors does not exceed one third of the total number of directors.

（理事の職務及び権限）
第23条　理事は，法令及びこの定款の定めるところにより，その業務を執行する。
２　代表理事は，当法人を代表し，その業務を統括する。
Article 23 Directors shall administer the business operation of the Association pursuant to the laws and regulations and the articles of incorporation.
2. A Representative Director shall represent the Association and supervise the business.

（役員の任期）
第24条　理事の任期は，選任後２年以内に終了する事業年度のうち最終のものに関する定時社員総会の終結の時までとする。
２　任期の満了前に退任した理事の補欠として選任された理事の任期は，退任した理事の任期の満了する時までとする。
３　増員により選任された理事の任期は，他の在任理事の任期の満了する時までとする。
Article 24 (The Tenure of Officers) Tenure of a director shall be until the end of the final annual meeting of the general assembly in a business year that ends within two years after his /her appointment.
2. Tenure of a Director who is appointed as a substitute for a Director who was terminated before the expiration of his/her tenure shall be until such time as the expiration of the director who was terminated.
3. Tenure of a Director who is appointed as an additional Director shall be until such time as the expiration of other incumbent Director.

（役員の解任）
第25条　理事は，いつでも社員総会の決議によって解任することができる。
Article 25 (Dismissal) Director may be dismissed at any time by resolution of the general assembly.

第５章　計算
CHAPTER 5 CALCULATIONS

（事業年度）
第26条　当法人の事業年度は，毎年１月１日から同年12月31日までの年１期とする。
Article 26 (Business year) The business year of the Association shall commence on

January 1st every year and end on December 31st of the same year.

（事業報告及び決算）

第27条　当法人の事業報告及び決算については，毎事業年度終了後，代表理事が次の書類を作成し，定時社員総会に提出し，第１号の書類についてはその内容を報告し，第２号及び第３号の書類については承認を受けなければならない。

(1)　事業報告

(2)　貸借対照表

(3)　損益計算書（正味財産増減計算書）

２　前項の規定により報告され，又は承認を受けた書類のほか，定款及び社員名簿を主たる事務所に備え置くものとする。

Article 27 (Business reports and Settlement of Accounts) With regard to the business report and settlement of account, the Representative Director shall prepare the following documents after the end of each business year and submit or provide to the annual meeting of the general assembly. And then the Representative Director shall report on the contents of the business report and the financial statements shall require the approval of the annual meeting of the general assembly.

(i)　Business reports

(ii)　Balance Sheets

(iii)　Profit and loss statement (Statement of changes in net properties)

2. The Association shall keep the documents reported to the annual meeting of the general assembly and received its approval pursuant to the provisions of paragraph(1), the articles of incorporation and its member registry at its principal office.

（剰余金の不分配）

第28条　当法人は，剰余金の分配を行わないものとする。

Article 28 (Non-Distribution of surplus) The Association shall not distribute the surplus.

第６章　定款の変更及び解散

CHAPTER 6 CHANGING THE ARTICLES OF INCORPORATION AND DISSOLUTION

（定款の変更）

第29条　社員総会の決議によって，当法人の定款を変更することができる。

Article 29 The Association may change its articles of incorporation by resolution of the general assembly.

（解散）

第30条　当法人は，社員総会決議その他法令で定められた事由により解散する。

Article 30 (Dissolution) The Association shall dissolve by a resolution at the meeting of the general assembly and on the grounds prescribed by laws and regulations.

（残余財産の帰属）

第31条　当法人が解散等により清算する際に有する残余財産は，社員総会の決議によって，国若しくは地方公共団体又は次に掲げる法人に贈与するものとする。

(1)　公益社団法人又は公益財団法人

(2)　公益社団法人及び公益財団法人の認定等に関する法律第五条第十七号イからトまでに掲げる法人

Article 31 (Ownership of Residual Assets) The residual assets which holds at the liquidation due to the dissolution etc. of the Association shall donate to a national or local government agency or a corporation listed as follows by resolution of the general assembly.

(i)　a public interest incorporated association or public interest incorporated foundation

(ii)　any of the juridical persons listed in Article 5, item (xvii), sub-items (a) to (g) of the Act on Authorization of Public Interest Incorporated Associations and Public Interest Incorporated Foundation

第７章　附則
CHAPTER 7 SUPPLEMENTARY PROVISIONS

（最初の事業年度）
第32条　当法人の最初の事業年度は，当法人の成立から　　年12月31日までとする。
Article 32（First business year）First business year of the Association shall commerce on the formation of the Association and end on December 31st, 2016.

（設立時社員の氏名及び住所）
第33条　設立時社員の氏名及び住所は，次のとおりである。

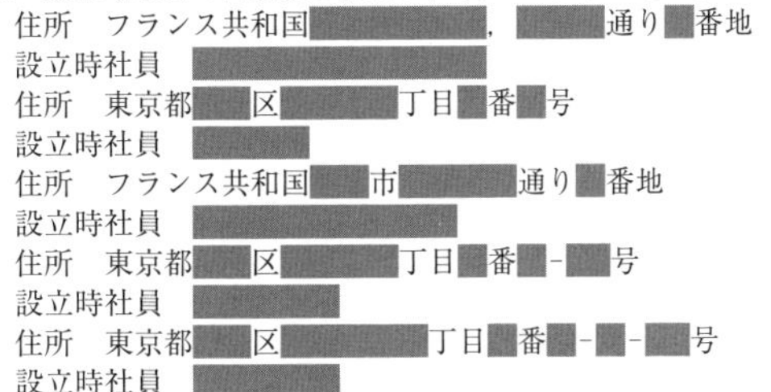

住所　フランス共和国　　，　　通り　番地
設立時社員
住所　東京都　区　　丁目　番　号
設立時社員
住所　フランス共和国　市　　通り　番地
設立時社員
住所　東京都　区　　丁目　番　-　号
設立時社員
住所　東京都　区　　丁目　番　-　-　号
設立時社員

Article 33（Names and addresses of members at incorporation）Names and addresses of members at incorporation are as follows:

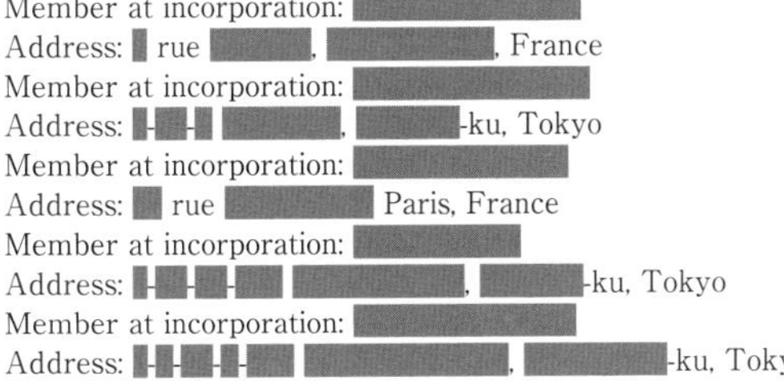

Member at incorporation:
Address: rue , , France
Member at incorporation:
Address: - , -ku, Tokyo
Member at incorporation:
Address: rue Paris, France
Member at incorporation:
Address: - - , -ku, Tokyo
Member at incorporation:
Address: - - - , -ku, Tokyo

（設立時役員）
第34条　当法人の設立時理事は，次のとおりとする。

設立時理事
設立時理事
設立時理事

２　当法人の設立時代表理事は，次のとおりとする。

住所　フランス共和国　　，　　通り　番地
設立時代表理事

Article 34（Officers at Incorporation）Directors at incorporation of the Association are as follows:

Director at incorporation:
Director at incorporation:
Director at incorporation:

2 Representative Director at incorporation of the Association is as follows:

Representative Director at incorporation:
Address: rue , , France

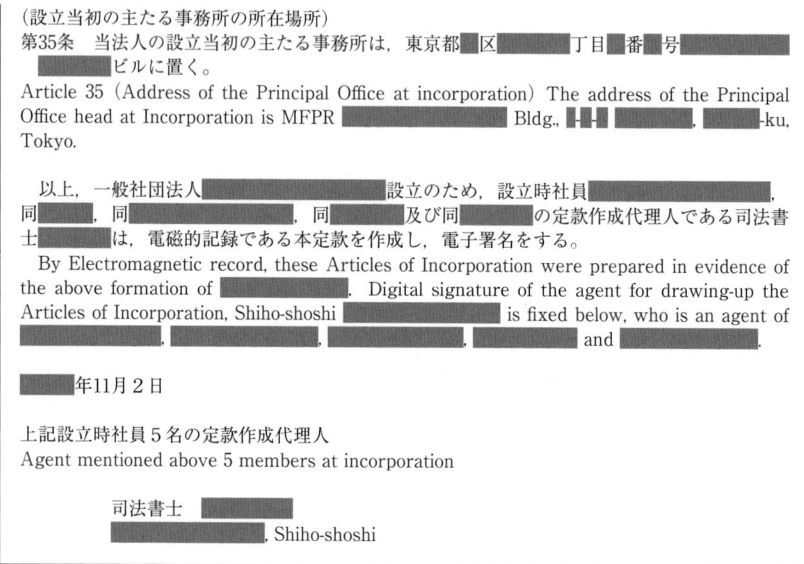

（設立当初の主たる事務所の所在場所）
第35条　当法人の設立当初の主たる事務所は，東京都■区■丁目■番■号■■ビルに置く。
Article 35 (Address of the Principal Office at incorporation) The address of the Principal Office head at Incorporation is MFPR ■ Bldg., ■-■ ■, ■-ku, Tokyo.

以上，一般社団法人■設立のため，設立時社員■，同■，同■，同■及び同■の定款作成代理人である司法書士■は，電磁的記録である本定款を作成し，電子署名をする。
By Electromagnetic record, these Articles of Incorporation were prepared in evidence of the above formation of ■. Digital signature of the agent for drawing-up the Articles of Incorporation, Shiho-shoshi ■ is fixed below, who is an agent of ■, ■, ■, ■ and ■.

■年11月２日

上記設立時社員５名の定款作成代理人
Agent mentioned above 5 members at incorporation

司法書士　■
■, Shiho-shoshi

〈例127　就任承諾書（抄，理事の就任承諾）〉

就任承諾書
Acceptance of Office as a Director at incorporation

私は，貴法人の定款において，貴法人の設立時理事に選任されましたので，その就任を承諾致します。
As I was elected as a Director at incorporation of the Association by the Articles of Incorporation, I hereby accept such appointment.

〈例128　承認承諾書（抄，理事・代表理事の就任承諾）〉

就任承諾書
Acceptance of Office as a Director at incorporation & a Representative Director at incorporation

私は，貴法人の定款において，貴法人の設立時理事及び設立時代表取締役に選任並びに選定されましたので，その就任を承諾致します。
As I was elected as a Director at incorporation and a Representative Director at incorporation of the Association by the Articles of

Incorporation, I hereby accept such appointment.

3　社員の入退者

一般社団法人の定款上の絶対的記載事項には，社員の資格の得喪に関する事項を規定しなければならない（一般法人11条1項5号）。ただし，社員の定義の規定はない。また，一般社団法人は，社員の氏名又は名称及び住所を記載した社員名簿を作成しなければならない（同法31条）。社員名簿は主たる事務所に備え置きをしなければならない（同法32条1項）。社員の入退社は登記事項ではないが，通常，社員の入社の際には，小規模の法人の場合，定款の規定により他の社員の同意書を徴求しているケースが多い。社員が多数の場合には，理事会の又は代表理事の承認を要件としているケースもある。

〈例129　同意書（入社につき他の社員の同意）〉

一般社団法人________
代表理事　________　殿
To: Mr. ________, Representative Director
____

同　意　書
Letter of Consent

一般社団法人________（"貴法人"）の社員である私，________は，以下の入社希望者が貴法人の社員になることついて同意いたします。
I, ________ who is a member of ________ (the "Association"), hereby agree that the following applicant for membership become a member of the Association.

記
Note

入社希望者住所：
(Address)

入社希望者氏名：
(Name)

入社希望者につき付記事項：
(Additional matter)

■■■■年　月　日
Date

社員氏名：
社員住所：

Name of Member: ______________________ (Signature)
Address of Member:

〈例130　退社届（抄，退社社員の退社の届）〉

退　社　届
Notice of Withdrawal of Members

貴法人定款第８条により，退社したく，お届け致します。
I do hereby give notice of my withdrawal as Member of ■■■■■■ under Article 8 of your Articles of incorporation.

〈例131　入社届（抄，入社社員の入社の届）〉

入　社　届
Enrollment Notice

私は，貴法人の目的に賛同し，定款を確認の上，入社を希望致します。
I hereby wish to become a member of your association on the approval of your purpose after confirming your Articles of Incorporation.

4　定時社員総会

定時社員総会は，毎事業年度の終了後一定の時期に招集しなければならない（一般法人36条１項）。定時社員総会においては，計算書類の承認並びに事業報告を行い，任期満了の理事の選任を決議することになる。

〈例132　定時総会議事録（計算書類承認・事業報告　理事選任）〉

一般社団法人 ■■■■ 定時社員総会議事録

Minutes of the Ordinary General Meeting of members of General Incorporated Association ■■■■

■■■■年３月15日午後５時00分，当法人の主たる事務所において，当法人定時社員総会を開催した。

The Ordinary General Meeting of members of the Association was held at the principal office of the Association from 5:00 p.m. on March 15, ■■■■.

議決権のある社員の総数　　　　　　４名
総社員の議決権の数　　　　　　　　４個
出席した社員数　　　　　　　　　　４名
この議決権の総数　　　　　　　　　４個

Total number of members entitled to exercise the right to vote at this members meeting: 4
Number of votes of members entitled to exercise the right to vote at this members meeting: 4
Number of members who are present at this members meeting: 4
Number of votes which members who are present at this members meeting hold: 4

出席理事：■■■■，■■■■，■■■■，■■■■
議長：　代表理事 ■■■■
議事録の作成に係る職務を行った理事：　代表理事 ■■■■

Directors present: ■■■■, ■■■■, ■■■■, ■■■■
Chairman: ■■■■, Representative Director
Director preparing minutes: ■■■■, Representative Director

上記のとおり社員が出席したので，本定時社員総会は適法に成立した。よって，定刻に，定款の規定により代表理事■■■■は議長席に着き，開会を宣し，議事の審議に入った。

Members being present as described above, the Ordinary General Meeting of the Members was duly convened. ■■■■, Representative Director, took the chair at the fixed time in accordance with the provision of articles of association, announced the opening of the meeting, and commenced the deliberation of the items on the agenda.

第１号議案　████度（自　████年１月１日　至　████年12月31日）計算書類の承認および事業報告の内容報告の件

議長は，当期における事業状況を事業報告書により詳細に説明報告し，下記の書類を提出して，その承認を求めた。

Item No.1 on the Agenda: Approval of the account documents and Reporting of the business report for the ███ Fiscal Term（From January 1, ███ to December 31, ███）

The Chairman explained the contents of the Business Report for the current business term in detail and submitted following documents to the members and asked for the approval thereof.

1．貸借対照表	The Balance Sheet;
2．損益計算書	The Profit and Loss Statement;
3．個別注記表	The Schedule of individual notes

総会は，別段の異議なく，承認可決した。

The Members meeting approved the proposal without opposition.

第２号議案　理事選任の件

議長は，理事の全員が本総会終了をもって任期が満了する旨を報告し，その後任の理事を選任する必要があることを説明した。ついで議長が本議案について賛否を議場に諮ったところ，以下の各氏が全員一致をもって理事に選任され，可決確定した。

【再任】理事　████████，████████，████████，████████

Item No.2 on the Agenda: Appointment of Directors

The chairman reported the attention of the meeting to the fact that the term of office of all directors of the Association would expire at the close of this meeting, and explained that it was accordingly necessary to elect their successors. On motion duly made and seconded, the persons stated below were unanimously elected serve as Directors:

（Reappointment）Directors：████████，████████，████████，████████

以上をもって本社員総会の議事を終了したので，議長は，午後５時30分閉会を宣した。

Whereupon, all matters before the present General Meeting of members having been completed, the Chairman presented his closing address, and declared this meeting dissolved at 5: 30 p.m.

上記決議の経過の要領およびその結果を明確にする為，本議事録を作成し，議事録の作成にかかる職務を行った代表理事■■■■が記名押印をする。

In order to confirm the above resolution, these minutes have been prepared, and the seal was affixed and the stamp beside printed name was appended by Representative Director ■■■■ who prepared them.

■■■■年３月15日
March 15, ■■■■
一般社団法人　■■■■　定時社員総会
The Ordinary General Meeting of Members of General Incorporated Association ■■■■

議長兼出席代表理事兼議事録作成者　■■■■
Chairman & Representative Director Present
& Person who prepared these minutes: ■■■■

Company Seal

Company Seal

〈例133　就任承諾書（抄，理事の就任の承諾）〉

就任承諾書
Acceptance of Appointment

私は，■■■■年３月15日付の貴法人定時社員総会において，貴法人の理事に選任されましたので，その就任を承諾致します。

I hereby accept the appointment that I was elected as a Director of the Association by the resolution of the Ordinary General Meeting of Members of General Incorporated Association ■■■■, held on March 15, ■■■■.

〈例134　理事決定書（抄，代表理事選任の決定）〉

理事決定書
WRITTEN DECISION OF DIRECTORS

1．代表理事選定の件
1．Concerning the Selection of Representative Director

住所　フランス共和国■，■通り■番地
Address　France ■ rue ■
代表理事　■
Representative Director: ■

上記の決定を明確にするため，この決定書を作成し，理事全員がこれに記名押印する。
In order to clarify the above decision, these written decisions have been prepared and the seal beside printed name was affixed by all directors.

〈例135　就任承諾書（抄，代表理事の就任の承諾）〉

代表理事就任承諾書
Acceptance of Appointment as Representative Director

私は，■年３月15日の貴法人の理事の一致において，貴法人の代表理事に選定されましたので，その就任を承諾致します。
As I was elected as the Representative Director of General Incorporated Association ■ by the decision of Directors of the Association, held on March 15, ■, I hereby accept such appointment.

〈例136　委任状（役員変更登記申請用）〉

委　任　状
Power of Attorney

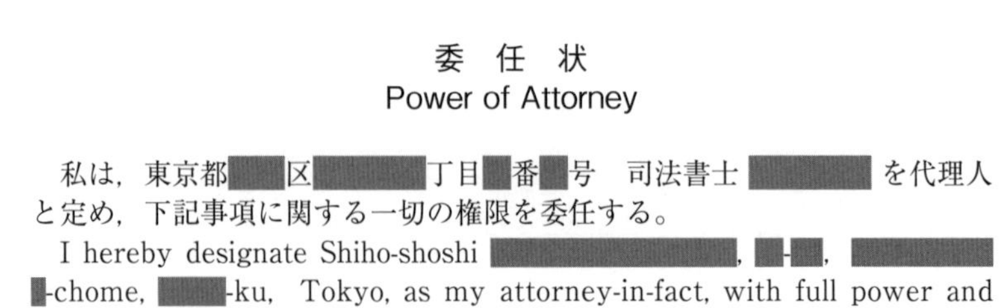
私は，東京都■区■丁目■番■号　司法書士 ■ を代理人と定め，下記事項に関する一切の権限を委任する。
I hereby designate Shiho-shoshi ■, ■-■, ■ ■-chome, ■-ku, Tokyo, as my attorney-in-fact, with full power and

authority to perform the following:

1．当会社の理事及び代表理事の変更登記申請に関する一切の件
1．To handle all matters relating to the application for our association registering of the change of Representative Director and Directors.

2．本件委任状の補完・訂正に関する件
2．Matters Regarding Amendments and Complements to the Power of Attorney.

3．原本還付請求及び受領に関する件
3．To request and receive original documents related to the above application.

5　臨時社員総会

社員総会は，必要があるときはいつでも招集できる（一般法人36条2項）ものであり，理事の辞任又は理事の増員よりその選任の必要性があるときは臨時の社員総会を招集し，その決議を行うことができる。

〈例137　臨時社員総会議事録（理事の選任のための決議）〉

一般社団法人 ■■■■ 臨時社員総会議事録
Minutes of the Extraordinary General Meeting of members of General Incorporated Association ■■■■

■■■■年10月5日午後5時00分，当法人の主たる事務所において，当法人臨時社員総会を開催した。
The Extraordinary General Meeting of members of the Association was held at the principal office of the Association from 5:00 p.m. on October 5, ■■■■.

議決権のある社員の総数　　4名
総社員の議決権の数　　4個
出席した社員数　　4名
この議決権の総数　　4個
Total number of members entitled to exercise the right to vote at this members meeting: 4
Number of votes of members entitled to exercise the right to vote at

this members meeting: 4
Number of members who are present at this members meeting: 4
Number of votes which members who are present at this members meeting hold: 4
出席理事：[REDACTED]，[REDACTED]
議長：　代表理事 [REDACTED]
議事録の作成に係る職務を行った理事：　代表理事 [REDACTED]
Directors present: [REDACTED], [REDACTED], [REDACTED]
Chairman : [REDACTED], Representative director
Director preparing minutes: [REDACTED], Representative director

上記のとおり社員が出席したので，本臨時社員総会は適法に成立した。よって，定刻に，定款の規定により代表理事[REDACTED]は議長席に着き，開会を宣し，議事の審議に入った。

Members being present as described above, the Extraordinary General Meeting of the Members was duly convened. [REDACTED], Representative Director, took the chair at the fixed time in accordance with the provision of articles of association, announced the opening of the meeting, and commenced the deliberation of the item on the agenda.

議案　理事選任の件

議長は，理事を選任する必要がある旨を述べ，議場に諮ったところ，全員一致により下記のものが選任され，可決確定した。

理事 [REDACTED]
理事 [REDACTED]

Agenda: Election of Directors

The Chairman stated that it was necessary to elect Directors. On motion duly made and seconded, the following persons were unanimously elected as Directors.

[REDACTED], Director
[REDACTED], Director

以上をもって本社員総会の議事を終了したので，議長は，午後５時30分閉会を宣した。

Whereupon, all matters before the present General Meeting having been completed, the Chairman presented his closing address, and declared this meeting dissolved at 5: 30 p.m.

上記決議の経過の要領およびその結果を明確にする為，本議事録を作成し，

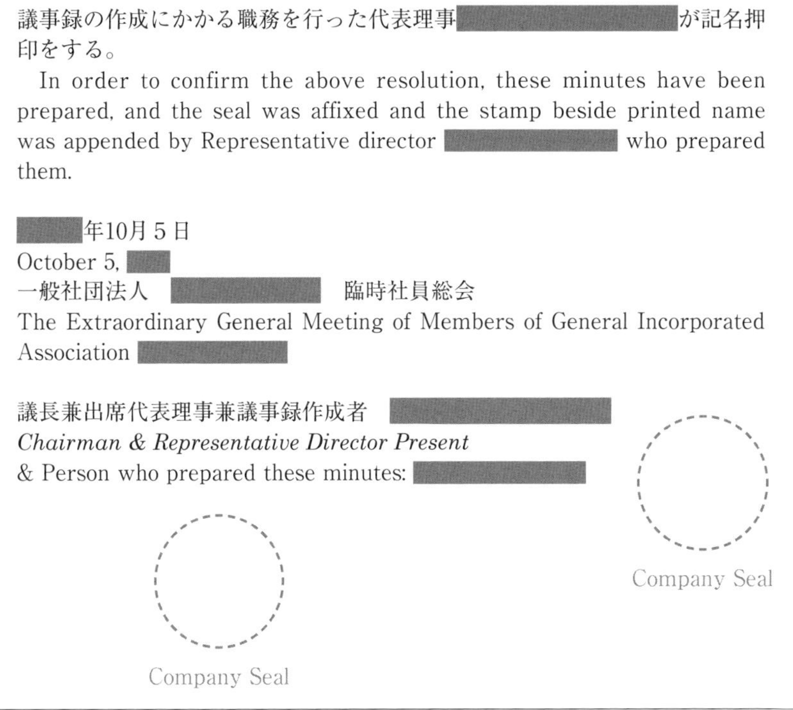

議事録の作成にかかる職務を行った代表理事■■■■が記名押印をする。

In order to confirm the above resolution, these minutes have been prepared, and the seal was affixed and the stamp beside printed name was appended by Representative director ■■■■ who prepared them.

■■年10月5日

October 5, ■■

一般社団法人　■■■■　臨時社員総会

The Extraordinary General Meeting of Members of General Incorporated Association ■■■■

議長兼出席代表理事兼議事録作成者　■■■■

Chairman & Representative Director Present

& Person who prepared these minutes: ■■■■

Company Seal

Company Seal

〈例138　辞任届（抄，理事の辞任の届け）〉

辞　任　届

Notice of Resignation

私は，■■年３月　日をもって，貴法人の理事を辞任したいので，お届けいたします。

I do hereby give notice of my resignation as a Director of General Incorporated Association ■■■■ as of March　, ■■.

〈例139　就任承諾書（抄，理事の就任の承諾）〉

> 就任承諾書
> Acceptance of Appointment
>
> 私は，████年　月　日付の貴法人臨時社員総会において，貴法人の理事に選任されましたので，その就任を承諾致します。
>
> I hereby accept the appointment that I was elected as a Director of the Association by the resolution of the Extraordinary General Meeting of Members of General Incorporated Association ████████ on 　　　, ████.

資料 用語集

株式会社	stock company
監査法人	audit corporation
合同会社	limited liability company（LLC）
一般社団法人	general incorporated association
一般財団法人	general incorporated foundation
公益財団法人	public interest incorporated foundation
公益社団法人	public interest incorporated association
合名会社	general partnership company
特例有限会社	special limited liability company
LLP	limited liability business partnership, limited liability partnership
合資会社	limited partnership company
学校法人	incorporated educational institution
宗教法人	religious corporation
水産業協同組合	fisheries cooperative
事業協同組合	business cooperative
農業協同組合	agricultural cooperative
代表取締役	representative director
取締役	director
監査役	company auditor（注1）
取締役会	board of directors
株主	shareholder, stockholder
株主総会	shareholders meeting
決算	settlement（of account）
定款	articles of incorporation
就業規則	rules of employment
会社法	Companies Act
労働基準法	Labor Standards Act

（注1） 原則としてcompany auditorであるが，前後関係から明らかである場合には，companyを省略し，auditorとするのも可。

（出典：法務省「日本法令外国語訳データベースシステム」（2020年6月1日現在）

著 者 紹 介

石 田 佳 治（いしだ　よしはる）

学　　歴：1956年　神戸大学法学部卒業
1979年　ワシントン州立大学ロースクール　サマーセッション
1989年　ウィスコンシン州立大学ロースクール　サマープログラム
1995年　サンタクララ大学ロースクール　サマープログラム

職　　歴：1956年-1976年　蝶理株式会社（主として法務・審査部門を担当，東京，大阪，ニューヨークに勤務）
1976年-1993年　日本ロシュ株式会社（法務部長）
1993年-1996年　ジボダン・ルール株式会社（常勤監査役）
1997年-現在　株式会社バベル　監査役
2000年-現在　バベル翻訳大学院プロフェッサー・ディーン（インターナショナルパラリーガル法律翻訳専攻）

関係団体：（一社）日本翻訳協会（1990年より理事）
経営法友会（1977年-1985年　幹事）
国際企業法務協会（1985年-1995年　理事）
著作権法学会
日本通訳翻訳学会

主要著書：『渉外相続・不動産登記・会社取引等で役に立つ　英文の法律・法的文書作成に関する実践と書式』（共著，日本加除出版，2018）
『リーガルドラフティング完全マニュアル』（バベル・インターナショナル）
『欧米ビジネスロー最前線』（民事法研究会，1991）
『シネマdeロー』（東京リーガルマインド，1997）
『訴訟の国のJACK＆BETTY』（共著，東京リーガルマインド，1992）

山 北 英 仁（やまきた　ひでひと）

司法書士・簡裁代理業務認定司法書士
行政書士・入国管理局申請取次行政書士

学　　歴：1970年　中央大学法学部法律学科　卒業

職　　歴：1987年　池袋国際司法行政書士事務所開設
1995年-1997年　東京司法書士会理事
1999年　４事務所と共に合同事務所リス・インターナショナルへ新設合併
2000年-2019年　日本司法書士政治連盟　副会長
2007年-2009年　日本司法書士会連合会　理事
2009年　合同事務所ジュリスター・インターナショナル新設

関係団体：NPO法人渉外司法書士協会　会長
日本司法書士政治連盟　相談役
（一社）民事信託推進センター　専務理事・事務局
（一社）国際行政書士協会　副会長

主要著書：『渉外相続・不動産登記・会社取引等で役に立つ　英文の法律・法的文書作成に関する実践と書式』（共著，日本加除出版，2018）
『渉外不動産登記の法律と実務２』（日本加除出版，2018）
『渉外不動産取引に関する法律と税金』（共著，日本加除出版，2016）
『渉外不動産登記の法律と実務』（日本加除出版，2014）
『不動産取引とリスクマネージメント』「第３章　物件調査，重要事項説明，契約書」（共著，日本加除出版，2012）など。

涉外取引・会社運営等で必要な
英文定款・議事録等の作成に関する実践と書式
―株式会社・合同会社・一般社団法人等で活用する定款，議事録，決算期変更，発行可能株式総数の変更，増資，減資，合併，清算，就業規則等における日英文例及び解説―

2020年8月21日　初版発行

著　者　石田佳治
　　　　山北英仁

発行者　和田　裕

発行所　日本加除出版株式会社

本　社　郵便番号 171-8516
東京都豊島区南長崎3丁目16番6号
TEL (03)3953-5757（代表）
(03)3952-5759（編集）
FAX (03)3953-5772
URL www.kajo.co.jp

営業部　郵便番号 171-8516
東京都豊島区南長崎3丁目16番6号
TEL (03)3953-5642
FAX (03)3953-2061

組版 ㈱郁文 ／ 印刷 ㈱精興社 ／ 製本 牧製本印刷㈱

落丁本・乱丁本は本社でお取替えいたします。
★定価はカバー等に表示してあります。

ISBN978-4-8178-4667-9